Multinationals and the National Interest

*Playing
by Different
Rules*

**Office of
Technology
Assessment
U.S. Congress**

Recommended Citation:

U.S. Congress, Office of Technology Assessment, *Multinationals and the National Interest: Playing by Different Rules,* OTA-ITE-569 (Washington, DC: U.S. Government Printing Office, September 1993).

For sale by the U.S. Government Printing Office
Superintendent of Documents, Mail Stop: SSOP, Washington, DC 20402-9328
ISBN 0-16-041943-3

Foreword

Over the past 25 years, technology differences have steadily decreased among competing firms of different nations. The technological superiority of an IBM, AT&T, or Boeing has been offset by the rise of capable competitors worldwide. The traditional U.S. advantages of privileged access to broad, deep, and liquid capital markets, as well as large economies of scale and scope, have similarly leveled off.

These changes reflect major shifts in the structure of the world economy. In the broadest sense, the globalization of business, communications, and transportation is transforming the post-WWII system of international trade and investment. At the same time, profound asymmetries have developed in the rules of different nations that influence and regulate the activities of multinational enterprises (MNEs).

In the post-cold war period, the structure of multinational industry is evolving far more rapidly than the rules that govern its conduct. The policy challenge is to manage and defuse escalating trade frictions in ways that promote growth and ensure a fair and sustainable distribution of advanced technology and manufacturing assets among competing national economies. MNEs are central to this process because they are international conduits of technology and goods and services; they also provide the quality jobs and capital that support economic growth and high standards of living.

The interests of MNEs, however, do not always conform to those of the United States. The United States wants MNEs to conduct core business operations here, to interact with local firms to create employment and wealth, and to retain the benefits of that wealth for U.S. citizens. But MNEs are understandably less concerned with advancing national goals (which may conflict among different nations) than with pursuing objectives internal to the firm—principally growth, profits, proprietary technology, strategic alliances, return on investments, and market power.

Surely there must be some balance or compromise that can be reached between maximizing efficiency at the level of the firm, and the need of host governments to ensure that firms act in ways that contribute to national well-being. Although companies and governments may pursue different objectives, there is no irreconcilable incompatibility between the interests of MNEs and those of nations.

This assessment was requested by the Senate Committee on Commerce, Science, and Transportation and the Senate Committee on Banking, Housing, and Urban Affairs. This is the first of two reports. It is intended as an introduction to and overview of the issues that affect multinational firms and the U.S. technology base. The final report, to be published in 1994, will present additional analysis and policy options related to issues raised in this report.

Roger C. Herdman, Director

Advisory Panel

Lawrence M. Friedman
Chairman
Marion Rice Kirkwood Professor
   of Law
Stanford Law School

Jay Chai
Chairman and CEO
Itochu International

Alfred Chandler
Straus Professor of Business
   History, Emeritus
Harvard Business School

Lance Compa
Administrative Officer
Washington-Baltimore
   Newspaper Guild

Stanley J. Fidelman
Senior Vice President, Engineering,
   Safety and the Environment
Merck

R. Scott Fosler
President
National Academy of Public
   Administration

William Greider
National Editor
Rolling Stone

Richard W. Heimlich
Corporate Vice President for
   International Strategy
Motorola

Robert J. Hermann
Vice President, Science and
   Technology
United Technology Corp.

Jeffrey Leonard
President
Global Environment Fund

Theodore J. Lowi
John L. Senior Professor of
   American Institutions
Cornell University

David A. Markle
Vice President, Advanced
   Technology
Ultratech Stepper

Oscar B. Marx, III
Vice President Automotive
   Components Group
Ford Motor Co.

William D. Mulholland
Bank of Montreal

Indra Nooyi
Vice President, Strategy and
   Planning
Asea Brown and Boveri

James F. Rill
Partner
Collier, Shannon, Rill, and Scott

Richard B. Samuels
Ford International Professor
Director of MIT Japan Program
Massachusetts Institute of
   Technology

Peter Schavoir
IBM Director of Strategy
IBM

Steven Schlossstein
President
SBS Associates

Harley Shaiken
Associate Professor, Department of
   Communication
University of California, San Diego

Raymond Vernon
Clarence Dillon Professor of
   International Affairs, Emeritus
John F. Kennedy School of
   Government

Andrew W. Wyckoff
Head of the Economic Analysis
   Section
Directorate for Science, Technology
   and Industry
Organisation for Economic
   Co-operation and Development

NOTE: OTA appreciates and is grateful for the valuable assistance and thoughtful critiques provided by the advisory panel members. The panel does not, however, necessarily approve, disapprove, or endorse this report. OTA assumes full responsibility for the report and the accuracy of its contents.

Project Staff

Peter D. Blair, *Assistant Director, OTA*
Energy, Materials, and International Security Division

Audrey B. Buyrn, *Program Manager*
Industry, Technology, and Employment Program

William W. Keller, *Project Director*

Kenneth E. Freeman
David Rosenfeld
Lucian Hughes

PRINCIPAL CONTRACTORS

Carol V. Evans
Louis W. Pauly
Simon Reich

CONTRACTORS

Paul N. Doremus
David J. Eichberg
Jacques Hymans
Takashi Mashiko
Elizabeth Sheley
Gregory S. Tsarnas

ADMINISTRATIVE STAFF

Carol A. Bock
Diane D. White

Contents

The Importance of Multinational Enterprises | 1

Multinational enterprises (MNEs) are business organizations that underpin much of the U.S. economy and the international system of trade and investment. They are increasingly global in their origins, sourcing, communications, production, and outlook. The foreign affiliates of MNEs control a substantial portion of the world economy, perhaps as much as one-quarter of all economic activity in their host countries. Intrafirm trade, that is, goods and services exchanged among parent companies and their foreign subsidiaries, may account for more than 40 percent of U.S. imports and 35 percent of U.S. exports.[1] Because they are so important and powerful, MNEs evoke a wide range of concerns from home governments, host governments, rival firms, and strategic partners.

Intensifying competition among firms in almost every sector of the international economy is changing the structure of multinational industry (see chapter 2). At the same time, **increasing competitiveness concerns and trade frictions among nations have led to a heightened awareness of the activities of MNEs. Because MNEs are the major force in international trade and are deeply enmeshed in local economies, they are influential in national politics and essential to industry. But because they span national borders, many MNEs are less concerned with advancing national goals than with pursuing**

---

[1] See notes 21, 22, and 23 below. In 1990, worldwide sales of foreign affiliates in host countries reached an estimated $5.5 trillion as compared with approximately $4 trillion in total world exports of goods and nonfactor services. See United Nations Conference on Trade and Development, Programme on Transnational Corporations, *World Investment Report 1993* (New York, NY: United Nations, 1993), p. 13.

objectives internal to the firm—principally growth, profits, proprietary technology, strategic alliances, return on investment, and market power. MNEs are highly flexible and can take many different forms (see table 1-1).

Congress is concerned about MNEs for several reasons. In the broadest sense, the globalization of business, transportation, and communications is disrupting the post-World War II system of international trade and, in the post-Cold War period, threatens to increase trade friction among nations to unmanageable levels. As tough talk on trade escalates between the United States and its principal trading partners, pressure builds for a coordinated response from Congress, the Administration, and U.S. business leaders. MNEs are increasingly the focus of this debate because they are international conduits of goods and services as well as major providers of the technology, jobs, and capital that support high standards of living in the industrialized nations.

At a more fundamental level, Congress should be concerned when **the interests of MNEs, both domestic- and foreign-based, increasingly diverge from those of the United States.** Foreign MNEs that penetrate U.S. markets, make few investments, and drive local firms from the marketplace cannot be considered national assets. Affiliates of foreign-based MNEs that import high percentages of complex parts for assembly operations, that do not provide commensurate pay, benefits, and training for American workers, and that extract excessive subsidies from state and local governments are not acting in the national interest. Similarly, if a U.S.-based firm principally operates screwdriver assembly plants in the United States, exports critical technology development functions, and moves most or all of its production facilities abroad to take advantage of low wages and lax environmental standards, it would not be acting in the Nation's interest.

As a further complication, the distinction between foreign and U.S. companies is breaking down. As U.S.-based MNEs commit ever more

Table 1-1—Types of Multinational Enterprises (MNEs)

For purposes of this report, OTA has identified and analyzed six principal types of MNEs. They are not intended to be rigid or mutually exclusive, but instead to capture the major differences that are relevant to the development of public policy. The six types of MNEs listed below are described in greater detail in chapter 2.

Resource-based MNEs
> organize around the extraction of natural resources, or agricultural products, and their processing for sale in the industrialized countries.

Export-oriented MNEs
> maintain the preponderance of their production and R&D base in their domestic market. Export high value-added products to other national markets, often through intrafirm trade. Typically establish final assembly, service, support, sales and marketing operations abroad.

Regional MNEs
> optimize their activities, including production, around a regional market but have not yet achieved significant sales and operations outside their region of origin.

Transnational MNEs
> have begun to locate production facilities globally, but still depend heavily on their domestic market and operations for their competitive position, economies of scale and scope, key production operations, and R&D.

Global MNEs
> replicate much of the full value-added chain, including substantial product development and research operations, in more than one national or regional market.

Distributed MNEs
> optimize the location of their sourcing, production, and R&D on a global basis.

SOURCE: Office of Technology Assessment, 1993.

resources to foreign affiliates, and foreign-based firms produce and invest in America, the question of what constitutes an American company for purposes of public policy becomes even more critical. The rapid expansion of the number and scope of international strategic alliances among MNEs adds complexity to this already difficult question (see chapter 5).

What do nations want from multinational enterprises? In the end, **the United States wants MNEs to conduct business here and interact with local firms in ways that generate and retain wealth and quality jobs within its** borders. This is what all nations generally want and increasingly demand from MNEs. For the United States, it translates most immediately into high-wage, high-value jobs for Americans, indigenous technology development, advanced manufacturing that draws on local talent, an expanding tax base, and ultimately, generalized economic well-being. **The connection between the location of technology leadership, both product and process, and the health of national economies and living standards is becoming ever more apparent to governments.**

The answer to the policy question of what should constitute an American company is tied not so much to the ownership or home base of particular MNEs, but rather to how a firm affects the well-being and standard of living in the local and national communities where it operates. In this view, **MNEs should be considered American if and when they act in the national interest, and as American companies, they should be entitled to a higher standard of consideration.**

The ultimate test of whether the United States should contemplate requiring standards of performance from foreign companies would be its willingness to see the same standards applied to U.S.-based firms operating abroad. In that case, the objective would not be to maximize benefits for the United States, but rather to reach a balance in trade and investment that did not confer large advantages on one nation at the expense of others. Some analysts note that creating such a regime would require joint development of performance standards among the principal trading countries, with the intent to avoid unilateral actions that might heighten trade conflict. Within that general approach, they suggest, it would then be appropriate to require foreign-based MNEs that enjoy the benefits of a nation's markets and national infrastructure to act in ways that contribute to the national interest of the host nation.

These concerns arise for two reasons. First, in some industrialized nations, increasing global-ization of research and development (R&D) and production is detaching firms from their national origins. As competition heats up within the Triad of North America, Europe, and Japan, many MNEs seek global economies of scale, and efficiencies of R&D, production, sales, and service, tied not to particular nations, but located within different national markets around the world. Because U.S. firms were first to globalize their operations in large numbers, this process is particularly pronounced for the United States.

Second, some very large firms organize their operations around what might be termed a "glo-calization" strategy, that is, around vertically integrated supplier networks, both in their home base and with respect to their foreign assembly operations. **These MNEs tend to retain higher value-added R&D and production functions at home, and to export sophisticated parts and components to their foreign subsidiaries.** Typically, they exert strong influence over their supplier networks, often requiring them to take on substantial design and engineering responsibilities, and help absorb losses when business is bad. Many analysts associate this model most closely with Japanese-based MNEs and their affiliated keiretsu business groups. (See chapter 4 for a discussion of the keiretsu system.)

Most corporate managers and analysts argue that setting up the full value-added chain in all principal markets—from R&D through manufacturing and after-sales service—would be highly inefficient and probably impossible, given existing networks of facilities and supplier relationships. The trend, they contend, is precisely the opposite, toward dispersed sourcing and greater international division of labor at all levels of business operations. **Many managers believe they cannot remain competitive unless they have access to low-cost components, high-quality labor, and flexible production arrangements—wherever and whenever these are available.** These concerns cannot and should not be taken lightly.

But these concerns can also be overemphasized. They reflect the needs of managers in particular companies to meet specific corporate objectives. And they do not give sufficient credit to the ability of MNEs to adjust and reconfigure to meet changing economic and political conditions. **The U.S. economy (or any other, for that matter) cannot remain competitive unless MNEs that sell and conduct business in America also contribute to its research and technology base, employment, manufacturing capabilities, and capital resources.** (See chapter 6 for a discussion of MNEs and international capital markets.)

Recognizing these requirements, many industrialized countries have imposed local content rules and have set up technology promotion programs that encourage companies to implement strong local commitments. Such rules have decreased penetration of key sectors in several European countries by Japanese exports, and have forced U.S. and Japanese companies to adopt more locally oriented production strategies as a condition of market access. Surely there must be some balance or compromise that can be reached between maximizing efficiency at the level of the firm, and the needs of host governments to ensure that firms act in ways that contribute to national well-being.

Although companies and governments may pursue different objectives, the interests of MNEs and those of nations are not necessarily incompatible. Governments can and do offer inducements or impose sanctions that encourage MNEs to act in ways that further the national interest. And companies, for their part, can adjust their approach, commitment, and investments to meet local economic and political conditions, particularly if constraints and opportunities are applied fairly and uniformly.

Problems occur when the rules of different nations that affect MNE behavior diverge from one another, or when one nation favors MNEs based in its own territory, or discriminates against the products and affiliates of foreign-based firms, and the target country does not. Solutions may lie

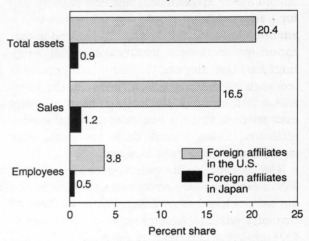

Figure 1-1—Percent Shares of Employment, Sales, and Total Assets of Foreign Affiliates in the United States and Japan, 1989

SOURCE: Ministry of International Trade (MITI), "Measures for Promoting Foreign Direct Investment in Japan," January 1992, chart 6; as taken from MITI, "Survey of Foreign Affiliates in Japan"; Ministry of Finance (MoF), "Corporate Business Statistical Annual Report"; U.S. Department of Commerce, *Survey of Current Business*.

either in no discrimination or in reciprocal and equal discrimination. **The key is to keep the system of MNE business from interacting with the system of nation states in ways that create unfair advantages for some national economies at the expense of others or, in the extreme, set one nation against another.** Despite recent progress at the 1993 G-7 Economic Summit, obstacles to harmonizing trade and investment regimes remain substantial.

The present system of international trade and investment can be characterized as one in which the interests of nations and MNEs have been drawn too tightly (as in Japan) or, conversely, have been allowed to drift too far apart (the U.S. case). This is the result of basic asymmetries, both in the different national systems of policy that regulate trade and investment, and in the organization of business (and business practice) within the Triad of modern industrial economies. **Ultimately, widely divergent policy systems and business practices among trading nations may disrupt the international economy.**

At one extreme, the United States has permitted and encouraged foreign companies to take advantage of extraordinary access to its markets for trade and investment purposes. Even in the automobile sector, for example, where voluntary export restraints were employed in the 1980s to limit Japanese imports, the United States permitted unfettered foreign direct investment (FDI), which helped the Japanese automakers capture even more of the U.S. car market. Thus, foreign affiliates in the United States account for a significant share of total U.S. assets, sales and, to a lesser extent, employment (see figure 1-1). In 1992, Japan's direct investment position in the United States reached $96.7 billion, exceeding that of any other nation.[2] (Chapter 3 discusses FDI and the special case of Japan.)

Moreover, the United States has constrained the cooperation of competing U.S. companies through pervasive antitrust legislation and litigation. For much of the post-World War II period, the United States championed the system of free and open trade, and to that end, tolerated some unfair trade practices of both developing and industrialized nations.[3] **Foreign-based MNEs, operating from a protected home base, have amassed capital and technology sufficient to mount highly sophisticated and successful assaults on key elements of important American industrial sectors and markets, such as** automobiles, machine tools, semiconductors, and consumer electronics. At the same time, they have also contributed to the quality and low cost of goods available in the United States. In the automobile sector, there is no doubt that the competitive challenge of Japanese auto companies has forced improvements in product quality and production efficiency at GM, Ford, and Chrysler.

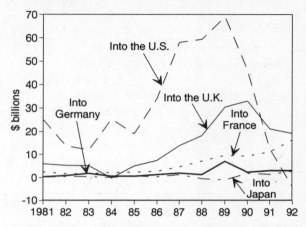

Figure 1-2—Inward Flows of Foreign Direct Investment into Selected Countries, 1981-1992

NOTE: Data are calculated on historical cost basis and are in nominal dollars. Reinvested earnings were not included in statistics for France, Germany, and Japan. Differences in data and calculation may account for discrepancies between OECD and Department of Commerce statistics.

SOURCE: Organization for Economic Cooperation and Development (OECD), *International Direct Investment Policies and Trends in the 1980s* (Paris, 1992), p. 15, table 3; OECD, *Financial Market Trends*, June 1993, p. 44, table 1.

At the other extreme, Japan has restricted foreign investment and imports, and has permitted foreign MNEs limited access to its markets, typically only through joint ventures with Japanese partners.[4] (See figure 1-2 for a comparison of FDI flows into Japan and several other Organization for Economic Cooperation and Development (OECD) countries, and figure 1-3 for a comparison of the domestic sales of foreign affiliates in the same countries.) Proprietary technology has often been extracted as a condition of market access. As a prominent Japanese industrialist wrote in 1993, **"Japan has much to do to open its domestic market . . . Although overt protectionism has been curbed, it is clear that many**

---

[2] U.S. Department of Commerce, Bureau of Economic Analysis, "U.S. Net Investment Position, 1992," press release, June 30, 1993, p. 8 and table 3. See fig. 3-3 in ch. 3 of this report.

[3] For a survey of foreign trade barriers, see Office of the United States Trade Representative, *1993 Trade Estimate Report on Foreign Trade Barriers*, Mar. 31, 1993.

[4] For a description of unfair trade practices directed toward Japan, see Industrial Structure Council, Uruguay Round Committee, Subcommittee on Unfair Trade Policies and Measures, *Report on Unfair Trade Policies by Major Trading Partners*, May 11, 1993. The Industrial Structure Council is the official advisory body to the Japanese Minister of International Trade and Industry.

Figure 1-3—Foreign Affiliates' Share of Domestic Sales in Selected Countries, 1986

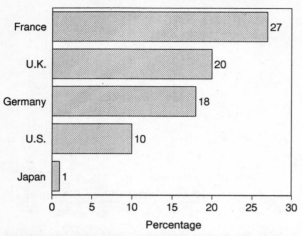

SOURCE: C. Fred Bergsten and Marcus Noland, *Reconcilable Differences? United States-Japan Economic Conflict* (Washington DC: Institute for International Economics), 1992, p. 66, table 3.3.

foreign products still have trouble with entry into and distribution in the Japanese market.''[5] Foreigners have often found it extremely difficult to invest in Japan, whereas Japanese investors have found many opportunities abroad. (See figure 1-4, which shows the trends in the position of inward and outward Japanese foreign direct investment, and figure 1-5, which offers a comparison of inward and outward direct investment in selected countries on a per capita basis.) In Japan, then, the conception of national interest is tightly coupled to preserving market and investment opportunities for Japanese-based companies, although in recent years, ''overt protectionism'' has played a less important role than nontariff and structural barriers to foreign products and investment.

The policy questions turn on two issues: 1) how to achieve a rough balance between the needs of MNEs to achieve global efficiency on the one hand, and the need of nations to retain technical and industrial competitiveness on the other; and 2) the exact mechanisms to be deployed for the distribution of advanced R&D and manufacturing capabilities among competing economies.

Greater coordination among the advanced industrial nations is probably required to harmonize the rules of business and of trade and foreign investment. Until that can be accomplished, however, Congress may wish to consider a range of policy instruments based on the notion of specific reciprocity. Such policies could facilitate the transition to a more global and internationally consistent set of rules for the conduct of international business. (Specific reciprocity is addressed in the Policy Discussion section at the end of this chapter.)

BACKGROUND AND ADDITIONAL CONSIDERATIONS

As technology and industrial power diffuse around the globe, fewer of the largest MNEs (as ranked by sales) are based in the United States (see figure 1-6). Since the late 1960s, U.S.-based companies have dropped steadily from the list of the 500 largest firms, at a rate of about 6 firms per year or about 150 firms altogether. They have been displaced largely by Japanese firms. During the same period, however, the number of European-based MNEs on the list increased moderately, and in 1991 edged past the number of U.S. firms. The aggregate sales of U.S.-based companies on the list were also exceeded in 1991 by the Europeans, and competition from the Japanese companies continued to escalate (see figure 1-7).

Foreign MNEs, primarily based in Japan and Europe, have thoroughly penetrated most sectors of the U.S. economy, putting pressure on indigenous firms, acquiring some, weakening many, and forcing others to become more efficient or exit the competition. This pattern is reminiscent of the extension of U.S.-based firms to European markets in the 1960s. Nevertheless, sustained concern has focused on the activities of Japanese-based MNEs in the United States, ranging from

---

[5] Akio Morita, ''Toward a New World Economic Order,'' *The Atlantic Monthly*, June 1993, pp. 90, 96.

Figure 1-4—Japanese Direct Investment Position Abroad and Foreign Direct Investment Position in Japan, 1980-1992

NOTES: Data are calculated on a historical cost basis and are not adjusted for inflation. Amounts for 1992 are Bank of Japan estimates.

SOURCE: MITI, "Measures for Promoting Foreign Direct Investment in Japan," January 1992, charts 1 and 3; Bank of Japan, *Balance of Monthly Payments*, March 1993.

Japanese investment in small, high-technology start-ups and university research programs, to the domination of whole industries by Japanese-based MNEs (see chapter 4). While U.S. firms are major players in most industries in Europe, they have, with some important exceptions, faced significant barriers to investing and gaining market share in Japan.

The competitiveness of U.S.-based MNEs is not necessarily the principal concern. Many analysts contend that the issue of national ownership or origin of firms is less important than the contributions that all firms, foreign and domestic, make to a nation's economy. In this view, governments should be concerned with funding basic research, educating a skilled workforce, improving infrastructure, and providing a stable fiscal and monetary environment attractive to MNEs. In practice, however, governments have structured trade, investment, financial, monetary, and industrial policies to benefit their economies and to create advantages for their firms, both at home and abroad.

This has led to broad asymmetries and increasing divergence in the national policy regimes of Europe, the United States, and Japan that, taken

together, constitute the rules of the game for the conduct of multinational business. In the area of foreign direct investment, to cite one example, the United States and Britain typically have applied free market principles to the inward and outward flow of investment capital. The other major trading nations, particularly Japan, have imposed a variety of restrictions and conditions on FDI. While France and Italy have consistently applied limitations, Japanese restrictions appear to be qualitatively different and even structural in character.

MNEs, for their part, have responded to asymmetries in market access or ease of investment by configuring their operations differently, for example, by engaging in minority joint ventures or licensing technology and marketing rights to indigenous firms in more exclusive national markets. But asymmetries in the rules of multinational business have not affected all firms to the same degree. MNEs based in Japan, for example, enjoy easy access to both Japanese and American markets, but many U.S.-based MNEs, while facing barriers in Japan, must still battle Japanese and European competition for market share in the United States. Such imbalances in market access

Figure 1-5—Per Capita Inward and Outward Direct Investment Position in Selected Countries, 1990

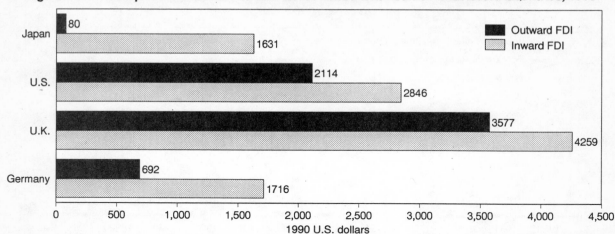

SOURCE: MITI, "Measures for Promoting Foreign Direct Investment in Japan," January 1992, charts 4; MITI, "Measures for Promoting Foreign Direct Investment in Japan," Sept. - Dec. 1992, charts 1.2 and 2.2; as taken from Bank of Japan, *Balance of Monthly Payments*; U.S. Department of Commerce, *Survey of Current Business*; Bank of England, *Quarterly Bulletin*; Deutsche Bundesbank, *Monthly Report*.

and in national treatment are partially reflected in the stubborn U.S. trade deficit with Japan, which has persisted despite substantial devaluation of the dollar against the yen. The concern is that in some nations, sanctuary markets have been preserved for indigenous firms, and that the participation of foreign-based companies, far from being free and open, has been structured to serve the host government's conception of the national interest.

The question arises: Why has the United States tolerated asymmetries in market access and investment with some of its trading partners, when such practices create disadvantages for U.S.-based MNEs and, in the long term, can inflict damage on important sectors of the U.S. economy and technology base? The answer is part history and part ideology, and goes beyond the question of MNEs. In the immediate post-World War II decades, the U.S. economy and technology base dominated the world. The United States championed the system of free and open international trade, in large measure by opening its own economy to imports and foreign investment, even if nations with less developed economies did not reciprocate. Since many companies in Europe and Japan could not have withstood head-to-head

competition with U.S.-based MNEs, foreign countries with recovering economies took steps to protect and subsidize infant industries, establish trade barriers, and regulate FDI.

Policymakers in the United States tended to view these developments as necessary for the recovery of the war-torn European and Asian economies, and for the establishment and maintenance of a global trading system that could support an increasing gross domestic product (GDP) and standard of living in both advanced and developing nations. For over three decades, the Bretton Woods system generally increased the wealth of the advanced industrial nations, and enabled remarkable economic progress among newly industrialized countries.

But since the early 1970s, the technology assets and industrial power of Japan, and to a lesser extent Europe, have grown to challenge and even surpass the United States in many areas. During the 1980s, the commitment to free and open trade, and the fear of igniting trade wars or a global recession, limited U.S. policy initiatives to a patchwork of ad hoc, protectionist policies. These were often designed to aid U.S. firms in industries like steel, textiles, automobiles, and machine tools, and culminated in the Super 301 provisions

Figure 1-6—World's 500 Largest Firms by Region of Origin, 1966-1991

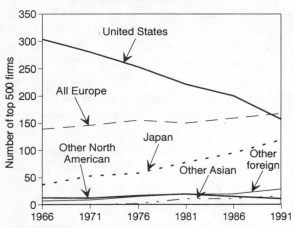

NOTE: Firms are ranked by sales as listed in the International Fortune 500. Some analysts suggest that this figure would be less dramatic if adjusted for exchange rate fluctuations.

SOURCE: OTA database compiled from annual reports, Fortune 500 International, and Standard and Poor's Register.

Figure 1-7—Sales of World's 500 Largest Firms by Region of Origin, 1966-1991

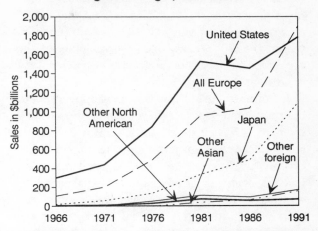

NOTE: Sales are calculated in nominal dollars. Some analysts suggest that this figure would be less dramatic if adjusted for exchange rate fluctuations.

SOURCE: OTA database compiled from annual reports, Fortune 500 International, and Standard and Poor's Register.

of the Omnibus Trade and Competitiveness Act of 1988.[6] Despite these measures, for most of the 1980s, the U.S. manufacturing base continued to erode and the U.S. standard of living slipped, both in absolute terms and relative to our major trading partners.[7]

Concern about MNEs is heightened when firms based in a single nation or region appear to win more than their expected or fair share of the global economy, and the suspicion persists that nationalist policies helped them to do so. In the late 1960s, for example, European journalists and policymakers warned that if the "invasion" of Europe by American MNEs was not stemmed, Europe would become a subsidiary, with industrial and technological development directed by MNEs based in the United States. In words echoed in recent

discussions of Japanese investment in the United States, one journalist described the "assault" in Europe by U.S.-based MNEs: "Most striking of all is the strategic character of American industrial penetration. One by one, U.S. corporations capture those sectors of the economy most technologically advanced, most adaptable to change, and with the highest growth rates."[8]

This view helped mobilize government policies intended to foster indigenous European technology development and industrial competitiveness. Most of the major industrial powers of Europe created national champions, protected their infant industries, restricted inward FDI, sponsored government-funded R&D programs, and subsidized essential industries. This pattern continues within the European Community (EC),

---

[6] Super 301 authorized the U.S. Trade Representative to retaliate against trading partners for persistent unfair trading practices, but has now lapsed due to sunset provisions in the 1988 legislation.

[7] On the erosion of the U.S. manufacturing base, see U.S. Congress, Office of Technology Assessment, *Making Things Better: Competing in Manufacturing*, OTA-ITE-443 (Washington, DC: U.S. Government Printing Office, February 1990); and on the relative decline of the U.S. economy, see U.S. Congress, Office of Technology Assessment, *Competing Economies: America, Europe, and the Pacific Rim*, OTA-ITE-498 (Washington, DC: U.S. Government Printing Office, October 1991).

[8] Jean-Jacques Servan-Schreiber, *The American Challenge* (New York, NY: Anthenium, 1968), p. 12.

with the implementation of EC directives that extend R&D subsidies and preferential government procurement to EC firms. That these policies encourage firms to establish production within the EC is supported by evidence of the continued high rate of FDI, despite recessionary conditions.[9]

In contrast, the U.S. Government appears not to have articulated a strategic concept of the national interest. It has, instead, continued to define the national interest in terms of the more global objective of promoting free and open trade and investment among the advanced industrial nations—and has deviated from these principles only under extreme pressure from special interests. As the U.S. technological and industrial lead diminishes relative to its trading partners, this approach is proving more difficult to sustain.

The interests of all nations ought to be fairly straightforward—quality jobs, a rising standard of living, technology and industrial development, ensured rights of workers and consumers, and a high-quality environment at home and globally. But the interests of nations diverge when there is a zero-sum economic game; for example, during a sustained global recession, or when one or more advanced industrial nations adopts a mercantilist perspective on world trade. They can also diverge over time when differences in the policy systems of disparate nations or regions become too extreme, when the principle of national treatment is applied by some states and not by others, and when MNEs doing business in one country can operate with considerably more latitude than in other countries.

As compared to nations, the interests of MNEs are far more situation-oriented and linked to opportunity. The specifics differ from industry to industry and from firm to firm within particular sectors. Because of their internal flexibility and ability to adapt to external circumstances, MNEs can reconfigure their operations and assets to meet the requirements of markets and host governments around the world. Increasingly they seek skilled labor, intellectual resources, finished components, capital, and physical infrastructure in different national jurisdictions. In this sense, they are well-equipped to deal with the various asymmetries among the policy regimes of Europe, Japan, and the United States. What they fear most is unpredictable change, change that can take the form of shifting market factors, government regulation, or labor relations—such as the violent labor upheavals in South Korea in 1988 and 1989. Such changes can force MNEs to abandon established strategies, and thereby internalize the costs of adjustment, either as direct financial losses or as lost opportunities. Firms desire what only nations can provide: a stable and predictable political and economic environment conducive to international business.

In specific cases, the interests of MNEs and nations may diverge sharply. From a firm's perspective, moving assets abroad may be necessary to meet competition that has access to lower-wage labor, less onerous taxes, government support for R&D, or even a protected home market. But from a policy perspective, the firm may represent part or all of a key national asset. Because of their ability to adjust to a wide range of external factors, many MNEs can play one national political jurisdiction off against another. Their motivation to do so may increase as global competition heats up and once-proprietary technologies become widely diffused around the world.

Some analysts believe that globalization of MNEs may collectively exert a steady downward pressure on wages, environmental standards, health and safety, and worker benefits. Some are concerned about the erosion of democratic principles, as decisions made in corporate boardrooms and among trade negotiators increasingly affect

---

[9] FDI flows into the EC from non-EC countries were approximately $86 billion in 1990, $67 billion in 1991, and $70 billion in 1992 (estimate). Bank for International Settlements, *63rd Annual Report*, 1993.

workers and consumers around the world.[10] This scenario echoes the more parochial conditions of 19th century America, when one state lost major firms or whole industries to another state. The difference today is that the winners might not reside in the United States.

While the social impact of MNEs is not the focus of this study, policymakers are finding that the debate increasingly extends beyond narrow questions of economic advantage. As the European nations are now discovering, the dynamics of cost competition in the global economy can set up a basic and continuing conflict with the social standards long advocated by governments in industrial societies. These include worker benefits, environmental quality, and progressive tax codes, among others. To the extent that global finance and production function in a relatively unregulated environment, this conflict may be inescapable, not just for the United States but for competitor nations as well. The Office of Technology Assessment (OTA) has recently addressed these issues with regard to the proposed North American Free Trade Agreement.[11]

The structure of multinational industry is undergoing a transformation, and it is transforming national economies with it. The change is characterized by globalization of markets and some firms, widespread excess capacity in mature industries, a tendency toward consolidation in many (but not all) sectors, deepening international cooperation and competition among firms, decreasing product-cycle times, and rapidly escalating costs of technology development. The potential consequences of these changes are unclear. Nevertheless, many MNEs appear to be moving toward a more widely distributed pattern of sourcing, foreign investment, and strategic alliances with other firms. (See chapter 5 for an overview of international strategic alliances.)

Their reasons are complex: some seek to optimize global resources, some to hedge against unfavorable national policies; others hope to reduce technical, financial, and market risks. Responding to these changes presents enormous challenges both to nations and to companies. **The principal concern is that MNEs are too important to national and global well-being to have this process proceed in a totally ad hoc manner, and that doing so could lead to economic dislocation and heavy costs of adjustment for nations and companies alike.**

ABOUT THIS REPORT

This report is the first publication of OTA's assessment of Multinational Firms and the U.S. Technology Base. It was requested by the Senate Committee on Commerce, Science, and Transportation and the Senate Committee on Banking, Housing, and Urban Affairs. The major findings of this report are presented immediately following this section. Although the findings suggest a number of policy options, this chapter does not propose specific policies for congressional consideration, but instead it presents a framework for a discussion of new and largely untried approaches to international trade and investment. The final report of this project, to be published in 1994, will propose specific policy options in the context of particular industries.

The goal of this assessment is not to formulate a series of unilateral national regulations, although that course should not be dismissed out of hand, but to suggest a framework for concerted multilateral action to construct a system of international commerce—one that constrains mercantilism, balances interests among nations and between nations and firms, and facilitates business conditions conducive to international commerce. Fundamental to such a system is the

---

[10] William Greider, *Who Will Tell the People: The Betrayal of American Democracy* (New York, NY: Simon & Schuster, 1992), pp. 377-378.

[11] U.S. Congress, Office of Technology Assessment, *U.S.-Mexico Trade: Pulling Apart or Pulling Together?*, ITE-545 (Washington, DC: U.S. Government Printing Office, October 1992).

maintenance of a high standard of living in the industrialized world and the continued improvement of less developed economies. This would have to be accomplished in the context of the protection of the rights of labor and convergence toward higher environmental standards throughout the world.

The problems besetting the system of international business and trade are exceedingly complex. The structure of multinational industry is evolving far more rapidly than the rules that govern its conduct. And, as already stated, the policy approaches of major industrialized nations have diverged significantly in ways that may ultimately undermine the post-World War II system of international trade and investment. With these thoughts in mind, this first report should be read as a primer, which develops a common understanding around which future policy issues and choices can be articulated.

The body of the report, chapters 2 through 6, describes and analyzes some of these issues, starting with an overview of the way in which multinational industry is organized and has developed over the past 25 years (ch. 2). Chapter 3 provides a comparative framework upon which to evaluate worldwide foreign direct investment. The chapter analyzes the critical policy differences between the United States, Japan, and the European Community, as well as the costs and benefits of the current U.S. policy of national treatment. The difficulties presented to foreign firms trying to invest in Japan are provided as a special case. Chapter 4 concentrates on the activities of Japanese MNEs in the United States—activities that have been the focus of discussion and congressional debate over the past several years. Chapter 5 addresses the growth of

strategic international business alliances, and their implications for the evolution and regulation of multinational commerce. The final chapter traces the emergence of global capital markets during the past two decades and examines some of the principal implications for MNEs and policymakers. Each of the chapters begins with a brief summary that is followed, when appropriate, by the major findings of the particular chapter.

This report concentrates on large-scale MNEs, many of which appear on the Fortune 500 international list, although it does not exclude analysis of smaller companies with overseas subsidiaries. The OTA database, on which several of the tables and figures rely, is comprised of basic statistics on the 500 largest MNEs in the world.[12] The emphasis on large MNEs stems from their ability to marshal tremendous economic, technological, and political resources. Some of these companies can mobilize technology on a scale matched by only a few nations. Individually, some MNEs are powerful enough to affect significantly the balance of trade among nations in particular industries.

The report also concentrates on manufacturing MNEs, although it does not exclude services or other sectors of international commerce.[13] This is due to the critical linkages among technology development, advanced manufacturing, and the competitiveness of nations, as well as the established concerns about the relative decline of manufacturing in the United States.[14] It is also partly in response to concerns expressed about manufacturing by the congressional committees that requested this assessment. This report draws extensively on the analysis and findings of previous OTA work, particularly on *Competing Economies*, which addressed America's com-

---

[12] The database, which contains about 40,000 data points, was drawn from three sources: statistics published from 1966 through 1991 in the International Fortune 500 List; data purchased from Standard & Poors; and data culled from over 500 annual reports of major corporations.

[13] For an overview of the services sector, see U.S. Congress, Office of Technology Assessment, *International Competition in Services*, OTA-ITE-328 (Washington, DC: U.S. Government Printing Office, July 1987).

[14] For more detail on problems associated with manufacturing in the United States, see *Making Things Better*, op. cit., footnote 7.

[15] *Competing Economies*, op. cit., footnote 7.

petitiveness problems as compared with Japan and the European Community.[15]

MAJOR FINDINGS

Finding 1:

The modern MNE is a highly flexible and adaptable form of business organization. It can take many different forms (see table 1-1). MNEs configure and reconfigure their operations to meet diverse requirements, including those imposed by different governments, or to take advantage of opportunities and inducements offered to them by governments.

Finding 2:

Technology differences have decreased among competing firms since the late 1960s. The absolute technology superiority of an IBM, AT&T, or Boeing has been offset by the rise of capable competitors worldwide. The traditional U.S. advantages of privileged access to broad, deep, and liquid capital markets, as well as large economies of scale and scope, have similarly leveled off. In this context, the policies and actions of governments may be decisive in determining which MNEs prosper in global competition. At a minimum, they will influence both which competitors will succeed and where state-of-the-art technology development and manufacturing take place.

Finding 3:

The structure of the MNE system is changing rapidly. Excess capacity and increasing competition are leading to consolidation and shakeout in many global industries such as consumer electronics, automobiles, pharmaceuticals, and steel. A coherent system of international trade, investment, and monetary polices has not emerged to meet the challenges of the global economy.

Finding 4:

Instead, broad asymmetries in the policy regimes of the major trading nations have developed—especially market access, foreign direct investment, financial, and industrial policies related to the activities of MNEs. These asymmetries, when combined with major shifts in the global economy and protectionist responses to them, contribute to increasing trade frictions and tensions in international relations.

Finding 5:

Public policies and private sector initiatives have combined to restrict foreign direct investment in some OECD nations to a level far lower than that of others. (See figure 1-8.) In Japan, for example, the ratio of outgoing to incoming FDI in 1990 was 20 to 1 as reported by Keidanren, Japan's premier business association.[16] The Japanese Government has acted both to assist domestic firms and to ensure that the domestic economy remains self-sufficient in designated industries and technologies. Some analysts suggest that the climate for FDI in Japan is improving, in part due to efforts by the Japanese Government. But the increase in FDI into Japan is moderate, and the evidence of real opportunities for foreign investors in Japan is inconclusive.[17]

Finding 6:

Governments remain influential in dealing with MNEs. The U.S. Government, however, has opted to minimize its influence over many aspects of MNE behavior in the United States. This attitude, as reflected in government policies, is in stark contrast to Japan and several EC member states. Twenty-five years ago, the United States was the center of gravity for world commerce and technology development. Today that center is slipping away, as foreign MNEs increase their penetration of U.S. markets and U.S.-based MNEs

---

[16] Keidenran Committee on International Industrial Cooperation, ''Improvement of the Investment Climate and Promotion of Foreign Direct Investment Into Japan,'' Oct. 27, 1992.

[17] See C. Fred Bergsten and Marcus Noland, *Reconcilable Differences? United States-Japan Economic Conflict* (Washington, DC: Institute for International Economics, June 1993), pp. 81-82.

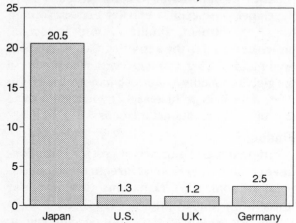

Figure 1-8—Ratio of Direct Investment Abroad to Inward Foreign Direct Investment in Selected Countries, 1990

NOTE: The ratios are derived by dividing outward by inward FDI.

SOURCE: MITI, "Measures for Promoting Foreign Direct Investment in Japan," Sept. - Dec. 1992, chart 3.

shift their attention and assets to expanding Asian markets and Europe. The U.S. Government has not developed sophisticated and flexible policy instruments or the institutional capacity to address this shift.

Finding 7:

Many MNEs are increasingly "multi" and less "national" than in the past; there appears to be a growing divergence of national needs and the needs of these MNE organizations. This finding is less true of Japanese and some European-based MNEs, where companies tend to retain a stronger national identity. In the European case, some major MNEs are owned or directly subsidized by the state. In Japan, formal government policies and informal administrative guidance—as well as the signals effectively embedded in the structure of business networks— have encouraged companies to consider and act in the national interest.

Finding 8:

The interests of U.S.-based MNEs frequently diverge from the U.S. national interest at least in part because the U.S. Government has not

specified what that interest is. In the past, the U.S. Government defined the national interest in abstract and international terms, as the maintenance of free and open trade, with the understanding that an expanding global economy means a rising standard of living for all major trading nations. Several high-ranking corporate officers told OTA that in order to survive, they are taking actions they believe are not in the national interest, including selling off key U.S. assets and placing R&D facilities and advanced manufacturing plants abroad.

Finding 9:

U.S.-based firms no longer dominate the list of the largest MNEs. This decline reflects in part the relative decline of the U.S. economy and the rise of Japan. Of the 500 largest MNEs in the world today, 157 are based in the United States, 168 in Europe, and 119 in Japan. In the late 1960s, 304 were U.S. companies, 139 were European, and 37 were Japanese. Of the 147 new foreign-based firms on the list, 82 are Japanese, 29 are European, and 36 are spread among 14 additional nations (see figures 1-6 and 1-7). The steady rise in the number of foreign-based MNEs is exerting pressure on U.S.-based companies and on the viability of important industrial sectors in the United States.

Finding 10:

The number and importance of international strategic alliances (ISAs) are increasing rapidly, but their overall significance is not well-understood. This trend is partly a result of intensifying international competition in many industries, and partly a result of dramatically escalating costs associated with technology development and bringing new products to market. There is concern that strategic alliances may weaken U.S. technology leadership in some industries by transferring technology to foreign-based firms. Conversely, some analysts cite the beneficial transfer of process technologies to the United States, particularly from Japanese-based manufacturing firms. In industries and product areas characterized by high barriers to entry and oligopolist competition, ISAs may present the potential for cartelization and even collusion among alliance partners. Until such time as egregious examples are brought to light, companies involved in strategic alliances will have to exercise a discipline of self-restraint.

Finding 11:

For an increasing number of firms, multinationalization represents a strategic response to a changing financial environment characterized by rising international capital flows, more open capital markets, expanded financing options, and volatile exchange rates. Because they have diversified operations in a number of national jurisdictions, many firms can take advantage of remaining regulatory and tax differences to hedge some of the risks created by increased financial uncertainty. Notwithstanding such strategies, productive new investments can still be undercut by the complexity of risk management in rapidly changing national and international markets.

Finding 12:

Many U.S.-based MNEs have learned to optimize their operations on a regional or global basis. It is, therefore, likely that movement toward a more managed trading system or a more highly regulated financial environment could force firms to adapt and reconfigure their operations.

Finding 13:

Japanese MNEs have used both domestic government support and the support of the keiretsu corporate ties to move aggressively into U.S. markets in numerous key sectors such as autos, semiconductors, and consumer electronics. They have drawn effectively on the technological resources of U.S. assets such as innovative small firms and world-class university research.

Figure 1-9—U.S.-European Community Direct Investment Position, 1980-1992

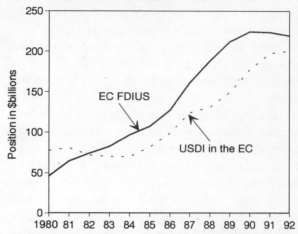

NOTES: FDIUS is foreign direct investment in the United States; USDI is United States direct investment abroad. All data are determined on a historical cost basis and are not adjusted for inflation. EC data after 1981 includes Greece and after 1986 includes Spain and Portugal.

SOURCE: U.S. Department of Commerce, *Survey of Current Business*, August issues, 1982-92; U.S. Department of Commerce, Bureau of Economic Analysis, "Net Investment Position, 1992," press release, June 30, 1993.

POLICY DISCUSSION

Asymmetry in the national policies that influence MNE trade, investment, and market access among Europe, Japan, and the United States is stark. European governments, caught in the intersection of national sovereignty and the evolving rules of the EC, often vacillate on trade and investment issues between promoting policies that tend toward closure and others that stress bilateral reciprocity.

It is difficult to generalize about a European position because countries vary in the policies they promote. French and Italian initiatives often place conditions or restrictions on trade and MNE investment, while the British seek greater access, at least in FDI. In the aggregate, however, the European direct investment position in the United States is comparable to the U.S. direct investment position in the European Community (see figure 1-9). Even though German governments have consistently advocated an open trade and investment system, they nevertheless often acquiesce to French and Italian demands for constraint of imports, foreign investment, and the activities of foreign-based MNEs. Many German firms have enjoyed the best of both worlds, as exporters and advocates of free trade on the one hand, and as beneficiaries of European protectionism on the other.

Japanese behavior bears little comparable ambivalence. Successive Japanese governments have favored or tolerated market closure in both trade and investment since 1945—to the increasing detriment of many foreign-based MNEs. In recent years, many formal legal barriers have come down, but structural ones have increased, offsetting the legal gains. Although Japan has liberalized outward FDI, joint ventures remain the principal avenue of market access for U.S.-based MNEs. These often involve minority investment positions for the U.S. partner, a significant transfer of American-origin technology to Japanese concerns and, on occasion, apparently preset limits on the market share the joint venture company can attain in Japan.[18] At the same time, some Japanese affiliates in the United States have transferred important management techniques and process-related technologies to U.S. companies. Figure 1-10 shows the disparity in the U.S.-Japan direct investment position over the past decade.

Both the structural impediments that exist in the private sector, and the reluctance of many foreign-based MNEs to commit resources to overcome de facto barriers to investment and trade, contribute to the failure of many U.S.-based MNEs to achieve a credible and commensurate presence in Japan. There is, nevertheless, growing

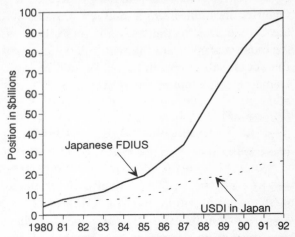

Figure 1-10—U.S.-Japan Direct Investment Position, 1980-1992

NOTES: FDIUS is foreign direct investment in the United States; USDI is United States direct investment abroad. All data are determined on a historical cost basis and are not adjusted for inflation.

SOURCE: U.S. Department of Commerce, *Survey of Current Business*, August issues, 1982-92; U.S. Department of Commerce, Bureau of Economic Analysis, "Net Investment Position, 1992," press release, June 30, 1993.

evidence that many problems faced by foreign firms in Japan could be alleviated by concerted action on the part of the Japanese Government, and there is increased interest in pursuing a more activist approach that includes quantitative goals for U.S. trade and investment with Japan, both in the U.S. Government and the private sector.[19] In a recent example, foreign-based firms achieved 20.2 percent penetration of the Japanese semiconductor market in the fourth quarter of 1992—in large measure due to administrative guidance promulgated by Japan's Ministry of International Trade and Industry (MITI).[20]

The relationship between transnational investment and trade is the subject of much recent

---

[18] Several companies told OTA that their Japanese joint venture operations have been limited to a specific market share.

[19] Council on Competitiveness, *Roadmap for Results: Trade Policy, Technology and American Competitiveness* (Washington, DC: June 1993), pp. 10-11.

[20] "Upon the conclusion of the [20 percent semiconductor] agreement, the Japanese Government attempted frantically a series of persuasions vis-à-vis the Japanese end-user industries." Yui Kimura, "Inward Foreign Direct Investment in the Semiconductor Industry in Japan," a paper presented at the Conference on Foreign Direct Investment in Japan at the School of Organization and Management, Yale University, May 14-15, 1993, p. 18. The critical role of MITI's administrative guidance in meeting the 20 percent goal by the end of 1992 was confirmed in discussions between OTA and staff of the U.S. Trade Representative.

analysis. Intrafirm trade may already exceed that of international trade among unaffiliated firms.[21] One authority calculates that, for both Japan and the United States, intrafirm trade combined with the exports of foreign-owned affiliates accounted for about half of all trade in the mid-1980s.[22] Using a more conservative measure, another authority estimates that in 1988, intrafirm trade accounted for approximately two-fifths of all imports to the United States, and for about one-third of all exports of U.S. firms.[23]

These figures indicate that, to an increasing extent, trade is closely coupled to and follows from investment by MNEs; that is, parent companies tend to supply their foreign subsidiaries and vice versa. Accordingly, if a nation closely controls or restricts the investments of foreign-based MNEs, then it also controls or restricts a significant proportion of related international trade. Conversely, a policy aimed at attracting inward FDI, if successful, would also attract more imported goods and services from foreign corporate investors. This helps to explain the simultaneous increase in Japanese direct investment in the United States and the increase in the balance of trade deficit with Japan, for example, in the automobile sector in the late 1980s.

The evidence of asymmetry in national FDI policies (documented extensively in chapter 3), and the structural importance of transnational investment to the global pattern of trade, raises the question of whether the United States might reconsider its present policy of national treat-ment.[24] Throughout the 1980s and into the 1990s trade tensions remained high, and "industrial countries resorted increasingly to non-tariff measures to protect trade-sensitive industries from foreign competition."[25] With a general propensity toward trade blocs and with the Uruguay Round unresolved, the issue of transnational investment takes on increased importance. As the foundation of intrafirm trade, such investments provide a safety valve against global market closure. The United States appears to be presented with three broad policy approaches.

▮ Three Possible Approaches

1. Unilateral National Treatment and Open Markets

The first approach, the currently employed policy of unilateral national treatment, is predicated on the principles of open markets, free trade, and unimpeded investment. The United States has tolerated defections from these principles by other nations that have employed overt industrial policies or more subtle, structural barriers to imports, trade, and investment. On the positive side, investments of foreign MNEs have helped compensate for the low savings rate in the United States, added financial liquidity, and instituted various organizational initiatives in manufacturing production. These benefits cannot be dismissed lightly.

In contrast, there is increasing evidence that a partially open system, characterized by asymmetries in national policy frameworks, may have

---

[21] John M. Stopford and Susan Strange, *Rival States, Rival Firms: Competition for World Market Shares* (Cambridge, MA: Cambridge University Press, 1991), p. 17; and *World Investment Report 1993*, op. cit., footnote 1.

[22] DeAnne Julius, *Global Companies and Public Policy: The Growing Challenge of Foreign Direct Investment* (New York, NY: Council on Foreign Relations, 1990), p. 74.

[23] Dennis J. Encarnation, *Rivals Beyond Trade: America Versus Japan in Global Competition* (Ithaca, NY: Cornell University Press, 1992), p. 28.

[24] The member states of the OECD formally subscribe to the principle of national treatment, which means that governments shall not discriminate against or in favor of any firm based on the nationality of its owners.

[25] International Monetary Fund, *Issues and Developments in International Trade Policy*, World Economic and Financial Surveys (Washington, DC: International Monetary Fund, August 1992). This report also noted that in the 1990s, ". . . protection persists in agriculture and declining sectors and has spread to newer 'high-tech' areas (aerospace, electronics, biotechnology) . . . .In this uncertain trade environment, countries are tending increasingly to address their concerns in the context of bilateral and regional trade arrangements," pp. 1-2.

significant disadvantages for U.S.-based MNEs, for technology development in the United States, and for the overall vitality of the U.S. economy. Over time, it may lead to the loss of many high value-added jobs in the United States. A primary question addressed in this report is whether the United States can afford to sustain an open, unilateral system of largely unregulated MNE access—both in trade and investment—while MNEs based in several OECD nations enjoy barriers that preclude or reduce comparable imports and investments, for example, in the automobile and electronics industries. The issue is a vital one if, as many now contend, trade and FDI are so inextricably linked in the 1990s that FDI has become "trade-creating," rather than "trade-destroying."

The competitive decline of many U.S. firms, and the increasing evidence that the U.S. economy has not benefited fully from the influx of trade and investment in the 1980s, suggests that a reconsideration of a unilateral policy of national treatment may be warranted. But the fear of advocates is that attempts by the United States to redress this imbalance could lead to a series of undesirable outcomes—for example, increased protectionism, prolonged global recession, or trade wars. Any adjustment in policy must address these legitimate concerns.

2. Enhanced Protection in the United States

The second possible approach would be to restrict foreign-based MNE investment and selected imports in the United States severely, as some appear to advocate. The introduction of wholesale sanctions against foreign direct investment in the United States (FDIUS), or an increase in protectionist trade practices, would likely generate domestic problems for the United States,

as well as problems for the effective functioning of an integrated capitalist system. Neoclassical economists call for maintaining a free trade and investment system because they fear any limitations will cause a spiraling descent into a 1930s-style depression.

Movement toward trilateral trading zones in Europe, Asia, and North America provides evidence of the allure of protectionist trade and investment practices, despite claims that reduced internal barriers are a sign of growing trade liberalization. The United States has worked diligently to avoid the growth of protectionist barriers through the GATT, although the problems of the Uruguay Round persist.

3. Specific Reciprocity

An intermediate approach embodies, more directly,[26] the notion of reciprocity in policy. Reciprocity emphasizes equivalence and contingency. Equivalence suggests a balanced exchange of benefits among nations, while contingency emphasizes conditional action to attain that balance.[27] Collectively, they might reasonably be expected to contribute to a doctrine of fairness, whose instruments are flexible and directed toward a policy of openness, but also amenable to greater closure in particular sectors if circumstances demand.

Some critics have equated reciprocity with mercantilism and protectionism.[28] Some even suggest that responding in kind to unfair foreign trade and investment practices would constitute a first step toward a descent into worldwide market closure and possibly global depression. In this view, the United States should maintain its stance as exemplar and defender of liberal trade, investment, and financial policies, even when significant damage is thereby inflicted on key sectors of

---

[26] The principle of national treatment encompasses the notion of "diffuse" reciprocity, which means that broad, unilateral action to open markets in one country should be reciprocated by other countries, although there is no direct requirement to do so.

[27] Robert Keohane, "Reciprocity in International Relations," *International Organization*, vol. 40, No. 1, winter 1986, pp. 5-8.

[28] See, for example, Jagdish N. Bhagwati and Douglas A. Irwin, "The Return of the Reciprocitarians-U.S. Trade Policy Today," *World Economy*, 10:1, June 1987, pp. 109-130; and Edmund Dell, "Of Free Trade and Reciprocity," *World Economy*, vol. 9, June 1986, pp. 125-139.

the U.S. economy and technology base. It is clear that specific reciprocity represents a distinct choice.

Specific reciprocity involves calculating a "careful equilibration of benefits" and rules that are "designed to achieve particular behavioral outcomes."[29] It may provide effective instruments for addressing the problem of asymmetry in policy—by obtaining compliance with the terms of bilateral or multilateral agreements through the implicit threat of reciprocal action. Because it can lead to the elimination of foreign barriers, it can expand free trade and investment.[30]

While reciprocity has sometimes been identified as protectionist, it may also serve as a principle of equity whose strategic instruments can promote greater free trade or comparable FDI rules. In the past, the United States has generally pursued unilateral principles in the realm of FDI that ignored transgressions by its trading partners.

Specific reciprocity emphasizes the contingent nature of the action of other countries with advanced industrial economies. It has its own advantages and disadvantages. Used prudently and conservatively, it could provide leverage for the U.S. Government to ensure access in other OECD countries for trade and investment by U.S.-based firms. Specific reciprocity has the strategic advantage that it can be applied in the context of bilateral negotiations or multilateral forums, and can carry sanctions that are unilateral in application. If used prudently, reciprocity emphasizes the capacity of the United States for flexibility, allowing appropriate policies tailored to particular market sectors. It supports more, and more varied, instruments of policy, while escaping the simplistic choice between free trade and protectionism.

Countervailing potential problems, however, could arise from implementation of a policy of specific reciprocity. Foremost is the possibility of a shift to closure rather than establishing reciprocity, if it is applied on a *quid pro quo* basis, or not employed with a degree of reserve and acumen. Threats of protectionism might, therefore, escalate in the absence of restraint and diplomacy. Indeed, reciprocity may often call for a less assertive tone, but more consultative forms of coordinated management between the U.S. Government and its major trading partners. Specific reciprocity requires competent management and effective diplomacy, but may present the basis for a constructive approach.

---

[29] Stephen D. Krasner, "Trade Conflicts and the Common Defense: The United States and Japan," *Political Science Quarterly*, vol. 5, 1986, p. 788.

[30] See, for example, Beth V. Yarborough and Robert M. Yarborough, "Reciprocity, Bilateralism, and 'Economic Hostages': Self-Enforcing Agreements in International Trade," *International Studies Quarterly*, (1986), 30, pp. 7-21, especially p. 19. Keohane, op. cit., footnote 27, discusses this possibility in more general terms, on p. 27.

Multinational Industry and National Differences | 2

This chapter examines the structure of multinational industry and how differences in the policies of national governments have affected that structure. It finds that differences in government policy and corporate behavior among nations may have broad implications for national sovereignty, for standards of living in the United States and other countries, and for international standards vis-à-vis wages, the environment, and workplace conditions.

This chapter is also intended as a primer for readers who may not have extensive experience with or knowledge of multinational enterprises (MNEs). Readers familiar with the complexities of MNEs and the policy environments in which they operate may wish to proceed to later chapters.

The development of the multinational enterprise is a logical extension of the rise of the modern industrial corporation in the 19th century. At first, businesses pursued scale and scope within their domestic markets. However, competition at home, opportunities abroad, the need to reduce financial and other risks, and foreign barriers to imports led increasing numbers of firms to establish and then expand overseas operations. These facilities have become important conduits for trade, investment, and technology flows.

At the same time, this expansion of business activity has brought companies and nations into ever more direct competition. As technology and management practices diffuse, workers in the Organization for Economic Cooperation and Development (OECD) countries increasingly find themselves in direct competition with one another, and with workers who are willing to accept lower wages, benefits, and workplace health and safety conditions. As they capitalize on these differences, multinationals can inadvertently become vehicles for declining standards.

As the structure and behavior of the world's leading industrial firms has changed, so too have the nations represented in their ranks. In the early 1960s, most MNEs were based in the United States. In 1966, for example, 61 percent of the world's largest companies were based here. By comparison, in 1991 firms based in the United States accounted for only 31 percent of these companies. Since the early 1970s, the number of large MNEs based in Europe, Japan, and South Korea has increased dramatically.

But the decline in dominance of U.S.-based MNEs is not due solely to impersonal market forces in other regions of the world. Many national governments actively intervene through such mechanisms as domestic content restrictions and tariffs to ensure that high value-added activities are conducted within their national boundaries. Indeed, many foreign governments systematically favor national champions and actively discriminate against foreign firms. Firms based in protected markets can use profits they might otherwise have been unable to achieve, along with government support, to underwrite expansion abroad and/or to exclude firms based abroad from their key domestic markets. Alternatively, if uncompetitive in technology, cost, or other factors, they can use their privileged position to forestall exit from the industry.

Taking into account such host government pressures and the traditional reluctance of the U.S. Government to intervene on their behalf, some U.S.-based companies have transferred operations and sourced abroad more than they otherwise might have. In the absence of effective government policies to the contrary, many U.S.-based firms can be expected to continue to respond to host government pressures in ways that may not contribute to their long-term interests and the strength of the U.S. economy and technology base.

The first section of this chapter describes what a multinational enterprise is and considers why a firm's managers might decide to locate distribution and production operations in foreign markets. Different corporate forms that function as de facto MNEs, such as strategic alliances and risk-sharing partnerships, are described. A typology of MNEs is offered, with attempts to explain the implications for national policy and international business of each type of enterprise identified.

In the second section, national differences among firms are analyzed, with the conclusion that government policy regimes strongly influence the behavior of their own national firms as well as foreign firms attempting to enter or conduct business in their national markets. The chapter finds that the dominance of U.S. firms among the ranks of the world's largest has diminished markedly over the past 25 years, and suggests that this is due in part to strategies that other nations deploy to enhance their domestic firms' competitiveness.

In the final section, some implications of MNE behavior are discussed. The analysis suggests ways in which MNEs can contribute to or reduce trade conflicts among nations. It addresses the influences that different kinds of MNEs exert on labor, wage, and environmental standards globally.

THE STRUCTURE OF MULTINATIONAL INDUSTRY

The development of the modern industrial corporation in the 19th century led firms to pursue economies of scale and scope.[1] Scale means the size (volume) of the production facilities. In

---

[1] See Alfred D. Chandler, Jr., *The Visible Hand: The Managerial Revolution in American Business* (Cambridge, MA: Belknap Press of Harvard University Press, 1977); Alfred D. Chandler, Jr., *Scale And Scope: The Dynamics of Industrial Capitalism* (Cambridge, MA: Belknap Press of Harvard University Press, 1990); Alfred D. Chandler, Jr., "The Enduring Logic of Industrial Success," *Harvard Business Review*, March-April 1990, pp. 130-140.

technologically advanced, capital-intensive industries, large facilities can usually manufacture less expensively than small ones because fixed costs can be shared among a greater number of units. Scope refers to the ability of large facilities to use similar raw, semifinished materials and intermediate production processes to make a range of different products.

Much of the cost advantage of large production facilities depends on a high rate of capacity utilization that enables investments and other fixed costs to be spread over a large number of units. To ensure a sufficient volume of sales, firms invest in national and international marketing and distribution organizations. Firms also invest in professional management to coordinate and monitor their operations, and to allocate resources. Modern management information systems and organizational design can drastically reduce the resources devoted to coordination and monitoring by the firm, providing potential advantages in response time and cost.

■ Why Firms Establish Foreign Operations

Initially, most firms serve their overseas and domestic customers from a single domestic production and research and development (R&D) base.[2] In a nearly perfectly competitive world, with no barriers to entry and very low transportation costs, it would be more attractive to expand existing facilities rather than establish new plants abroad. In the real world, however, transportation costs are often substantial, currency values fluctuate, and governments actively intervene to influence market outcomes. In addition, competitors seek to gain market power—for example, by exploiting advantages of scale and scope, product differentiation, political influence, government financial support, strategic alliances among two or more companies, and differential pricing.

A firm may establish overseas operations to attract local capital, limit risk from currency fluctuations, serve its foreign customers, or reduce the manufacturing costs of products intended for its domestic customers. Such an action can take place in response to competitive pressures, as a means of reducing risk or enhancing profitability, and as a direct result of government policies intended to force firms to locate part of their value-added chain within the host country.

Overseas production and R&D operations can enhance a firm's efficiency if they are located in a region particularly strong in a desired capability. Locating facilities in areas with low-cost labor, energy, or other inputs may significantly reduce costs.[3] In some cases, overseas manufacturing can significantly reduce transportation and inventory costs of finished products. Local operations may help a firm adjust its products or services to meet distinctive differences in consumer taste, as well as regulatory or other requirements.[4]

Overseas operations can facilitate the penetration of markets controlled by entrenched firms. They can also be used to rapidly develop new markets and preempt foreign or local competition. Overseas operations may be used to deny opposing companies a protected domestic base from which to subsidize an export drive into key markets in the United States or elsewhere.

Host government policies often influence both the decision to establish overseas facilities and their nature. Governments and businesses engage in dynamic and iterative relationships. Govern-

---

[2] Christos N. Pitelis and Roger Sugden, *The Nature of the Transnational Firm* (London: Routledge, 1991).

[3] For example, the assembly of automobile wiring harnesses and windshield wiper systems is very labor-intensive. U.S. tariffs on completed assemblies are low. Not surprisingly, such work has migrated to low-labor cost areas such as Mexico. U.S. Congress, Office Of Technology Assessment, *U.S.-Mexico Trade: Pulling Together or Pulling Apart?*, ITE-545 (Washington, DC: U.S. Government Printing Office, October 1992), p. 147.

[4] Michael Porter, ''The Competitive Advantage of Nations,'' *Harvard Business Review*, March-April 1990, pp. 73-93.

ments often seek to induce firms to transfer into the country more of the value-added chain than the domestic market would otherwise support, while firms seek to shape and respond to government policies in the most cost-effective manner.

Government-imposed barriers to entry, such as tariffs and local content requirements, provide firms the opportunity to participate in protected markets. If the market is large enough, such policies can lead firms to set up facilities, transfer technologies to local suppliers and competitors, and establish joint ventures that would otherwise not have taken place.

As discussed in box 2-A, companies consider a wide variety of issues when adding or rationalizing capacity. Some countries impose trade-balancing requirements as part of the price for participating in a protected market. A firm may be willing to build a product in a potentially lucrative protected market, and export it to its home market to meet trade-balancing laws—even if the cost of supplying the product to the firm's domestic market is increased. For example, if transportation, inventory, and investment costs are taken into account, U.S. automobile manufacturers building for U.S. markets often find it more expensive to manufacture in Mexico than in the United States. However, to meet the requirements of the Mexican Auto Decrees and thereby participate in Mexico's profitable protected market, they export vehicles from Mexico to the United States, even when this is more costly.[5]

Previous expenditures can lock in a firm, reducing its ability to respond to change. Industries with large capital investments and low profit margins are more susceptible to lock-in than those with high margins and low capital commitments. Plant and equipment that become rapidly obsolete can be abandoned more readily than those with a long productive life. Accordingly, the automobile

industry is more locked in by its investments than the semiconductor industry.

▌ Strategic Alliances and Risk-Sharing Partnerships

Strategic alliances and risk-sharing partnerships often are attempts by firms to expand their scale and scope. (For discussion of strategic alliances, see chapter 5.) These alliances can extend the financial, technical, and political reach of the firm. They can enhance market access, distribution networks, and manufacturing capabilities, or impose market discipline. They can speed products to market, reduce financial and technological risk, lower investment requirements, add or streamline capacity, and lower costs. Such alliances can increase flexibility by expanding the boundaries of the firm. In some circumstances, they can facilitate the development of legal cartels or serve as vehicles for tacit or explicit collusion to fix prices or allocate markets.

The strategic alliance formed by IBM, Siemens, and Toshiba, for the design of dynamic random access memory semiconductors (DRAMS), represents an alliance to reduce joint costs among three large powerful MNEs in a highly competitive industry. The industry is characterized by intense competition, short product lifecycles, escalating R&D and manufacturing investments, and prices that fall rapidly over time. Profitability depends upon getting to market before price erosion starts and then cutting costs faster than the price erodes. At the same time, costly investments are necessary to expand capacity fast enough to capture sufficient market share to maintain the cycle. Although demanding and expensive, the technology is relatively well-understood, limiting the useful life expectancy of proprietary knowledge. As a result, new firms with access to

---

[5] *U.S.-Mexico Trade*, op. cit., footnote 3.

Box 2-A—Rationalizing Production: Considerations Vary

Many observers mistakenly suggest that firms seek low labor costs to the exclusion of other considerations when either adding capacity or restructuring their operations. Firms balance many factors in reaching such decisions, including manufacturing philosophy, product quality, workforce quality and costs, transportation costs, capital costs, competitive position, market characteristics, capacity utilization, labor relations, plant corporate cultures, and the local supplier base. No single factor can be expected to dominate.

Legal and other requirements make it difficult and expensive to lay off workers in France and the Netherlands, Britain's lower wages and benefits notwithstanding.[1] Plants located in Europe, especially Britain, often have restrictive work rules and union demarcation lines that hinder productivity. British workers are often less productive because of their relatively low levels of education and training. Despite all this, Hoover recently chose to close a plant in Dijon, France and transfer the work to its plant in Scotland where excess capacity existed, labor costs were less, and the union made concessions to improve productivity in exchange for financial compensation to the workers.[2]

GM intends to transfer automobile production from a joint venture with Valmet, a Finnish Government-owned company, to its German operations. The move will increase capacity utilization in Germany and reduce transportation costs for components.[3] Hitachi has closed television assembly facilities in the United States and transferred some of the work to Mexico and Malaysia.[4] Hyundai has transferred its personal computer operations to the United States to facilitate timely product development and delivery.[5]

As these examples show, labor costs do not always outweigh other considerations. Nevertheless, firms can and do attempt to balance differences in labor and social costs, workplace practices, and the regulatory environment. The greater the competition, the more interested the firm will be in reducing costs. In the absence of transnational standards, regulatory bodies and enforcement, such activities, in aggregate, are not unlikely to exert downward pressure on wages, benefits, and workplace practices that are unrelated to plant efficiency.

[1] This discussion is based on: Robert Taylor, "Hoover Unveils Tough Deal at Glasgow Plant," *Financial Times*, Jan. 26, 1993, p. 6; Robert Taylor, "Hoover Workers Get Lump Sum for Deal," *Financial Times*, Feb. 3, 1993, p. 9; David Goodhart, "Social Dumping: Hardly an Open and Shut Case," *Financial Times*, Feb. 4, 1993, p. 2; David Buchan, "French Promise to Make Hoover Pay Dear," *Financial Times*, Feb. 4, 1993, p. 2; and Robert Taylor, "Dijon Cleans Up Scottish Jobs in Reversal of Hoover Move," *Financial Times*, Feb. 5, 1993, p. 12.

[2] To ensure efficient operation of the Glasgow plant, Hoover was forced to compensate its workers for the abandonment of restrictive work rules, demarcation lines, and a reduction in the premium rate paid to third shift workers. These payments ranged between 2,650 and 3,150 pounds per worker. See: Taylor, "Hoover Workers Get Lump Sum for Deal," op. cit., footnote 1.

[3] Kevin Done, "GM Ends Finnish Production," *Financial Times*, Jan. 29, 1993, p. 14.

[4] "Company News: Hitachi Closing California Plant," *The New York Times*, Jan. 15, 1992, p. D4.

[5] John Markoff, "Hyundai to Move Its PC Unit to U.S.," *The New York Times*, Apr. 20, 1992, p. D3.

substantial financial resources are still able to enter, even as unprofitable competitors depart.[6]

The IBM-Siemens-Toshiba alliance appears to provide its members with important advantages, including reduced financial and technological risk, lower individual firm R&D and investment costs, a quicker development cycle, and enhanced profitability. The coalition may provide the possibility of at least tacit market discipline.

[6] Many new and some existing semiconductor producers receive considerable financial support from their national governments. Their pursuit of market share at the expense of short-term profits has a depressing effect on prices, lowering the profitability of other participants. Poor profitability can drive out participants dependent on the private sector for capital.

Operational control of development is vested with IBM, probably the most capable player, reducing technological risk for the participants. Three firms pooling their investment and resources in an alliance with clear operational control and lines of responsibility should be able to develop the product more quickly than any could alone. If the venture is well-managed, the costs to each of the participants will be less than if they had proceeded alone, even if total development costs are greater.

Reduced development times make it likely that the individual member's DRAMS will get to market sooner, commanding a premium prior to the entry of new competitors. Early production should give important cost advantages over later entrants, an advantage that could be accentuated if at least two of the partners share manufacturing experience, leading to faster joint cost reductions than would otherwise have been possible.

Significant cost advantages on the part of the three partners should support an aggressive campaign to add capacity. This should, therefore, reduce the incentive for competitors to add capacity ahead of demand and to initiate price warfare to gain market share. Any resulting increase in market discipline would further enhance the coalition's profitability in the product.

MULTINATIONAL FIRMS TAKE DIFFERENT FORMS

The Office of Technology Assessment (OTA) has identified six types of multinational firms. In the case of large diversified MNEs, different divisions or subsidiaries may fit into different categories. As a result, the categories are not intended to be rigid or mutually exclusive. Rather, they capture the major differences that are relevant to the development of public policy. (See also table 1-1.) The six types of MNEs may be described as:

- resource-based,
- export-oriented,
- regional,
- transnational,
- global, and
- distributed.

Resource-based firms were the earliest widespread form of MNE. They are oriented to agricultural products or the extraction and processing of natural resources, and their processing for sale in the industrialized countries. Firms set up operations where the natural resources are found and/or can be produced cheaply. Minimal processing is undertaken, generally to reduce transportation costs or to ensure quality. Oil companies, mining companies, and firms that market products that include inputs based on tropical agricultural commodities often take this form.

Export-oriented firms have their principal production operations located in their domestic market and export to other national markets, although they may have final assembly, service, support, sales, and marketing operations abroad. R&D and design activities are usually concentrated in the domestic base. Firms pursue such a strategy for four major reasons. First, sales abroad may be too low to provide the economies of scale for the establishment of efficient-sized overseas units. Second, higher factor costs can discourage the establishment of production operations abroad. Third, government policies in the home base,[7] coupled with relatively open target markets, make it desirable to export rather than establish production facilities in additional countries. Fourth, the firm may enjoy a monopoly that makes it unnecessary to respond to or preempt competitors.

Export-oriented firms that receive protection or direct government support at home can pose a severe threat to competitors located in more open

---

[7] This may include a protected national market and financial assistance (e.g. subsidies, R&D contracts, export financing, and low-cost capital).

markets, and accordingly may contribute significantly to rising trade friction. If the position of these firms depends on a technological monopoly or economies of scale, they may find themselves targeted by other governments eager to ensure that domestic firms participate in the industry.

Regional MNEs are firms that have optimized their operations, including production, around a regional market, but have not yet achieved significant sales and operations outside the region. Declining barriers to entry and intensifying competition have made this an increasingly tenuous strategy in industries such as mainframe computers, minicomputers, central office digital switch equipment, and automobiles. However, firms can grow and prosper when: products have high transportation costs; strong regional differences in product specifications and/or consumer preferences exist; there are high regional barriers to entry (perhaps associated with regional trading blocs); and global competitors are evenly matched, precluding expansion outside of traditional markets. Relatively weak companies may find themselves confined to this role and under attack from larger global competitors.

Traditionally, many European MNEs and U.S. firms fit this description. Government ownership, with its emphasis on employment, may severely inhibit companies' attempts to move beyond this role. Regional companies often resort to international strategic alliances as a means of expanding the resources available to them.

Transnational MNEs are firms that have begun to locate production operations globally, but depend heavily on their domestic market and operations for their competitive position, key production operations, and R&D. Such a firm would be unable to sustain its competitiveness if these operations were significantly reduced. Overseas operations usually do not include the most

technologically and organizationally difficult portions of the production process. R&D outside the domestic base is limited at best, and primarily intended to customize the product to local requirements and taste. Firms assume the transnational form for a variety of reasons. These include:

- Matching costs and revenues.
- Transportation costs, factor inputs, manufacturing philosophy, or market growth that make it more efficient to manufacture, or at least assemble, in the regional market.
- Barriers to entry, such as tariffs and established brand preferences.
- Government restrictions intended to induce the firm to establish operations or to exclude imports.

Global MNEs have replicated the full value-added chain, including substantial product development and often research operations, in more than one national or regional market. In theory, such a firm might survive if it sustained the loss of its operations in its domestic market. In many cases, this form of organization reflects the long-term consequences of host government policies intended to exclude or limit imports. As international sales and assets increase, the firm may no longer depend on its domestic national market for scale and scope. This is most likely to occur in firms whose domestic base is in small but technologically advanced nations, such as Canada and some European countries. Development of regional trading blocs in Europe and North America could over time further reduce the importance of the domestic base and increase the importance of the regional base for such firms.

Distributed multinationals are firms that have optimized their sourcing, production, and R&D

base globally.[8] In some circumstances, this can provide the firm with advantages in factor costs, economies of scale and scope, and experience curve effects that outweigh government interventions to restrict or impose conditions on market access and subsidize or support national champions. As a result they can be thought of as MNEs that have limited the influence of both their domestic base and host government's policies on their organizational structure. The actions of distributed MNEs are driven by the global markets and global competition. In its purest form, such a firm would have little allegiance to its historic domestic base beyond advantages relating to the size and openness of the market, the availability and cost of scarce factors, and government policies.

Distributed MNEs are particularly responsive to the policies of host governments, although the response can take the form of exit from a particular market or geographic location. Countries with more restrictive FDI and trade policies are likely to receive a greater proportion of work and manufacturing facilities from distributed MNEs than might otherwise have been the case. This is emphasized when local markets are strong or expanding.

In many cases, the decisions that influence the nature of the firm are affected by economies of scale and other advantages that can lead firms to center specific activities, products, or processes in either national or regional markets from which they serve their regional and/or global markets.[9] Where they exist, agglomeration economies of scale reinforce such decisions on a firm or industry-wide basis.[10] Organizing the firm on a distributed basis is less attractive if barriers to entry are high, governments effectively intervene to shape business resource allocation decisions, transportation costs are prohibitive, or there are factors specific to the market.

∎ Factors That Influence Form

When economies of scale allow (and the policies of the domestic base government do not preclude), firms expanding overseas can be expected to locate an increasing proportion of their assets in their major overseas markets. Determining an appropriate form for a firm is a complex process with numerous factors. Table 2-1 seeks to compare the relative importance of selected criteria that determine the form of organization that an MNE will gravitate toward over time. Domestic government policies—especially protected national markets—are often relatively more important to the *export oriented* MNE. Host government policies—including protected markets—make an important contribution in the *regional, transnational, global* and *distributed* forms of MNEs.

As competition intensifies, minimum efficient economies of scale grow larger, customers become more demanding, and firms become more sophisticated in their relationships with their

---

[8] Nike is an example of such a company. Design and marketing expertise is centered in the United States. Manufacturing is provided by subcontractors in the Far East. Working capital is provided by Nissho Iwai, a trading company. Subcontractors, with Nike's assistance, are constantly being relocated to take advantage of the best cost and quality available. Nike closed its manufacturing operations in the Philippines, Malaysia, Britain, and Ireland when these sites proved uncompetitive, and manufacturing is shifting from Taiwan and South Korea to lower-cost sites in China, Indonesia, and Thailand. See: Mark Clifford, ''Spring in Their Step,'' *Far Eastern Economic Review*, Nov. 5, 1992, pp. 56-57.

[9] For example, Philips has recently decided to concentrate global production of cathodes at a single plant in Blackburn, Lancashire in the United Kingdom. In 1993, 60 percent of its global production was located at this site and the balance at Sittard in the Netherlands. ''UK to Get All Philips Cathode Work,'' *Financial Times*, Feb. 3, 1993, p. 9.

[10] For example, the size of the market and rapid technological change provided by the Japanese, Korean, and Taiwanese consumer electronics industry and the strength of the Japanese semiconductor manufacturing machinery sector provide additional incentives to locate semiconductor manufacturing facilities in the region. Each such facility located in the region reinforces the advantages of locating facilities there.

Table 2-1—Factors Influencing Type of Multinational Enterprise

	Resource	Export	Regional	Transnational	Global	Distributed
Domestic base market size	High	Low	Medium	Medium	Low	Medium
Transport costs	High	High	Medium	Medium	Medium	Low
Low-cost inputs	High	Low	Medium	Medium	Medium	High
Economies of scale	Medium	High	Medium	Medium	Medium	High
Technology	Low	High	Medium	Medium	Medium	Medium
Government financial assistance ...	Low	High	Medium	Medium	Medium	Medium
Government ownership	Low	High	Medium	Low	Low	Low
Currency risk	Low	Low	Medium	Medium	Medium	Medium
Domestic government policy	Low	Medium	Medium	Low	Low	Medium
Protected national market	Low	Medium	High	Medium	Medium	Low
Protected regional market	Low	Medium	High	Medium	Medium	Medium
Host government policy	Low	Low	High	High	High	High
Host country market size	Low	Low	Medium	High	High	High

SOURCE: Office of Technology Assessment, 1993.

domestic and host governments. In these conditions, the overall structure of international business may tend toward a more *distributed* mode. For some products, generally those characterized by low transportation costs and/or large economies of scale, firms may source from a single location. For products where coordination, transportation costs, inventory costs, government-induced barriers to entry, and differences in taste and standards prove prohibitive, a firm may organize its operations on a regional basis.[11] Diffusion of technology means that competitiveness will increasingly depend on the effectiveness of the process of research, development, design, production, distribution, and marketing rather than on any single element of the process. This heightens the importance of the firm correctly identifying which configuration is the most appropriate for each of its operations. As chapter 5 suggests, international strategic alliances are one available avenue to help meet these requirements.

NATIONAL DIFFERENCES

MNEs resist sudden changes in their structure and organization. Previous investments in plant, equipment, technology, people, corporate culture, distribution channels, and organizational structure all tend to limit their freedom of action. In the absence of dramatic differences in government policies or rapid technological change, MNEs can be expected to evolve gradually from one form of organization to another.

However, each of the three regions—Europe, North America, and East Asia—tend to produce different characteristics in their MNEs. For example, firms based in Japan and South Korea are more likely to be *export-oriented* MNEs. Firms based in Europe are more likely to correspond to the *regional* or *transnational* form. Many MNEs based in the United States are either *global* or *distributed*. This section examines some of the factors that account for strong regional tendencies in the dominant types of MNEs.

---

[11] Louis T. Wells, Jr., *Conflict or Indifference: US Multinationals in a World of Regional Trading Blocs*, Technical Papers No. 57 (Paris: Organization For Economic Co-operation and Development, 1992), pp. 26-27.

Table 2-2 identifies some historical factors that may help to explain these regional variations. There are important differences in several factors, including the time at which industrialization took place and the relative size of the domestic market. Table 2-2 also suggests important differences in government policies and the support provided to domestically based firms. Asymmetries in government policies have had a profound influence on the differences in firm organization by region.

■ The Influence of Location

Traditionally, U.S. firms first established themselves in their domestic market before expanding abroad. Capital markets have been very efficient in the United States, encouraging a focus on short-term results. Until recently, sufficient economies of scale were present in the domestic market to ensure competitiveness without need of scale and scope in foreign markets. When U.S. firms ventured abroad, they faced numerous restrictions on their operations, which encouraged them to produce in local markets. As a result many U.S.-based MNEs historically viewed their international facilities as an adjunct to their domestic operations and chose to expand internationally in one of three ways: licensed production; joint ventures and distribution arrangements; and production in the host market.

More recently, U.S. firms have sought to configure themselves around regional markets. This can give them an advantage relative to competitors whose primary market is a single national market. It does not, however, automatically provide an advantage over *export-oriented* and *distributed* MNEs that compete globally.

Firms based in more open markets may find it uneconomical to remain horizontally and vertically integrated. They frequently respond to competitive pressures by shedding less critical operations, or exiting an industry segment. The relative openness of the U.S. market ensures U.S.-based companies will often face intense competitive pressure in their core domestic market. Often, companies based abroad enjoy a sanctuary home market. As a result, U.S.-based MNEs tend to be relatively more specialized than their international competitors of comparable size.

Firms that compete globally but lack a sanctuary home base often choose to source from direct or potential competitors.[12] As they gain economies of scale and scope, suppliers based in protected markets may exploit such relationships to compete directly with the purchaser in its core markets. The long-term consequences of relationships with suppliers based in protected markets must be weighed carefully if the firm based in the more open market is to avoid undermining its own competitiveness.

In some industries, such as automobiles, protectionist policies in various national or regional markets forced U.S. firms to replicate virtually the entire value-added chain, or to export products to gain credits to import. European and some Japanese firms also have been forced at times to undertake similar operations. For example, both Nissan and VW (as well as the U.S.-based MNEs of GM, Ford, and Chrysler) manufacture and export from Mexico. The threat of protectionism was a major factor in the timing of the decision by such firms as Honda, Toyota, and Nissan to assemble vehicles in the United States.

Managers must weigh the costs and benefits of responding to host government pressures. In their calculations, U.S. business leaders are aware of the traditional reluctance of the U.S. Government to intervene with host governments to offset local pressure on their foreign affiliates. They must also consider the penetration of the U.S. market by

---

[12] Firms based in sanctuary markets may also be forced to source from direct or potential competitors. For example, manufacturers of 486 PC clones based in Asia until recently have been forced to buy their microprocessors from Intel because there were no other suppliers available.

Table 2-2—Historical Factors Influencing Firm Organization

	Europe	United States	Japan
Present dominant form of MNE	Regional/ transnational	Transnational/ distributed	Export
Period of peak competitiveness	Pre-1945	1945-80	1980+
Period of modern industrialization	Early 1900	Early 1900	Post 1945
Domestic market			
Size	Medium	Large	Medium
Accessibility	Medium	High	Low
Attractiveness of regional market			
Size	Medium	Small	Medium
Accessibility	Low	Low	Medium
Government protection	High	Low	High
Overall level of government support	High	Low	High
Incentives to export	Medium	Low	High
National treatment of FDI	Medium	High	Low
Present efficiency of capital markets	Medium	High	Low

SOURCE: Office of Technology Assessment, 1993.

imports, U.S. national treatment of FDI, and the relative lack of export incentives for U.S.-made products. In such circumstances, management could be expected to respond to host government restrictions and inducements, when not unprofitable to do so, at the expense of their U.S. operations. This in turn can lead to important industrial capabilities being relocated faster or to areas other than what a free market might dictate.

With few exceptions, European-based MNEs have received a greater degree of protection and direct government support than have U.S. firms. A major exception is the defense aerospace sector, in which levels of support provided by national governments are similar. However, even here the commercial aircraft built by European aerospace firms generally have received greater levels of government support than have their U.S. competitors. Japanese aerospace companies have

also benefited from high levels of government support.[13] In certain countries, most notably France and Italy, firms are often at least partly owned by the government, or are explicitly designated as national champions.[14] Relatively protected markets have encouraged firms to engage in a wider range of activities than their U.S. competitors, both horizontally and vertically. European MNEs tend to have a strong regional focus, although where products are transportable and distinctive competence is intact, worldwide export of finished goods is common.

European firms are powerful competitors in telecommunications, often due to their ability to exploit domestic protected markets and other government assistance. They are still powerful in consumer electronics, although many find the transition to the *distributed* MNE form from *regional, global,* and *transnational* forms to be

[13] For a discussion of government support of the commercial aircraft industry, see chapter 8, ''Government Support of the Large Commercial Aircraft Industries of Japan, Europe, and the United States'' in U.S. Congress, Office of Technology Assessment, *Competing Economies: America, Europe and the Pacific Rim* (Washington, DC: U.S. Government Printing Office, October 1991), pp. 341-362.

[14] In 1992 there were 10 French, 3 Italian, and 3 Spanish government-owned companies in the Fortune 500 International list. There were no British, German, or Japanese government-owned corporations in the group.

traumatic. European companies remain important competitors in machine tools and electrical systems, and are first-rank contenders in petrochemicals and pharmaceuticals. In most areas of aerospace, European firms, often making heavy use of government subsidies and components sourced in the United States, remain contenders. European firms are competitive in consumer products and durables, although rationalizing these industries on a regional basis is proving a challenge, leading toward further consolidation in the industry.

In industries characterized by rapid change, state sponsorship has often led firms to fail to expand globally in time to compete effectively with U.S. and Japanese companies pursuing global economies of scale and scope. European semiconductor companies, for example, remain relatively weak despite a 14-percent tariff on semiconductors and billions of dollars in subsidies and support. As competition has intensified, European computer firms, such as Bull and Siemens-Nixdorf, have fared poorly against U.S. and Japanese-based rivals.[15] Financial support of national champions can be massive. For example, since the early 1980s, the French Government has provided Bull, its national computer champion, with financial support equal to 15 billion French francs.[16] Several national champions have been acquired by U.S. or Japanese-based MNEs.[17]

Historically, European firms have followed two major approaches to their international operations. The first was to organize as *export-oriented* MNEs, that is, to manufacture domestically and sell globally. The second was to set up a full value-added chain, generally excluding corporate R&D, in major national or regional markets. European firms often purchase subsidiaries that are then run as autonomous units. Historically, European MNEs have been the largest source of foreign direct investment (FDI) in the United States.

In the post-World War II period, Japanese and South Korean firms have enjoyed substantial protection from imports and FDI.[18] They have benefited from government financial and regulatory assistance, infant industry policies, outright protection, and government targeting of selected industries. At the same time, their governments have encouraged and directed domestic firms to seek economies of scale from exports. Until recently, the predominant form of organization has been as *export* MNEs. Many firms, however, are beginning to establish international operations and have begun to draw on the international capital markets, reducing the influence of the domestic government. Despite this, many of these firms have shown a much greater reluctance to transfer higher-value activities to their overseas operations than have either U.S. or European firms. Some Japanese automakers grant their U.S. operations less autonomy and source a higher percentage of components from their domestic operations than do U.S. automobile companies in Europe.[19]

---

[15] Both NEC and IBM have equity stakes in Bull.

[16] Richard L. Hudson, "Bull Weighs Expanding Ties to Other Firms," *The Wall Street Journal*, May 28, 1993, p. A5D.

[17] For example, ICL has been acquired by Fujitsu and Phillips computer operations by DEC.

[18] See chapters 6 and 7 of *Competing Economies*, op. cit., footnote 13, pp. 237-337.

[19] Honda was the first Japanese automobile company to begin assembly of automobiles in the United States. Domestic content for corporate average fuel economy (CAFE) standards exceeds 70 percent. However, on a component basis it may be as low as 50 percent. (See box 4-A.) The average European content of GM and Ford vehicles, according to the automakers, exceeds 95 percent, in large measure because the vehicles are engineered, designed, and sourced in Europe.

ASYMMETRIES IN GOVERNMENT POLICIES, OWNERSHIP, AND CONTROL

In 1971, the world of multinational enterprises was dominated by U.S.-based firms.[20] Today competition from firms based in Europe and Asia, most notably Japan, may threaten the survival of key U.S.-based MNEs in a range of industries. As discussed below and in chapters 3 and 6, important differences in government policies, capital markets, and industry structure have influenced the rise of large numbers of new competitors based in Asia and Europe.

Asian firms, especially those in Japan and South Korea, have increased their share of the Fortune 500 International list the fastest, reflecting the advantages of both a rapidly growing protected domestic market and government policies intended to encourage exports and target selected global industry segments.[21] In several key industries—such as consumer electronics, automobiles, and mainframe computers— considerable excess capacity exists on a global basis. As consolidation takes place, asymmetries in government policies can influence the probability of survival and the distribution of potential gains among otherwise evenly matched competitors or facilities.

The decline in relative importance of the U.S. economy has been matched by a decline in the relative importance of U.S.-based MNEs. International competitors are much more numerous and their relative size has placed them on a much more even footing. Japan now has the second greatest number of large multinationals, comparable to the United States or the European Community (EC) as a whole. Asymmetries in government policies among Europe, the United States, and Japan have led firms to configure themselves in very different ways.

The United States has pursued a policy of national treatment of foreign investors. With some important exceptions, such as quotas on textiles and agricultural products and the ''voluntary restrictions'' on imports of Japanese manufactured automobiles, the United States has been relatively open to imports and FDI. Moreover, it has not intervened to prevent firms from reconfiguring themselves in response to the policies of other governments.

As noted above, many European governments have protected national markets and limited imports.[22] The extraordinary support they provide their national champions can include direct cash infusions, preferential access for government procurement, the creation or tolerance of national cartels, and other market allocation mechanisms. In some industries, such as telecommunication digital switches, the government may even own the primary customer. This strengthens the linkage between public policy and domestically based MNEs.

In Asia, governments have pursued three major strategies toward industrialization. The first is import substitution. The second is to provide an attractive location for MNE global export platforms. The third is to nurture domestically based, export-oriented MNEs.

Countries that traditionally pursued import substitution policies, such as India, sought to use protected national markets and other government assistance to supply the domestic market with local production. Among policies to support this strategy are the exclusion of international competitors, import licensing, domestic content require-

---

[20] Raymond Vernon, *Sovereignty at Bay: The Multinational Spread of U.S. Enterprises* (New York, NY: Basic Books, Inc., 1971). As early as 1902, concern was expressed in Europe regarding the invasion of American-based firms. Overseas investment of U.S.-based firms as a percent of GNP was the same in 1966, at 7 percent, as it was in 1914. See Alfred Chandler, *Scale and Scope*, op. cit., footnote 1, p. 369.

[21] *Competing Economies*, op. cit., footnote 13, pp. 7-13.

[22] Office of the U.S. Trade Representative, *1993 National Trade Estimate Report on Foreign Trade Barriers* (Washington, DC: U.S. Government Printing Office, 1993).

ments, government ownership of major domestic firms, foreign exchange controls, and the granting of monopolies to favored domestic or international firms. Because of inadequately sized national markets, isolation from the global economy, and a lack of leading edge technology, import substitution has been unsuccessful on its own, leading an increasing number of countries to seek alternative solutions. However, as both Japan and South Korea have demonstrated, it can be an important component of government industrial policy.

Some countries, such as Malaysia, Singapore, and Thailand, have concentrated on providing an attractive environment from which MNEs can serve both regional and global markets. Their policies include facilitating access to existing pools of low-cost and increasingly skilled labor, targeting of specific industries for encouragement and support, aggressively investing in education and training, and providing financial and tax incentives. They have also allowed relative freedom of operation for the MNEs and their supporting suppliers and subcontractors in movements of goods, services, and capital. With some exceptions, most notably the automobile industry, relatively little effort has been invested in developing domestic firms to compete abroad with large MNEs. These countries contribute few firms to the Fortune 500 International. However, the lack of direct domestic competitors heightens the attraction for foreign-based MNEs, in part because technology leakage to competitors is less likely.

The governments of Japan and Korea have pursued industrialization through promoting competition among domestic firms, protected domestic markets, direct government intervention and assistance, the aggressive pursuit of exports to achieve economies of scale and scope, and acquisition of technology from abroad. Support has included industrial targeting, provision of low-cost capital to favored firms, restricted government procurement, restrictions on FDI, import licensing, aggressive investments in education and worker training, government-led research consortia, and the encouragement of cartels and other market sharing mechanisms.[23] Box 2-B discusses one of the most famous examples of a U.S.-based firm, Texas Instruments, being forced to trade proprietary technology for unequal market access.

In general, European firms' sales have traditionally been more concentrated in domestic and regional markets than their Asian counterparts.[24] Large U.S. firms, by contrast, have a greater percentage of their assets outside their national and/or regional base. Japanese and Korean firms are more likely to be substantial net exporters from their domestic base of operations, and to have a lower ratio of overseas assets to overseas sales.

Ownership and control also varies by nationality of the firm.[25] Different types of investors have different objectives and financial performance requirements, leading to differences in MNE cost of capital, patience of capital, and planning horizons. If the true cost of capital converges, then differences in MNE behavior on the basis of national origin should begin to close. Differences in government policies will affect both the degree and the rate of convergence.

In the United States, ownership is often concentrated in large institutional investors, such as pension fund managers under pressure to maximize short-term profitability. U.S. capital mar-

---

[23] See chapters 6 and 7 of *Competing Economies*, op. cit., footnote 13, pp. 237-337.

[24] Roger Abravanel and David Ernst, ''Alliance and Acquisition Strategies for European National Champions,'' *McKinsey Quarterly*, 1992, No. 2, pp. 44-62; and OTA MNE database.

[25] The discussion of the influence of ownership, control, and cost of capital that follows is based on Michael Porter, *Capital Choices* (Washington, DC: Council on Competitiveness, June 1992).

Box 2-B—Trading Technology for Unequal Market Access in Japan: Texas Instruments

One of the most famous examples in which a U.S.-based company struggled to gain even unequal access to the Japanese market is provided by Texas Instruments (TI).[1] TI held fundamental patents, was politically influential, and was both a market and technological leader in its industry. Nevertheless, lengthy negotiations were required with the Japanese Government before TI gained permission to establish wholly owned manufacturing operations in Japan. TI agreed to license key technologies to Japanese firms and to consult with the Japanese Ministry of International Trade and Industry (MITI) on a regular basis regarding its plans and future operations in Japan.

Texas Instruments enjoyed important patent rights due to its ownership of Kilby's patents, which made the integrated circuit possible. Early efforts to establish first a wholly owned physical presence and then a manufacturing facility in Japan were rebuffed. TI's 1960 application for Japanese patents was delayed as a result of industry pressure until 1989.[2]

In 1966, manufacture of integrated circuits began in Japan. Intervention by the U.S. Secretary of Commerce proved fruitless. As production volumes and experience grew, the major domestic firms became more willing to countenance limited competition in their home market. This, coupled with the threat of legal retaliation for patent infringement on planned exports, led the major electronics firms, acting through their trade organization, to fashion a new strategy to deal with TI.

Negotiations between MITI and TI continued. Official appeals on the part of the U.S. Government were rebuffed. In late 1966, TI was able to force both Sony and Sharp to withdraw products from the U.S. market.

In April of 1968, over 4 years after the process began, an agreement was reached. This required that TI establish a 50/50 joint venture with Sony for 3 years. At the end of the 3 years TI could seek government permission to buy out Sony, and TI received formal assurances from Sony, and informal assurances from the Japanese Government, that it would be able to do so. TI was also forced to negotiate with and license as a group its major Japanese competitors, substantially reducing its relative bargaining power and future royalties. Because it already had a license for Fairchild's patents, NEC was able to obtain a license from TI at even more favorable rates, further reducing TI's royalty income. In addition, TI was required to " 'consult' with MITI about production levels from its Japan-based venture."[3] Market access has remained limited and TI has been unable to achieve a market share in Japan that corresponds to its position in the rest of the world.

---

[1] This discussion draws on Mark Mason, *American Multinationals And Japan* (Cambridge, MA: Harvard University Press, 1992); and *Competing Economies: America, Europe and the Pacific Rim*, (Washington, DC: U.S. Government Printing Office, October 1991), pp. 341-362.

[2] The granting of the patents in 1989 seems to have strengthened TI in its subsequent ongoing negotiations for patent royalty income with Japanese semiconductor manufacturers. See: Andrew Pollack, "A Chip Maker's Profit on Patents," *The New York Times*, Oct. 16, 1990, p. D1.

[3] Mason, op. cit., footnote 1, p. 186.

kets are extremely liquid, enabling investors to shift their holdings very rapidly in search of small increases in the risk-adjusted rate of return. Foreign participants enjoy national treatment in U.S. financial markets and face few restrictions on the import of capital or the repatriation of profits, making it relatively easy to acquire both successful and unsuccessful U.S.-based firms.

Except for certain favored defense contractors, there is relatively little government intervention to allocate credit and subsidize the cost of capital. Neither antitrust nor national security considerations have proven significant barriers to FDI.

Capital markets in Europe are less liquid than they are in the United States, making the pursuit by an investor of short-term advantage more difficult. Governments are more willing to intervene to rescue unsuccessful competitors or to prevent the foreign acquisition of domestically based firms. The time horizons of large institutional investors are significantly longer than in the United States, leading to more patient capital.[26] Controlling interests are often concentrated in a small number of shareholders, making the firms very resistant to unfriendly takeovers.

■ Eroding Dominance of U.S.-Based MNEs

Following World War II, U.S. firms achieved commanding advantages in scale, scope, and technology over the vast majority of their foreign competitors. Foreign opportunities, coupled with rising competitive pressures at home, led industrial firms to expand internationally.[27] By the late 1960s, the success of U.S. MNEs led many observers to conclude that they posed a direct threat to the independence and prosperity of their host countries.[28] Many governments actively sought to offset the competitive advantages of U.S.-based multinationals. They responded with policies intended to shield domestically based competitors from foreign, mainly U.S.-based, MNEs, and to force, or at least encourage, MNEs to replicate their value-added chain and transfer technology within the domestic economy. The U.S. Government provided few countervailing pressures and even encouraged U.S.-based MNEs to cooperate with host governments.

Since the early 1970s, global diffusion of technology has greatly reduced or eliminated an important competitive advantage of many U.S. firms. In many industries, the number of and capabilities of competitors at both the supplier and original equipment manufacturer level have increased dramatically. As a result, product life cycles have become shorter, the benefits of vertical integration have been reduced, and it has become more difficult to sustain advantages in product differentiation and manufacturing technology. Increased competition has, in turn, often reduced profitability and raised investment costs. For these reasons, most large-scale firms now seek access to all major markets on a timely basis, to ensure profitability and to defray rising investment requirements.

Intensifying competition within the U.S. market—from new domestic entrants, transplants, and foreign-based exporters—has forced an increasing number of U.S. companies to pursue product and process development, sourcing options, and manufacturing strategies intended to minimize short-term costs rather than build long-term competitive positions.[29] This often means relying on competitors to manufacture key components or final products.

In 1966, U.S. firms dominated the Fortune 500 International list, with European firms running a distant second, and Asian firms a remote third (see box 2-C). With the exception of certain raw materials producers, relatively few of the Fortune 500 International firms depended on their international operations for a greater share of their

---

[26] Ibid. At least some of this difference in time horizon may be attributable to the less liquid capital markets.

[27] Vernon, op. cit., footnote 20.

[28] J.J. Servan-Schreiber (translated by Ronald Steel), *The American Challenge* (New York, NY: Atheneum, 1968).

[29] For example, for a discussion of how GE came to source microwave ovens from Samsung in Korea rather than continue to manufacture them, see Ira C. Magaziner and Mark Patinkin, "Fast Heat: How Korea Won the Microwave War," *Harvard Business Review*, Jan./Feb. 1989, pp. 83-92.

Box 2-C—The International Fortune 500: Steady Erosion of U.S. Dominance

Since 1966 there has been a steady erosion in the percentage of the International Fortune 500 firms based in the United States. As figure 1-6 demonstrates, in 1966 the United States accounted for 61 percent (304) of these firms. In 1991, only 31 percent (157) of the 500 largest manufacturing firms were based in the United States. In comparison, firms based in Europe grew from 28 percent (139) in 1966 to 34 percent (168) in 1991. In the same period, firms based in Japan grew rapidly from 7 percent (37) in 1966 to 24 percent (119) in 1991.

Figure 1-7 shows that in 1966, U.S.-based firms in the Fortune 500 International had sales of $299 billion, or roughly 67 percent of the $441 billion in total sales of the International Fortune 500. Firms based in Japan accounted for less than 5 percent ($21 billion) and firms based in Europe accounted for 25 percent ($111 billion). In comparison, in 1991 total sales of the International Fortune 500 were $5,188 billion. U.S.-based firms accounted for 34 percent ($1,785 billion). Firms based in Japan accounted for 21 percent ($1,097 billion) and firms based in Europe accounted for 36 percent ($1,901 billion), exceeding sales of U.S.-based MNEs.

Overall employment of the International Fortune 500 grew from 21 million

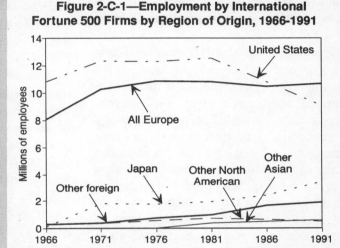

Figure 2-C-1—Employment by International Fortune 500 Firms by Region of Origin, 1966-1991

SOURCE: OTA data base compiled from annual reports, Fortune 500 International, and Standard and Poor's Register.

in 1966 to 26 million in 1991. Most of this growth took place in the period 1966-1971. Figure 2-C-1 shows that U.S.-based firms increased their employment by 1.5 million workers between 1966 and 1971. Between 1971 and 1991, U.S.-based firms shed 3.2 million workers. In comparison, employment for firms based in Japan has grown from 1.2 million to 3.5 million. Other Asian-based firms saw their employment grow from 0 to 581,000 during this period. Between 1966 and 1971, employment for firms based in Europe grew from 8.1 million to 10.3 million. It has remained relatively stable since. Firms based outside Asia, Europe, and North America saw employment grow from 271,000 to 1.9 million.

revenues and profits than their domestic operations.[30] However, in some cases non-U.S.-based MNEs, most notably those headquartered in small but economically advanced countries, had the bulk of their sales and production outside their domestic market.

---

[30] For example, one study was able to profile the international sales of 93 U.S.-controlled MNEs for 1964. Only 6 reported international sales greater than 50 percent of total sales; 36 reported international sales that were less than 20 percent of total sales. See: N.K. Bruck, and F.A. Lees, "Foreign Content of U.S. Corporate Activities," *Financial Analysis Journal*, Sept./Oct. 1966, pp. 1-6, cited in table 4-1, "One Hundred Forty U.S.-Controlled Multinational Enterprises Classified by Foreign Content of Operations, 1964," in Vernon, op. cit., footnote 20, p. 122.

From the 1950s to the 1970s, U.S.-based MNEs tended to use their domestic production base to supply products for a significant proportion of their international sales. Overseas operations were created for several reasons: to serve local and regional markets; to seek low-cost factor inputs, usually raw materials or unskilled assembly labor; and to improve the competitive position in markets located in industrially advanced countries.

The typical U.S.-based MNE developed new products for and introduced products in its domestic market.[31] Once the domestic market was saturated, additional growth would be pursued abroad. The steady diffusion of technology and the reduction of barriers to entry in many major markets have rendered this "product life cycle" strategy obsolete for an increasing range of industries.[32] Today MNEs tend to introduce products globally to preempt competition from local firms and other MNEs. This shortening of the product life cycle requires that firms place greater emphasis on speed and flexibility. It has forced them to reconsider manufacturing, sourcing, and distribution strategies, and to forge new relationships with both their domestic and host governments. Strategic alliances, often with firms based overseas, have become integral in this quest for advantage (see chapter 5).

IMPLICATIONS FOR TRADE FRICTION AND PUBLIC WELFARE

MNEs are the primary mechanism through which international trade and investment are conducted and, as a result, have become increasingly important building blocks of the international economy. They pursue advantage (market power) through the quest for economies of scale and scope. They export and import, invest and acquire, manufacture and source, develop, license and transfer technology around the globe. In the mid-1980s, the sales of MNEs represented between 25 and 30 percent of the combined gross domestic product of the market economies.[33] MNEs account for about three-quarters of the world's commodity trade, and four-fifths of the trade in technology and managerial skills of these economies. MNEs may now account for one-third of all global manufactured exports. A similar proportion of global trade in goods and services is intrafirm trade, that is, trade among parent MNEs and their foreign subsidiaries.

In many sectors, international competition is primarily organized around large oligopolist companies that compete globally, although not necessarily equally, in trade and investment. Leading MNEs are believed, on average, to receive 30 to 40 percent of their total sales outside their home country, although the 50 largest have 54 percent of their revenues from outside their domestic base.[34] Overseas production by such firms often exceeds their share of international trade.

This section briefly examines how the action of MNEs can contribute to or alleviate trade friction among nations. It shows how the different types of MNEs described above can strengthen or weaken their domestic base and the host country's

---

[31] Vernon, op. cit., footnote 20, pp. 65-106; Also see Louis T. Wells, Jr. ed., *The Product Life Cycle and International Trade* (Boston, MA: Division of Research, Graduate School of Business Administration, Harvard University, 1972).

[32] Christopher A. Bartlett and Sumantra Ghoshal, *Managing Across Borders: The Transnational Solution* (Boston, MA: Harvard Business School Press, 1991), p. 115.

[33] John H. Dunning, *Multinational Enterprises and the Global Economy* (New York, NY: Addison-Wesley Publishing Company, 1993), pp. 14, 386-387.

[34] John Dunning, "Dunning on Porter: Reshaping the Diamond of Competitive Advantage," *University of Reading Discussion Papers in International Investment and Business Studies 152*, 1991; as cited in Laura D'Andrea Tyson, *Who's Bashing Whom* (Washington, DC: Institute For International Economics, 1992), footnote 5, p. 4; and "The Non-Global Firm," in "The Economist Survey: Multinationals," *The Economist*, Mar. 27, 1993, p. 10.

economy, technology base, labor markets, and regulatory environment.

Many MNEs are able to seek capital and government financial assistance on a global basis. As a result they can make use of and are influenced by both global and national capital markets. This can reduce the influence of government policies in both home and host nations. Firms may shift work from one facility to another in pursuit of export financing. For example, the failure of Britain's Export Credit Guarantee Department to provide export insurance, and the willingness of the U.S. Eximbank to do so, led the British-based MNE Trafalgar House to transfer a 200-million-pound contract to its U.S. subsidiary.[35] The British-based MNE John Brown transferred a large contract from its U.K. operations to its French and Dutch subsidiaries for the same reason.

The efficiency of MNEs, and their ability to mobilize resources, including political support, is matched by their ability to reconfigure their operations to meet changing market conditions, seek out low-cost alternatives, and respond to government initiatives. Accordingly, their activities may place into contact and competition different national labor forces, financial institutions, product markets, and systems of public policy.[36] Firms may relocate high value-added activities to take advantage of more permissive regulatory regimes.[37]

Governments unwilling to rely on the impersonal working of the market may encourage or foster the creation of economies of scale. Carefully orchestrated government policies, combined with aggressive business practices, can create a critical mass of technology, trained workers, and production economies of scale within a specific region and provide a protected sanctuary from which favored firms operate. Such conditions may create a self-reinforcing cycle that eliminates facilities located in less favored locations. This can lead to substantial trade friction.[38]

The *resource-based* MNE may pose considerable dangers for its host government because of the economic and political influence it may be able to mobilize. However, if such firms' activities are confined to the exploitation of natural resources for which alternative independent sup-

---

[35] David Dodwell, "Jobs and Exports 'Lost Because of Credit Terms,' " *Financial Times*, Feb. 5, 1993, p. 6.

[36] For example, BMW's decision to establish an assembly plant in the United States may have been motivated in part by the desire to improve its bargaining position vis-a-vis its traditional workforce and supplier base. See: Barbara Harrison, "High Hopes for New Plant," *Financial Times*, Oct. 20, 1992, p. 34; John Templemen and David Woodruff, "The Beemer Spotlight Falls on Spartenburg, USA," *Business Week*, July 6, 1992, p. 38; Ferdinand Protzman, "BMW Details Plan to Build Cars in South Carolina," *The New York Times*, June 24, 1992, p. D4; Diana T. Kurylko, "BMW Poised to Build in U.S.," *Automotive News*, Mar. 30, 1992, pp. 1, 38; James R. Crate, "Special Convertible May Be 1st Model," *Automotive News*, June 29, 1992, pp. 1, 38; Lindsay Chappell, "South Carolina Is a Surprising Fit for BMW," *Automotive News*, June 29, 1992, pp. 1 and 40; Diana Kurylko, "Von Kunheim Drives BMW Beyond Continent," *Automotive News*, June 29, 1992, p. 38; Diana Kurylko, "Costs Drove Decision to Build in U.S.," *Automotive News*, June 29, 1992, p. 39; and Lindsay Chappell, "Plant Quest Began in '70s," *Automotive News*, June 29, 1992, p. 39. For an example of how MNEs and governments can work in concert to defeat attempts to organize a national electronics union in Malaysia, see Michael Vatilkiotis, "Credibility Gap: Union Issue Mars Image as Third World Leader," *Far Eastern Economic Review*, July 16, 1992, p. 18.

[37] For example, the German chemical company Bayer is relocating much of its biotechnology R&D from Germany to the United States to take advantage of the more favorable regulatory environment.

[38] For example, consumer VCRs are mostly manufactured in Asia, despite Phillips, the Dutch firm, and Ampex, a U.S. firm, having pioneered much of the technology.

pliers are available, they pose relatively little risk to the major industrialized nations.[39]

A variation of the *resource-based* MNE that has the potential to create trade friction is the MNE that exploits low-cost labor pools for manufacturing and service operations.[40] This creates direct competition in wages and benefits between workers in the industrialized countries and their less fortunate counterparts. Such activities are precluded where poor infrastructure, transportation, coordination, and communication costs exceed productivity-adjusted differences in worker compensation costs. Where they do not, and where other barriers to entry are low or nonexistent, work can be expected to migrate rapidly to the lower labor cost areas.[41] This in turn can exert considerable downward pressures on wages and benefits, raising social tensions in the industrialized countries.

The *export-oriented* MNEs—coupled with domestic government policies that favor local production for export, provide a protected sanctuary, and/or actively inhibit inward FDI—have the greatest potential for provoking trade friction among the industrialized nations. This is pronounced when a national system organized in such a fashion runs large, visible trade surpluses. Such surpluses, even when fairly earned, can cause surviving competitors to seek relief from their domestic and host governments. Unless equivalent jobs are readily available, displaced

workers are likely to raise vocal protests against declining wages and benefits or the closing of their place of employment. Alternatively, large trade surpluses can induce governments to seek to establish new competitors to share in the rewards.[42]

Regional MNEs often arise and persist as a result of barriers to entry and host government policies.[43] They may also arise when: 1) MNEs take advantage of low-cost labor to manufacture products for sale in their domestic base, displacing the traditional workforce; 2) MNEs manufacture and source substantially less in the host country than they sell, contributing visibly to a balance of trade deficit; and 3) MNEs transfer work from the established workforce to facilities located in the host country, often in response to protected foreign markets or trade balancing requirements.

Transnational and global MNEs generally increase the proportion of their assets abroad as their international sales expand relative to their domestic sales. To minimize financial risk over time, firms seek to match costs and revenues, provided that doing so does not put them at a competitive disadvantage. Where government policies impose only small distortions in markets, movements toward *transnational* and *distributed* MNE forms are unlikely to worsen trade friction. On the other hand, *transnational*, *global* and *distributed* MNEs can contribute substantially to

---

[39] In some cases, such as copper mining, advantages in transportation costs, technology, supporting infrastructure, and workforce capabilities can offset seemingly insurmountable advantages in such factors as ore quality and wage rates. See: U.S. Congress, Office of Technology Assessment, *Copper: Technology and Competitiveness*, OTA-E-367 (Washington, DC: U.S. Government Printing Office, September 1988). Nevertheless, the import of significant quantities of low-cost natural resource products from abroad may render uncompetitive domestic facilities leading to their closure. Trade friction may result if those threatened with displacement seek protection or compensation.

[40] Stride-Rite Corp. is an example of a firm that has moved rapidly in this direction. See: Joseph Pereira, "Split Personality: Social Responsibility and Need for Low Cost Clash at Stride Rite," *The Wall Street Journal*, May 28, 1993, pp. A1, A6.

[41] A major constraint is the availability of skilled managers and technicians in the host country.

[42] The establishment of the AIRBUS consortium represents such an example. See chapter 8, "Government Support of the Large Commercial Aircraft Industries of Japan, Europe, and the United States," in *Competing Economies*, op. cit., footnote 13, pp. 341-362.

[43] Barriers to entry involving transportation costs are unlikely to provoke friction unless these costs are made artificially high. For example, transportation costs could be raised artificially by requiring that imports be shipped on favored carriers, or by delaying certification, inspection, and customs clearance.

trade friction when government policies distort markets or where economies of scale and limited technology diffusion lead to large and visible trade imbalances.

The development of *distributed MNEs* may in part demonstrate that firms have become increasingly sophisticated at avoiding restrictions intended to force them to duplicate the complete value-added chain within each national market. In the absence of effective international oversight, this form of organization, because it facilitates the arbitraging of national differences, may create additional downward pressure on labor markets and regulatory regimes. Greater organizational freedom may raise the importance of both production and agglomeration economies of scale, possibly leading to greater concentration of certain types of work in specific countries or regions.

Foreign
Direct
Investment | 3

O nly in recent years has the U.S. Government become concerned with the ways that foreign-based multinational enterprises (MNEs) affect the national interest. The main stimulus for this new interest has been the extraordinary economic achievements of large Japanese firms and their pervasive penetration of U.S. markets, particularly in industries such as automobiles, electronics, and banking. The apparent inability of U.S.-based MNEs to invest on a comparable scale in Japan has magnified this concern. Other, less dramatic policy asymmetries exist between the United States and Europe. Therefore, this chapter considers two issues: 1) the existing government rules and private sector practices governing foreign direct investment (FDI) in the United States, Europe, and Japan; and 2) the role of major foreign multinational enterprises—from Europe as well as Japan—in the U.S. economy.

The chapter examines the U.S. policy environment for FDI and compares it to the policy regimes of other major trading nations. Ideally, the United States wants FDI to provide well-paid, skilled jobs, responsible corporate citizenship, and enhancement of the Nation's industrial and technology base. Clearly, it makes sense to object to the presence of foreign firms in the U.S. economy only to the degree to which they do undesirable things. If they provide good jobs, add value to U.S. products, and contribute to the U.S. technology base, they should be encouraged. There may, however, be grounds to object if America's leading trade partners do not reciprocate in providing U.S.-based MNEs with similar opportunities to invest overseas and derive the benefits from those investments.

The chapter reviews the benefits and problems associated with foreign direct investment in the United States (FDIUS). It

43

elaborates on many themes initially examined in OTA's report, *Competing Economies*,[1] and discusses the findings presented below. The analysis suggests that rather than encouraging or discouraging FDIUS indiscriminately, it would be more productive to develop an approach that benefits foreign investors and maintains technological development and high value-added jobs in the American economy.

CHAPTER FINDINGS

1. The significant expansion of FDIUS in the 1980s brought a number of benefits to the Nation. The first major benefit was macroeconomic: the influx of FDIUS helped compensate for the low rate of domestic savings that had adversely affected domestic investment rates.[2] Foreign investors stimulated the U.S. economy, first by providing liquidity to the financial system through large purchases, and second by constructing greenfield wholesaling operations and manufacturing plants. The second major benefit was microeconomic: foreign investors, often Japanese-based MNEs in the manufacturing sector, introduced innovative managerial and organizational techniques to their U.S. competitors, joint venture partners, and suppliers. Consumers subsequently benefited from improved products and services.

2. The lack of more than minimal provisions regarding the foreign acquisition of U.S. high-technology firms—in contrast to the restrictive rules and private sector practices governing foreign acquisitions in some European Community (EC) countries and Japan—may have major implications for the U.S. technology base. Acquisition of U.S. high-technology firms has helped improve the competitiveness of the manufacturing affiliates of foreign producers in the United States and/or their parent producers in Japan or Europe. At the same time, it may have increased reliance on foreign-owned sources of technologies critical to the sustained success of many domestic manufacturing firms. In many industries, technological diffusion has not been reciprocal.[3]

3. At present, U.S. Government policy cannot distinguish between questionable FDI and that which clearly benefits the national interest. Current policy allows foreign-based MNEs to implement strategies based on rational and intelligent business practices, whether or not they benefit the U.S. economy. Foreign-based MNEs cannot be faulted for acting in their own interests. Fault may lie instead in the lack of clear national goals expressed through flexible but explicit legislation.

4. FDI may be becoming less important to MNEs relative to strategic alliances. Statistical data provide ample evidence that the rates of growth in both global FDI and FDIUS have fallen significantly since 1990, as demonstrated in table 3-1 and figure 3-1.[4] It is unclear whether this tendency will reverse course in the near term. While no thorough, accurate data exist to estimate the amount invested by MNEs in

[1] U.S. Congress, Office of Technology Assessment, *Competing Economies: America, Europe, and the Pacific Rim*, OTA-ITE-498 (Washington, DC: U.S. Government Printing Office, October 1991). See especially ch. 3.

[2] Edward M. Graham, "Foreign Direct Investment in the United States and U.S. Interests," *Science*, vol. 254, Dec. 20, 1992, pp. 1740-1745.

[3] For data on technology trade among the United States, Japan, and the EC see "Major Indices of Japanese R&D Activity," JPRS-JSP-73-003, Jan. 21, 1993, pp. 40-53. See also General Accounting Office, *U.S. Business Access to Certain Foreign State-of-the-Art Technology*, September 1991.

[4] John Rutter, "Recent Trends in Foreign Direct Investment in the United States: The Boom of the 80s Vanishes," Department of Commerce, International Trade Administration, December 1992. However, it should be noted that more recent reports suggest, for example, that there has been a net disinvestment during 1992. See "Japan Keeps Cash at Home," *Financial Times*, June 15, 1993, p. 4; as taken from Bank for International Settlements, *63rd Annual Report* (Basle, Switzerland: BIS, 1993); see also U.S. Department of Commerce, Bureau of Economic Analysis, "Net International Investment Position, 1992," press release, June 30, 1993.

Table 3-1—Inward Flows of Foreign Direct Investment, by Host Country per Annum, 1981-1992 (in billions of dollars)

	1981	1982	1983	1984	1985	1986	1987	1988	1989	1990	1991	1992
United States	25.2	13.8	11.9	25.4	19.0	34.1	58.1	59.4	69.0	46.1	12.6	3.9
United Kingdom	5.9	5.3	5.1	–0.2	5.0	7.3	13.9	18.2	30.4	33.1	21.1	19.1
Netherlands	1.5	1.0	0.8	0.6	0.6	1.9	2.3	4.1	6.4	8.7	5.1	5.2
(West) Germany	0.3	0.8	1.8	0.6	0.6	1.2	1.9	1.2	7.0	2.3	2.9	3.0
Japan	0.2	0.4	0.4	0.0	0.6	0.2	1.2	–0.5	–1.1	1.8	1.4	2.7
France	2.4	1.6	1.6	2.2	2.2	2.8	4.6	7.2	9.6	9.2	11.1	16.3

NOTE: All figures are calculated on historical cost basis and are not adjusted for inflation.

SOURCE: Organization for Economic Co-operation and Development (OECD), "Inward Direct Investment Flows," *International Direct Investment Polices and Trends in the 1980s* (Paris: OECD, 1992), table 3; OECD, *Financial Market & Trends*, June 1993, table 1.

Figure 3-1—Foreign Direct Investment in the U.S., Annual Growth Rate and Position, 1962-1992

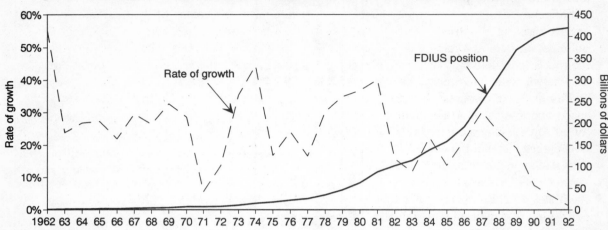

NOTES: All data are calculated on historical cost basis and are not adjusted for inflation. Differences in data and calculation may account for disparities between Department of Commerce and Organization for Economic Cooperation and Development (OECD) statistics.

SOURCE: U.S. Department of Commerce, Bureau of Economic Analysis, *Business Statistics, 1963-91* (Washington, DC: U.S. Government Printing Office, June 1992), p. A-120; U.S. Department of Commerce, Bureau of Economic Analysis, "Net Investment Position, 1992," press release, June 30, 1993.

that MNEs increasingly prefer strategic alliances because they allow greater flexibility and less commitment than strategies associated with FDI.

5. A discrepancy exists between the comparatively open-door, national treatment policy towards foreign multinational corporate investment adopted by the United States and the United Kingdom and those policies adopted by other major trading nations. Only the United Kingdom (since the early 20th century) and the United States (in the post-WWII period) have applied free trade principles to the inward and outward flow of investment capital. U.S. policy has actively encouraged such practices.[5] As table 3-1 indicates, from 1986 to 1990, FDI into the United States and the United Kingdom increased to record levels. During the same

period, FDI into Germany and Japan remained low; for Japan, in 1988 and 1989 (the peak years for FDI in the United States), net inward investment was negative.

6. Since the 1970s, some Organization for Economic Cooperation and Development (OECD) countries have liberalized their rules on the outflow of investment capital; during the same period, there has been an increased inflow of FDI in some countries. But historically this inflow has been regulated to provide limited market access for foreign producers, sometimes in exchange for the transfer of proprietary technology. It remains small relative to outflows. In some European states (e.g., France and Italy) government policies on inward FDI have been consistently restrictive. The constraints in Japan are more systematic; they are

[5] For a comparative historical analysis of FDI in Europe, Japan, and the United States, see Simon Reich, *The Fruits of Fascism: Postwar Prosperity in Historical Perspective* (Ithaca, NY: Cornell, 1990). As an illustration of these policies in practice see, for example, Mira Wilkins and Frank E. Hill, *American Business Abroad: Ford On Six Continents* (Detroit, MI: Wayne State University Press, 1964); for the case of policy in Japan, see Mark Mason, *American Multinationals and Japan: The Political Economy of Japanese Capital Controls, 1899-1980* (Cambridge, MA: Council on East Asian Studies, Harvard University, 1992). For a European assessment of the constraints on FDI in the United States, see Services of the Commission of the European Communities, *Report on United States Trade and Investment Barriers: Problems of Doing Business With the U.S.* (Brussels, Belgium: Commission Services, April 1993), pp. 82-90.

also more often a product of private sector initiatives.[6]

7. MNEs based in countries with restrictive FDI policies may enjoy strategic advantages over their U.S. competitors. These advantages are associated with the generation of artificial profits in home markets[7] and the capacity to reach economies of scale. Senior officers of major American companies told OTA that such advantages threaten the degree of competitiveness and even the continued existence of some large-scale U.S.-based MNEs.

8. Japanese and European policymakers have concluded that they must maintain a domestic presence in some sectors even when it seems expensive in the short run. These governments have reached an understanding with their MNEs; business has agreed to sustain some production that may be unprofitable in the short term but that is essential to the productivity of several crucial sectors. Furthermore, MNEs in these countries have agreed to maintain as much high value-added production in their home base as possible. Some governments among the OECD nations have instituted a variety of subsidies and structural adjustment policies to assist their own MNEs.[8]

FDI IN THE UNITED STATES

■ What is Foreign Direct Investment?

There are two types of private overseas investment, portfolio investment and foreign direct investment. Portfolio investment involves the purchase of bonds of U.S. firms or the U.S. Government, or holdings in U.S. banks. Portfolio investment accounts for more than 60 percent of transaction flows into and out of the United States.

According to the International Monetary Fund:

Direct investment refers to investment that is made to acquire a lasting interest in an enterprise operating in an economy other than that of the investor, the investor's purpose being to have an effective voice in the management of the enterprise.[9]

Foreign direct investment in the United States, however, has a more specific legal and statistical definition. The *International Investment and Trade in Services Survey Act* says it is the ownership by a foreign person or corporation of 10 percent or more of the voting equity of a firm located in the United States. Such an investment is considered evidence of a long-term interest in, and a reflection of influence over, a company's affairs.[10] This definition has advantages and disadvantages, and is open to a variety of exceptions. An individual or company owning less than 10 percent might still be the largest and most influential shareholder; one owning more may remain a passive investor. Either way, the behavior of the company or its strategic significance might remain unaffected by a change in ownership of this type.

This report is less concerned with the formal definition of FDI than the influence that foreign

[6] See Office of the United States Trade Representative, *1993 National Trade Estimate Report on Foreign Trade Barriers* (Washington, DC: 1993), pp. 79-94, 143-170; for a Japanese perspective in support of this finding, see The Report of the Ad-Hoc Committee on Foreign Direct Investment in Japan, Keidanren Committee on International Industrial Cooperation, Committee on Foreign Affiliated Corporations, *Improvement of the Investment Climate and Promotion of Foreign Direct Investment into Japan*; see also House Wednesday Group, *Beyond Revisionism: Towards a New U.S.-Japan Policy for the Post-Cold War Era* (Washington, DC: Congress of the United States, March 1993).

[7] House Wednesday Group, ibid., p. 18.

[8] For related discussion, see Laura D'Andrea Tyson, *Who's Bashing Whom? Trade Conflict in High Technology Industries* (Washington, DC: International Institute for Economics, 1992).

[9] IMF definition cited in DeAnne Julius, *Global Companies and Public Policy: The Growing Challenge of Foreign Direct Investment* (London: Royal Institute of International Affairs, 1990), p. 15.

[10] See U.S. Department of Commerce, Bureau of Economic Analysis, *Foreign Direct Investment in the United States, 1987 Benchmark Survey, Final Results* (Washington, DC: U.S. Government Printing Office, August 1990).

direct investors exert on the behavior of corporations. Such influence can alter a firm's standard practices relative to other companies in a particular industry. Moreover, foreign ownership can have major strategic implications for the welfare of the U.S. economy, in terms of technological development, balance of trade flows, employment training and practices, and national security requirements.[11]

Foreign direct investment includes the purchase of resources, such as knowledge, managerial expertise, plant facilities, or real estate, and the building of greenfield plants. FDI is not defined by the source of the capital used, but rather by ownership, even if foreign persons or corporations used domestic sources to finance their transactions. Although FDI accounts for less than 25 percent of all investment flows, it can be of strategic importance to the U.S. economy because of the types of jobs it generates, its impact on domestic industry, and its effect on the balance of trade, especially in industries like autos and computers.

With some exceptions, the United States has generally applied national treatment to foreign investors.[12] National treatment articulates the principle that foreign investors, whatever form their investment takes, should be treated as if they were domestic investors. This approach encourages the influx of FDI. The U.S. Government's approach to FDI comes much closer to the position of the advocates of FDIUS than that of its critics, as was clearly articulated in 1991 by the Bush administration:

The Administration supports maintaining an open foreign investment policy, with limited exceptions related to national security. This policy produces the greatest possible national benefits from all investments made in the U.S. economy. The United States has long recognized that unhindered international investment is beneficial to all nations, that it is a "positive sum" game.[13]

Prior to the mid-1970s, the principle of national treatment had little practical consequence in the United States. The inflow of investment funds was minimal, largely because other industrial powers lacked the necessary capital. A second important barrier to entry was the peculiarity of U.S. markets, for example, until the first gas crisis American consumers were uniquely unconcerned with fuel economy and preferred large, comfortable automobiles. Most U.S.-based MNEs did not face serious competition from foreign-based MNEs, either through the import of finished products or through foreign investment.

U.S.-based MNEs therefore prospered in relatively insulated consumer markets. This insularity lent itself to the development of historically unparalleled wealth and strength. The surplus was so large that U.S. citizens enjoyed the highest per capita income in the world, while its corporations benefited from technological leadership and economies of scale. Together, these factors afforded many domestic firms the capacity to build or acquire overseas facilities, and thus produced many multinational enterprises.[14] The high value of the dollar made U.S. real estate expensive, and meant there were significant disincentives to

---

11 Julius, op. cit., footnote 9, p. 14.

12 See Edward M. Graham and Paul R. Krugman, *Foreign Direct Investment in the United States* (Washington, DC: Institute for International Economics, 1989), pp. 95-109. Critics contend that existing laws and the proposed NAFTA Agreement Annexes provide a legal framework that could support a decision by the U.S. Government to implement policies that moved away from national treatment of FDI. For example, see Edward M. Graham and Christopher Wilkie, "Multinationals and the Investment Provision of the NAFTA," to appear in *The International Trade Journal*, vol. 8, No. 3 (winter 1993-1994). However, there is no evidence to date that the U.S. Government intends to do so.

13 *Economic Report of the President*, Transmitted to Congress, February 1991, together with the *Annual Report of the Council of Economic Advisors* (Washington, DC: U.S. Government Printing Office, 1991), p. 262.

14 Raymond Vernon, "International Investment and International Trade in the Product Cycle," *The Quarterly Journal of Economics*, May 1990, No. 2, pp. 190-207.

manufacturing, wholesaling, or real estate investments by foreign-based MNEs. This approximated the conditions for a sanctuary market; accordingly, some people contend that U.S. criticism of Japan for having a comparable situation today is inappropriate. But, if the United States did indeed enjoy a sanctuary market, it was by force of circumstance, not by the design of the public or private sector, as is the case in Japan.[15]

The issue of national treatment started to assume importance in the 1970s. The U.S. Government responded to the influx of FDI favorably, with only nominal institutional constraints on investment flows. At the Federal level, the institution directly responsible for addressing issues relating to FDIUS is the Committee on Foreign Investment in the United States (CFIUS). Created by President Gerald Ford in 1975 as an oversight body, CFIUS monitors and regulates FDIUS from the standpoint of protecting the national security. It is an interagency body composed of officials from the Departments of State, Commerce, Defense, and Justice, the Office of the United States Trade Representative, the Office of Management and Budget, and the Council of Economic Advisers; it is usually chaired by a Treasury official.

Most CFIUS authority comes from the Exon-Florio provision in the *Omnibus Trade and Competitiveness Act of 1988*, which empowers the President to veto any takeover of a U.S. firm on national security grounds. Agency officials see the mandate of CFIUS as being consistent with a broader U.S. policy "to welcome direct investment and to support free and open foreign direct investment among all nations."[16] They have stated that the Exon-Florio Provision is a statute that protects national security without compromising an open investment policy.[17]

The Treasury officials who have headed the agency have adopted a narrow position in defining threats to national security.[18] One prominent critic, for example, noted in a 1992 congressional hearing that U.S. foreign direct investment policy does not distinguish between purchases made by foreign investors from the private sector and those made by foreign governments, whose motives might not be "market-driven." She recommended that the U.S. Government routinely examine all prospective purchases involving foreign governments. She also suggested that the definition of national security be clarified to include a list of critical military technologies that would not be available for foreign purchase, while the definition of national security be expanded to include elements of economic security.[19]

However, with very few notable exceptions, CFIUS has adopted a passive role. Agency officials have "received over 700 notices since the inception of Exon-Florio in August 1988. Of that total, 13 transactions have been subject to a 45-day extended review. Nine of those reached the President's desk for decision. In eight of those nine transactions, he decided to take no action."[20]

---

[15] House Wednesday Group, op. cit., footnote 6.

[16] Statement by Stephen J. Canner, Treasury Official Director for International Investment, before the Defense Policy Panel and Investigations Subcommittee of the Armed Services Committee, U.S. House of Representatives, May 14, 1992.

[17] See statement by Olin Wethington, Assistant Secretary for International Affairs, U.S. Department of the Treasury, at Hearing before the Subcommittee on International Finance and Monetary Policy on June 4, *Foreign Acquisition of U.S. Owned Companies* (Washington, DC: U.S. Government Printing Office, 1992), pp. 5-6.

[18] For example see Statement of Peter Mills, Former Chief Administrative Officer of Sematech, at Hearing before the Subcommittee on International Finance and Monetary Policy on June 4, ibid., pp. 15-18. Some analysts argue that without change the Exon-Florio legislation would support much more restrictive policies towards FDIUS. See Edward M. Graham and Michael E. Ebert, "Foreign Direct Investment and U.S. National Security," *The World Economy*, vol. 14, No. 3, September 1991, pp. 245-268.

[19] Statement by Laura D'Andrea Tyson, at Hearing before the Subcommittee on International Finance and Monetary Policy on June 4, op. cit., footnote 17, pp. 18-19.

[20] Statement by Stephen J. Canner, op. cit., footnote 16.

In the case of the attempted purchase of General Ceramics Ltd. by the Tokuyama Soda Co., CFIUS recommended that the acquisition be blocked because the U.S. firm was a supplier of nuclear defense technology. The sale went through after the nuclear weapons component was sold to another firm. The only recorded case of a sale being blocked after CFIUS review was the proposed purchase of Mamco Manufacturing of Seattle by the China National Aero-Technology Import and Export Corp. According to the director of CFIUS, the agency "is achieving its goal of protecting the national security without discouraging foreign direct investment."[21]

The limited use to date of the legislative provisions under which CFIUS operates does not appear to represent a significant barrier to foreign direct investors. Moreover, many observers note that informal limitations on foreign investors are minimal or nonexistent in the United States.[22] However, some contend that the very existence of CFIUS has had a chilling effect on FDIUS.

The loss of both market insularity and U.S. technological superiority has heightened competition from many European and Japanese firms and their affiliates operating in the United States. Formerly, the issue of mutual openness for trade and investment was treated by U.S. policymakers as relatively unimportant. In the context of U.S. economic dominance, policymakers often considered America's primary economic role to be that of a locomotive for global prosperity. But the successful regeneration of the economies of Europe and the emergence of Japan as an economic superpower, coupled with a relative decline in U.S. economic strength and technological advantage, has put new competitive pressures on U.S.-based MNEs.[23]

During the 1980s, the United States was the largest single recipient of FDI, accounting for over 30 percent of global FDI that totalled about $1 trillion, with Britain in second position at 15 percent.[24] This was a dramatic change for the United States, whose MNEs have been the largest overseas investors for most of the post-WWII period.

In the early 1970s, U.S. scholars worried that large overseas investment by America's largest and most powerful MNEs might contribute substantially to a decline in U.S. competitiveness, and to the growth in the budget deficit, particularly if the profits were not repatriated. At the same time, Europeans feared that Europe would be dominated by the subsidiaries of U.S.-based MNEs, and that European companies might not develop sufficient scale and scope to compete on a European or global basis.[25]

In the late 1980s, the focus of debate changed dramatically, as the huge surplus of U.S. direct investment abroad (USDIA) over FDIUS reversed course. Based on book value calculations, FDIUS exceeded U.S. foreign investments for the

---

[21] Ibid. For details of the review process itself undertaken by CFIUS, see statement of Frederick Volcansek, Acting Assistant Secretary for Trade Development, U.S. Department of Commerce, in Hearing before the Subcommittee on International Finance and Monetary Policy on June 4, op. cit., footnote 17, pp. 10-11.

[22] For an alternative view, see Services of the Commission of the European Communities, op. cit., footnote 5, pp. 82-90.

[23] This issue was a central one addressed in *Competing Economies*, op. cit., footnote 1.

[24] In contrast, the Federal Republic of Germany attracted investments totaling $19 billion in this period. See "Study: U.S. Leads, Germany Trails, in Attractiveness to Direct Investors," *This Week in Germany*, Oct. 23, 1992, p. 5.

[25] For a discussion of these issues see C. Fred Bergsten, Thomas Horst, and Theodore H. Moran, *American Multinationals and American Interests* (Washington, DC: Brookings Institution, 1978); Robert Gilpin, *U.S. Power and the Multinational Corporation: The Political Economy of Foreign Direct Investment* (New York, NY: Basic Books, 1975); Fred Block, *The Origins of International Economic Disorder: A Study of the United States International Monetary Policy from World War II to the Present* (Berkeley, CA: University of California Press, 1977); and Jean-Jacque Servan Schreiber, *The American Challenge* (New York, NY: Athenium, 1968).

first time in 1989; foreign MNEs invested more in the United States than did U.S. MNEs abroad.[26]

Although global FDI rose from $208 billion in 1973 to $1,403 billion in 1989, FDIUS increased much faster, from $21 billion (10 percent of the total) to $401 billion (29 percent of the total) in the same period. The flow of direct investment into Japan, however, remained low.[27] Table 3-2 compares the shares of total global inward FDI of several host countries and regions.

The United States thus became the world's largest importer of capital in the 1980s. The gross total of FDIUS grew from $83 billion to $185 billion between 1981 and 1985, increasing at an annual rate of 17 percent. The rate of FDIUS growth accelerated between 1985 and 1989, averaging 21 percent. In 1990 and 1991, however, the rate of FDIUS slowed dramatically and may even have become negative in 1992, although OECD and U.S. Department of Commerce data do not agree on this last point (see figure 1-2 in chapter 1 and figure 3-1 in this chapter).

Some economists argue that a decline in new FDI in 1990 and 1991 may have signaled a break in new FDIUS; they postulate that the flow of net lending from parents to affiliates declined and the stock of retained earnings of U.S. affiliates fell because affiliates paid dividends to their parents despite negative earnings.[28] Figure 3-1 graphically illustrates the cumulative position and growth rate of FDIUS. While there has been a dramatic decline in the growth rate in the early 1990s, the total of FDIUS has grown, despite a recession and slow recovery.

■ Measuring Foreign Presence

Measuring the importance of foreign firms in the domestic economy is complex.[29] On the face of it, foreign-controlled production does not loom large in the landscape of the U.S. economy. Despite the sometimes contentious public debate surrounding FDIUS, foreign firms accounted in 1988 for a relatively small share of the U.S. economy—no more than 4.1 percent of total employment and 4.1 percent of total domestic product.[30] As one Commerce Department analyst observed, ''the role of foreign-owned firms in the U.S. economy—in terms of proportion of domestic sales, assets or employment—remains the lowest, except for Japan, among industrial countries.''[31] In 1988, U.S. affiliates of foreign firms did, however, account for a larger share of the domestic manufacturing economy, with 14.7 percent of the assets, 12.2 percent of the sales, and 10.5 percent of the gross product. (See box 3-A.)[32]

These figures, however, underestimate the importance of foreign multinationals in the U.S. economy. To appreciate the full impact of foreign-based firms, all foreign-owned production—both FDI and imports—should be considered together. In specific industries—many of them related to critical technologies—the foreign position is much larger than the averages suggest. For example, in the automotive industry, foreign

---

[26] U.S. Department of Commerce, Office of the Chief Economist, *Foreign Direct Investment in the United States: Review and Analysis of Current Developments* (Washington, DC: U.S. Government Printing Office, August 1991), p. 4. It should be noted that the U.S. book value of the net foreign direct investment position has been positive since 1990 (see figure 3-A-3 in box 3-A). U.S. Department of Commerce, ''Net International Investment Position, 1992,'' op. cit., footnote 4.

[27] U.S. Department of Commerce, *Foreign Direct Investment in the United States*, ibid., p. 21.

[28] Graham, op. cit., footnote 2, p. 1740.

[29] For discussions on the issue of alternative measures of FDI see Julius, op. cit., footnote 9, pp. 14-24; Robert Eisner and Paul J. Pieper, ''The World's Greatest Debtor Nation?,'' *North American Review of Economics and Finance*, 1 (1), pp. 9-32; U.S. Department of Commerce and Bureau of Economic Analysis, *Survey of Current Business*, May 1991, especially p. 41.

[30] Gerald R. Moody, ''Role of Foreign-Owned U.S. Affiliates in the U.S. Economy, 1977-88,'' U.S. Department of Commerce, *Foreign Direct Investment in the United States*, op. cit., footnote 26, p. 30.

[31] Sumiye Okubo McGuire, ''Summary and Conclusions,'' U.S. Department of Commerce, ibid., p. 84.

[32] Moody, op. cit., footnote 30, p. 30.

Table 3-2—Host Country Share of Global Foreign Direct Investment, Selected Years (percent of world total)

	1967	1973	1980	1989
U.S	9.4	9.9	16.5	28.6
EC	23.5	32.7	37.0	34.5
Japan	0.8	0.8	0.7	0.7
LDCs	30.6	26.1	22.0	19.2
Other	29.4	24.8	18.7	13.0

NOTES: All figures are EC-12, regardless of year. LDCs denote lesser developed countries, as defined in the source.

SOURCE: U.S Department of Commerce, Bureau of Economic Analysis, *Foreign Direct Investment in the United States: Review and Analysis of Current Developments* (Washington, DC: U.S. Government Printing Office, August 1991), table 4-2.

producers control about 31 percent of the U.S. market. In the merchant semiconductor market, the figure was about 30 percent in 1991,[33] and in the chemical industry, the foreign share was about 26 percent.[34]

Significant foreign production is conducted in the United States. Foreign firms provide an estimated 72,200 automotive industry jobs in the United States,[35] 280,800 jobs in the chemical industry,[36] and 51,500 jobs in the steel industry.[37] This accounts for a significant share of total domestic employment in major industries, as shown in figure 3-2.

The pattern of FDIUS that developed during the 1980s was characterized by an increase in Canadian, Japanese, and European investment.[38] In the aggregate, Europe remained the leading foreign investor,[39] accounting for approximately 65 percent of all FDIUS in the 1980s, but the Japanese position rapidly expanded. Figure 3-3 charts these investment positions. Japan's rise from the fourth to the largest single investor is particularly striking.

Japan's investments have received intense scrutiny for a number of reasons. These include the accelerated rate of growth of Japanese direct investment (in the context of the competitive challenge of the Japanese economy), the asymmetry in trade and investment access by U.S. firms to Japan, and the burgeoning U.S. trade deficit. In addition, there is a widespread perception—right or wrong—that Japanese investors are better able to maximize market share and absorb technology than other foreign investors. Furthermore, Japan is the most diversified of the major foreign direct investors in the United States, and often all their major producers in a sector—such as automobiles or steel—invest in the United States, giving critics a sense that Japanese investment is enveloping the U.S. economy.

The breadth of Japanese investment is reflected in employment figures for manufacturing industries by sector. Table 3-3 profiles foreign affiliate employment in the manufacturing and wholesale trade sectors, covering the seven largest investors in the United States during the early 1990s. While Britain and Canada remain the largest two manufacturing employers, the table shows significant employment levels for Japanese affiliates. The table also illustrates the comparatively broad

---

[33] Semiconductor Industry Association, *Annual Data Book*, 1991, p. 12.

[34] U.S. Department of Commerce, Bureau of Economic Analysis, *Survey of Current Business*, various issues 1992; *U.S. Industrial Outlook* (Washington, DC: U.S. Government Printing Office, January 1992 and January 1993).

[35] As of 1988; Economic Strategy Institute, "The Case for Saving the Big Three," interim report (Washington, DC: Economic Strategy Institute, 1992), p. 56.

[36] As of 1988; U.S. Department of Commerce, *Foreign Direct Investment in the United States*, op. cit., footnote 26, p. 68.

[37] Ibid., p. 62.

[38] Ibid., p. 23.

[39] KPMG Peat Marwick, "European Investment in the United States," report for The European Institute, 1991, p. 1.

Box 3-A—Three Ways To Calculate Foreign Direct Investment in the United States (FDIUS)

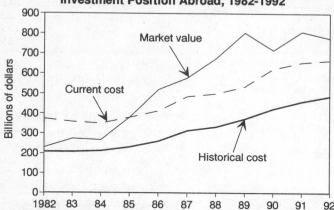

Figure 3-A-1—Alternative Valuations of U.S. Direct Investment Position Abroad, 1982-1992

SOURCE: J. Steven Landefeld and Ann M. Lawson, "Valuation of the Net U.S. International Investment Position," *Survey of Current Business*, May 1991, p. 40, table 1; Russell B. Scholl, Raymond L. Mataloni, and Steve D. Bezirganian, "The International Investment Position of the United States in 1991," *Survey of Current Business*, June 1992, p. 53, table 4; U.S. Department of Commerce, Bureau of Economic Analysis, "Net International Investment Position, 1992," press release, June 30, 1993.

Measuring global foreign direct investment (FDI) is a contentious issue. Depending on how FDI is calculated, very different outcomes can be reached in identifying the ratio of U.S. direct investment abroad (USDIA) to FDIUS, and second, the relative significance of foreign investment in the United States. The most widely used method is the "book value" or "historical cost" approach. This approach calculates the value of FDI from the initial cost of the investment, ignoring subsequent changes in the value of the investments. There are two major problems with the book value approach: it usually understates substantially the current value of investments; and it can be distorted by currency fluctuations.

One alternative to calculating by book value is to calculate by stock or current cost. This approach calculates the current value of an investment, not its original value. This method also has problems, principally because it is very laborious to update repeatedly the values of numerous investments.

A third method is the "replacement cost adjustment" or "market value" method. This is similar to the stock value method, but focuses on investment goods prices rather than on share prices. This approach has two major deficiencies. First, the current value of many investments has little to do with the replacement cost of the original capital goods, much of which may be outdated; second, the value of an investment may have less to do with the market value of physical capital assets than with the value of intangible assets such as skills, knowledge, or goodwill.[1]

There are two practical implications of the distinctions among the book (historical cost), stock (current cost), and replacement (market value) methods. The first concerns the ratio between the outflow of FDI from the United States (USDIA) and the inflow of capital (FDIUS). According to Department of Commerce estimates, based on book value, FDIUS exceeded USDIA for the first time in 1989.[2] This method prompted some economists to contend that the United States had become the "world's greatest debtor nation," based on its net international investment position. Others, relying on stock estimates that recalculate old investment at present values, have reached a different conclusion, especially when other resources such as gold are added to equity ownership.[3]

---

[1] For a general discussion of the merits of all three approaches see Robert Eisner and Paul J. Pieper, "The World's Greatest Debtor Nation?," *North American Review of Economics and Finance*, vol. 1, No. 1, pp. 9-32. The market value figures are available in BEA, "Valuation of the U.S. Net International Investment Position of the United States," *Survey of Current Business*, June 1992, p. 53, table 4.

[2] U.S. Department of Commerce, Office of the Chief Economist, *Foreign Direct Investment in the United States: Review and Analysis of Current Developments* (Washington, DC: U.S. Government Printing Office, August 1991), p. 4.

[3] Eisner and Pieper, op. cit., footnote 1, p. 11.

(continued on next page)

Box 3-A—Continued

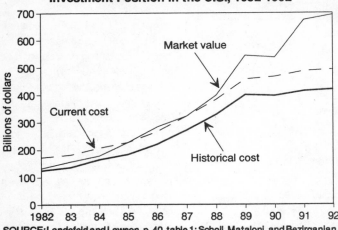

Figure 3-A-2—Alternative Valuations of the Foreign Direct Investment Position in the U.S., 1982-1992

SOURCE: Landefeld and Lawson, p. 40, table 1; Scholl, Mataloni, and Bezirganian, p. 53, table 4; U.S. Department of Commerce, Bureau of Economic Analysis, "Net International Investment Position, 1992," press release, June 30, 1993.

Using Bureau of Economic Analysis (BEA) data and all three methods of calculating USDIA, FDIUS, and the net position, Department of Commerce economists in 1991 concluded that only the book method showed the United States as a net debtor in 1989. Both the stock and the replacement methods yielded a net direct investment surplus. (Figures 3-A-1, 3-A-2, and 3-A-3 show the results of the different measurements of USDIA, FDIUS, and the net direct investment positions.)

Using assigned stock or replacement value as an indicator suggests that USDIA is still greater than FDIUS by a large margin. Even the book method shows the net investment position of the United States in surplus after

1989. However, the replacement value figures are affected by the high value of the U.S. dollar in the 1950s and 1960s relative to its value between 1985 and 1990. In addition, the figures are potentially distorted by stock market fluctuations.

The second practical implication concerns the investment positions of different countries in the United States. Critics suggest that book value understates the position of historical European, particularly British, investment and overstates the extent of the Japanese position because it is more recent. This view holds that Japanese FDI is overstated on a global scale as well as in the United States.[4] On the other hand, some analysts argue that too much emphasis is placed on the timing of FDIUS. The distortion of the position of the major bilateral investors is much smaller than critics suggest because the vast majority of both European and Japanese FDI occurred in the 1980s.[5]

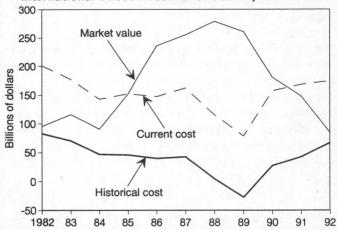

Figure 3-A-3—Alternative Valuations of the Net U.S. International Direct Investment Position, 1982-1992

SOURCE: Landefeld and Lawson, p. 40, table 1; Scholl, Mataloni, and Bezirganian, p. 53, table 4; U.S. Department of Commerce, Bureau of Economic Analysis, "Net International Investment Position, 1992," press release, June 30, 1993.

[4] DeAnne Julius, *Global Companies and Public Policy: The Growing Challenge of Foreign Direct Investment* (London: Royal Institute of International Affairs, 1990), p. 38.

[5] See Eisner and Pieper, op. cit., footnote 1, p. 17, table 5B.

Figure 3-2—Percent of U.S. Workforce Employed by Foreign-Owned Affiliates in Selected Manufacturing Sectors, 1990

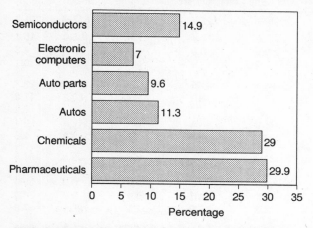

SOURCE: U.S. Department of Labor, Bureau of Labor Statistics, "Employment and Wages in Foreign Owned Businesses in the United States, Fourth Quarter 1990," press release, October 20, 1992, table 2.

Figure 3-3—Foreign Direct Investment Position in the U.S. by Selected Country, 1980-1992

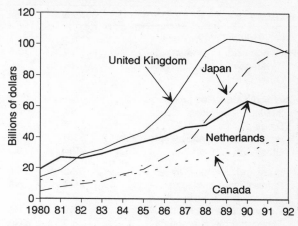

NOTE: All data are calculated on a historical cost basis and are not adjusted for inflation.

SOURCE: U.S. Department of Commerce, Bureau of Economic Analysis, *Foreign Direct Investment in the United States: Review and Current Developments*, August 1991, table 2-4; U.S. Department of Commerce, Bureau of Economic Analysis, *Foreign Direct Investment in the United States: An Update* (Washington, DC: U.S. Government Printing Office, June 1993); U.S. Department of Commerce, Bureau of Economic Analysis, "Net Investment Position, 1992," press release, June 30, 1993, table 3.

distribution of Japanese affiliates, as well as the relatively high levels of Japanese affiliate employment in wholesale trade. In comparison, Canadian affiliates, which have approximately the same number of workers in aggregate, employ only 13.5 percent as many workers in the wholesale trades. British investors employ nearly a quarter-million more people, yet they employ some 90,000 fewer in wholesaling. Given that wholesale trade is directly related to the import of goods, rather than their domestic manufacture, this statistic suggests that Japanese investors employ a large percentage of workers among affiliates that are primarily devoted to importing. This issue is returned to later in this chapter.

Japanese manufacturing investment in the United States also differs from traditional investment patterns because of its strategic nature. Japanese firms have invested heavily, for example, in steel, rubber, and autos as one complex, or triangle, of investment (consumer electronics, semiconductors, and computers are another). These horizontally and vertically integrated groups appear to be more coherent, comprehensive, and strategic than European patterns of FDIUS, such as heavy British investments in chemicals, medical instruments, and publishing, and have thus tended to generate more concern among critics. Figure 3-4 shows Japanese affiliates' assets in several manufacturing sectors.

Overall, Japan's FDIUS rose from $4.7 billion in 1980 to $69.7 billion in 1989, increasing at an average annual rate of 32.5 percent between 1980 and 1985, and accelerating to 37.8 percent between 1985 and 1989. The rate of Japanese FDIUS declined between 1990 and 1992,[40] because of a recession in Japan and an increase in the cost of capital in Japan.

Putting these figures in perspective, the EC countries' expansion of FDIUS, although notable, was much slower than Japan's. European FDIUS rose from $47.3 billion in 1980 to $234.8 billion

[40] "Japan Keeps Cash at Home," op. cit., footnote 4, p. 4.

Table 3-3—Employment of Affiliates by Industry of Affiliate and by Country of Ultimate Beneficial Owner, 1990 (in thousands of employees)

Industries	Canada	France	Germany	Netherlands	Switzerland	Britain	Japan
Total manufacturing	305.5	181.1	249.7	127.7	178.6	538.7	291.7
Food and kindred products	NA	12.5	2.9	17.4	NA	105.0	15.1
Beverages	NA	5.5	0.5	0.0	*	2.4	4.3
Other	21.0	7.0	2.4	17.4	NA	102.8	10.7
Chemicals and allied products	NA	22.8	94.4	41.5	60.4	129.2	23.7
Industrial chemicals	NA	NA	70.1	NA	1.1	80.3	11.2
Drugs	*	NA	4.2	*	53.6	32.0	7.2
Soap, cleaners, and toiletries	1.5	0.5	18.0	NA	NA	NA	2.7
Other	0.4	0.9	2.2	NA	NA	NA	2.6
Primary and fabricated metals	32.2	35.3	21.8	10.5	8.2	39.5	61.8
Primary metal industries	24.2	NA	6.0	0.0	5.7	10.4	54.0
Ferrous	9.3	3.1	2.0	0.0	0.3	0.5	50.0
Nonferrous	14.9	NA	4.1	0.0	5.4	9.9	4.0
Fabricated metal products	8.0	NA	15.8	10.5	2.5	29.1	7.8
Machinery	41.3	34.5	59.9	NA	49.3	92.1	89.6
Machinery, except electrical	6.1	15.1	20.9	1.6	NA	44.7	54.7
Computer and office equipment	0.7	NA	2.7	0.7	NA	10.3	25.2
Other	5.4	NA	18.2	1.0	18.3	34.4	29.5
Electric and electronic equipment	35.2	19.4	39.0	NA	NA	47.4	34.9
Audio, video, and commercial	NA	NA	NA	NA	NA	7.5	3.4
Electronic components	2.1	NA	12.6	2.7	0.4	11.1	24.1
Other	NA	5.5	NA	0.5	NA	28.8	7.4
Other manufacturing	90.2	76.0	70.8	NA	NA	172.7	101.6
Textile products and apparel	10.7	1.9	7.7	0.4	1.5	20.0	8.6
Lumber and furniture	2.4	0.7	5.5	0.0	0.4	6.2	1.0
Paper and allied products	5.9	0.5	1.6	NA	NA	5.9	4.2
Printing and publishing	51.1	NA	NA	NA	NA	33.7	NA
Rubber products	NA	NA	NA	NA	*	NA	NA
Misc. plastics products	3.5	4.8	3.4	NA	0.5	10.8	3.5
Stone, clay, and glass products	NA	29.9	10.1	NA	5.3	30.7	11.2
Transportation equipment	NA	10.9	6.1	0.7	0.5	22.4	26.2
Motor vehicles and equipment	7.6	NA	4.5	0.0	0.5	4.0	26.2
Other	NA	NA	1.6	0.7	0.0	18.4	0.0
Instruments and related products	1.1	6.6	9.4	0.3	7.1	30.9	5.6
Other	1.3	3.0	0.7	*	2.4	NA	3.8
Total wholesale trade	20.7	43.4	65.6	16.2	14.9	59.9	152.9
Motor vehicles	1.4	NA	18.4	0.1	0.0	5.0	38.1
Professional/commercial equipment ..	0.2	0.4	4.0	2.2	5.7	6.1	18.7
Metals and minerals	NA	2.4	6.8	0.7	0.1	3.6	7.1
Electrical goods	0.9	0.8	NA	0.1	0.4	2.1	68.3
Machinery and equipment	3.1	0.7	4.6	2.8	3.0	4.3	9.2
Other durable goods	0.7	2.4	1.5	2.5	1.2	19.5	5.7
Groceries and related products	NA	NA	NA	1.4	0.2	7.6	1.2
Farm product raw materials	0.1	11.9	0.1	0.6	NA	0.3	1.5
Other nondurable goods	7.4	11.4	4.2	5.8	NA	11.5	3.1

NOTES: Ultimate Beneficial Owner is that firm, moving up a U.S. affiliate's ownership chain, and beginning with and including the foreign parent, that is not owned more than 50 percent by another firm. An asterix indicates fewer than 50 employees. NA indicates data is not available.

SOURCE: U.S. Department of Commerce, Bureau of Economic Analysis, *Foreign Direct Investment in the United States, Operations of U.S. Affiliates of Foreign Companies, Preliminary 1990 Estimates* (Washington, DC: U.S. Government Printing Office, August 1992), table F-3.

in 1989,[41] at an average annual increase of 17.8 percent between 1980 and 1985, and 21.6 percent between 1985 and 1989. In other words, the growth rate of Japanese FDIUS was much higher than the European growth rate of FDIUS, although cumulative EC FDIUS is still much higher than that of Japan. Japanese FDIUS is also much higher than U.S. investment in Japan. (See figure 1-10 in chapter 1, which compares Japanese investment in the United States to U.S. direct investment in Japan through the 1980s. See also figure 1-9, which compares U.S. investment in the European Community to EC investment in the United States.[42])

▌ Reasons for Reversal

What explains the shift in flows toward FDIUS? Traditional economic theory postulates that foreign investors make decisions based on two sets of considerations. Classical macroeconomic investment theory points to the significance that investors attach to the marginal returns on capital relative to its cost, motivated by the desire to maximize returns while hedging against interest and exchange rate fluctuations.[43] The alternative, microeconomic or industrial organization approach, focuses on the strategic behavior of the multinational enterprise. It claims that MNEs set up foreign subsidiaries because of their desire to sustain profits in the face of stiffer competition; to gain access to a market or expand share; to sustain or create a comparative advantage enjoyed by the firm; to service the particular needs of a customer or its market; or for political reasons.[44]

Dating from the late 1970s, foreign firms— most particularly Japanese firms—began to follow the pattern traditionally associated with U.S. firms as they became MNEs. Besides the large and persistent U.S. balance of trade deficits, which itself is caused in part by barriers to trade and investment in certain key markets, analysts have identified at least six possible reasons for the growth of FDIUS in the United States. These reasons are not mutually exclusive and varied in importance for MNEs from different countries.

The first reason was *changes in the cost of capital*. U.S. debt and equity markets had traditionally been a source of relatively cheap capital, and American firms benefited from this system. However, during the late 1970s and 1980s, the pattern changed. The traditional U.S. advantage of access to liquid capital markets of unrivaled scope disappeared. Exacerbated by the rising budget deficit, high inflation levels raised domestic interest rates. These factors, when combined with the globalization of some financial markets, meant that foreign producers could benefit from comparable and often lower interest rates than their U.S. counterparts.[45] This development is reflected in figures 3-5 and 3-6, which show the nominal corporate and prime interest rates in the United States and Japan between 1970 and 1991.

As the figures indicate, the beginning of the boom in Japanese FDIUS in the early 1980s coincided with the period of greatest disparity between U.S. and Japanese interest rates, whether corporate or prime. How are these interest rate differentials and the growth of Japanese FDIUS

---

[41] Ibid.

[42] When these investment levels are considered in real terms, despite slight discrepancies the same patterns emerges in both cases.

[43] See, for example, Gary Hufbauer, ''The Multinational Corporation and Direct Investment,'' in Peter B. Kenen, ed., *International Trade and Finance: Frontiers for Research* (Cambridge: Cambridge University Press, 1975).

[44] The most noted proponent of this view is Stephen H. Hymer. See his two books: *The International Operations of National Firms: A Study of Direct Foreign Investment* (Cambridge, MA: MIT Press, 1976) and *The Multinational Corporation: A Radical Approach* (Cambridge, MA: MIT Press, 1979). More recent versions of this argument have evolved into the theory of internationalization. For example, see John Cantwell, ''A Survey of Theories of International Production,'' in Christos N. Pitelis and Roger Sugden, *The Nature of the Transnational Firm* (New York, NY: Routledge, 1991), pp. 16-63 and especially pp. 23-26. Dunning makes similar arguments in his eclectic paradigm. For a recent version see John H. Dunning, *Multinational Enterprises and the Global Economy* (New York, NY: Addison Wesley Publishing Co., 1993).

[45] For a discussion of this point see, for example, ''Capital Punishment,'' *The Economist*, May 23, 1992, p. 1.

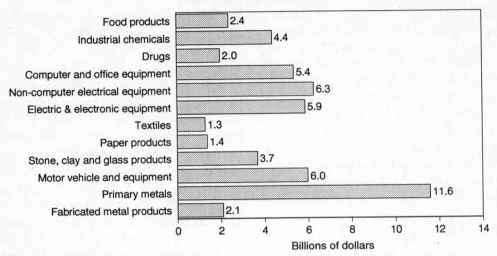

Figure 3-4—Assets of Japanese Manufacturing Affiliates in the U.S. by Selected Industry, 1990

NOTE: Data are calculated in 1990 dollars.

SOURCE: U.S. Department of Commerce, Bureau of Economic Analysis, *Foreign Direct Investment in the United States, Operations of U.S. Affiliates of Foreign Companies, Preliminary 1990 Estimates*, August 1992, table B-5.

related? As the cost of money falls (adjusted for inflation and currency fluctuations), the incentive to invest grows. Thus, as long as inflation remains low and currency exchange rates remain favorable, interest rate disparities encourage Japanese investors to pursue opportunities abroad. This is what they did.

Correspondingly, as the difference between interest rates in the United States and Japan shrank and all but disappeared in the early 1990s, so too did the propensity towards Japanese FDIUS.[46] Indeed, it has been suggested that Japan has suffered from a capital cost disadvantage since 1992.[47] These figures support the proposi-

tion that the cost of capital affected the propensity toward foreign investment; as it becomes cheaper in the investing country, the prospect of FDI becomes more attractive.[48]

The expansion of Japan's equity market during the 1980s caused new sources of cheap capital to develop, as Japanese firms benefited from leveraged loans. However, the subsequent decline of the Japanese stock market in the early 1990s did much to offset this advantage.[49] In the early 1990s, therefore, while the growth rate in foreign investment in the United States has declined, Japanese as well as European investment has levelled off after the fast growth of the previous

---

[46] For details in the decline in major investments in the United States, see "Fewer Deals, Less Investment," *Forbes*, July 20, 1992.

[47] Richard P. Mattione, "Capital Cost Disadvantage for Japan?" (Tokyo: Morgan Guaranty Trust Co., Apr. 6, 1992).

[48] This slow-down in the rate of increase of Japanese FDIUS was part of a general deceleration or possible decline of FDIUS among OECD countries (see footnote 50), which suggests one of three possibilities: first, that the cost capital differential shrank among the United States and all major investors in the United States at about the same time; second, that the cost of capital issue only appertained as an incentive to Japanese investors because the differential was so great; or third, that the cost of capital differential is only a partial explanation of the changes in rates of Japanese FDIUS. Finally, there is also an argument, and appropriate supporting evidence, contradicting the claim that there is a relationship between the cost of capital and patterns of FDI. For a summary discussion of this debate, see ch. 6.

[49] James Sterngold, "Japan's Cash Fountain Has All But Dried Up," *New York Times*, Dec. 6, 1991, p. D1.

Figure 3-5—Nominal Prime Interest Rates in the U.S. and Japan, 1970-1991

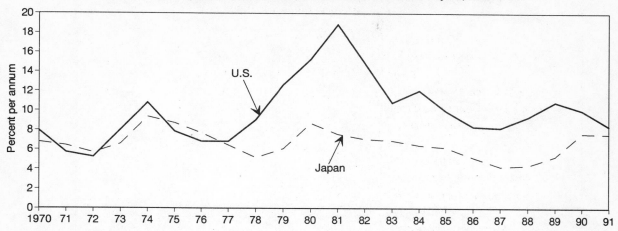

SOURCE: Adapted from Richard P. Matteone, "A Capital Cost Disadvantage for Japan?" Morgan Guaranty Trust, Tokyo, April 1992, p. 3.

decade.[50] The decline can be attributed largely to the U.S. recession of the late 1980s, but problems in the Japanese economy during the early 1990s also contributed. As the Japanese stock market bubble deflated, industrial firms that engaged in heavy financial engineering suffered heavy losses, as did many Japanese banks that might have provided loans to replace equity financing.[51]

The 1970s and 1980s also saw the impact of three distinct systems of capital among leading OECD countries. While the American and British economic systems continued to rely on equity markets, some countries (like Germany) developed a credit-based system run by national banks, and others (like France) had a state-run system.[52]

Both the national bank-led and state-run systems were characterized by greater patience and a willingness to make long-term capital available at lower interest and on a more liquid basis to domestic firms than to foreign-owned firms.[53]

In Germany, for example, national banks usually serve on the boards of the companies to which they provided loans, ensuring a measure of fiscal prudence as well as coordinating company behavior through interlocking directorates. In Japan, a similar function is performed by banks associated with specific keiretsu or groups of companies.[54] In France, state-owned banks facilitated investment by providing capital at lower interest rates. France reversed its net FDI position

---

[50] James Sterngold, "Japan's 'Recycling' of Its Trade Surplus Declines," *New York Times*, Feb. 22, 1993, p. A1. Due to the preliminary nature of the 1992 data, Department of Commerce, OECD, and Bank for International Settlements estimates of FDI inflows show either a slight increase or decrease in FDIUS. This small discrepancy, when compared to aggregate FDIUS and the lower direct investment outflows from Japan and Europe, still supports the general evidence of a slowdown in FDIUS in the early 1990's. See ''Japan Keeps Cash at Home,'' op. cit., footnote 4; U.S. Department of Commerce, ''Net International Investment Position, 1992,'' op. cit., footnote 4; and OECD, *Financial Market Trends*, June 1993, table 1, p. 44.

[51] Anthony Rowley, ''Ebbing Streams; Japanese Firms Curtail Their Overseas Forays,'' *Far Eastern Economic Review*, June 18, 1992; also see Sheridan Tatsuno, ''Japanese Redirect Electronics Investments to Asia,'' *New Technology Week*, Nov. 16, 1992, p. 6.

[52] For a full discussion of this issue see John Zysman, *Governments, Markets, and Growth: Financial Systems and the Politics of Industrial Change* (Ithaca, NY: Cornell, 1983).

[53] For an analysis of this issue see Michael E. Porter, *Capital Choices: Changing the Way America Invests in Industry* (Washington, DC: Council on Competitiveness, 1992).

[54] For a discussion see Robert J. Ballon and Iwao Tomita, *The Financial Behavior of Japanese Corporations* (Tokyo: Kodasha International, 1988), especially pp. 58-63.

Figure 3-6—Nominal Corporate Bond Rates in the U.S. and Japan, 1970-1991

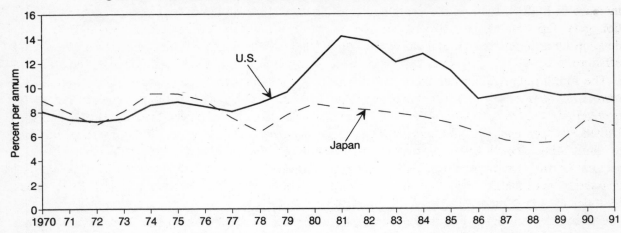

SOURCE: Adapted from Richard P. Matteone, "A Capital Cost Disadvantage for Japan?" Morgan Guaranty Trust, Tokyo, April 1992, p. 3.

and became a net FDI exporter for 8 of the 9 years between 1983 and 1992.[55]

These institutional arrangements encouraged foreigners to invest in the United States. The influence of capital shortages, one of the traditional impediments to investment on the scale required to compete in the United States, had been alleviated, creating incentives for a variety of foreign firms to expand their manufacturing or resource base to the United States.

The second reason for the shift in FDI flows is the *liberalization of rules governing the outward flow of capital in some OECD countries* in the 1970s and 1980s. The most prominent examples included countries that had previously restricted outbound FDI, such as France, Italy, and Japan. Of these, Japan was initially perhaps the slowest to respond.[56] Yet when capital liberalization in 1972 finally replaced the Foreign Exchange Control Law of 1949, Japanese overseas investment grew quickly. Reflecting its importance,

Japanese officials often refer to liberalization as the "gannen" of overseas FDI, a term usually reserved for the first year of the reign of a Japanese emperor.[57] Overseas investment by Japanese firms almost doubled in the early 1970s, to a total of $345 million,[58] and continued to increase dramatically. By the end of the 1980s, Japanese global external direct investment totaled $201 billion, with $69.7 billion invested during 1989 in the United States alone.

The third major reason was *the shift in exchange rates between the dollar and the yen.* The dramatic fall in the value of the dollar against the yen between 1985 and 1988, under the terms of the Plaza Agreement in 1985, encouraged the influx of FDIUS. During this period the yen rose against the dollar by about 90 percent. This rapid strengthening of the yen brought about a sharp, widespread decline in the cost of production in host countries relative to the cost in Japan, including the initial costs of investment. Thus the

---

[55] Julius, op. cit., footnote 9, p. 24.

[56] Japan's rules regarding both inbound and outbound FDI are chronicled in Dennis Encarnation, *Rivals Beyond Trade: America Versus Japan in Global Competition* (Ithaca, NY: Cornell University Press, 1992), pp. 36-146.

[57] Ryutaro Komiya, *The Japanese Economy: Trade, Industry and Government* (Tokyo: University of Tokyo Press, 1990), p. 118.

[58] Ibid., p. 112.

strong yen is an important factor behind the sharp increase in FDIUS. Further, the yen's appreciation gave Japanese firms a strong incentive to develop labor-intensive manufacturing facilities offshore.[59]

The fourth major reason for the shift was the *institution of a series of formal and informal protectionist barriers*. During the 1980s, the United States extended its protectionist measures to limit direct competition in manufacturing sectors for the first time since 1945, a pattern characteristic of the EC as a whole and many of its member states. Increased U.S. protectionism was accomplished through a variety of formally negotiated agreements or informally negotiated, self-imposed restraints, such as voluntary export restraints and orderly marketing agreements in such areas as the automobile, machine tool, textiles, and steel industries.[60] As a result, many firms transferred some part of their manufacturing or sales to the United States. They did so either to ensure continued access to what was, in many sectors, the world's largest market, or to maintain price competitiveness in the face of possible tariffs.

A fifth factor affecting the growth in FDIUS was *pressure from the Japanese Government* designed to encourage some of their largest domestic corporations to invest in the United States. Often these firms were initially reluctant to do so, being concerned about the political, cultural, and economic implications of trans-

planted investments. Officials of Japan's Ministry of International Trade and Industry (MITI) were often vocal proponents of FDIUS and believed that it would mitigate the friction between the United States and Japan generated by the burgeoning trade deficit. This was most evident in the case of the automobile industry, where Toyota and Nissan initially resisted MITI's prompting and were subsequently disciplined by having their market share of exports to the United States reduced under the terms of the Voluntary Export Restraint Agreement of 1981.[61] (See chapter 4.)

A final factor was *the tendency to follow the leader for fear of the opportunity cost of not doing so*. Companies, as risk-averse actors, fear that their competitors will gain a significant advantage. This is particularly true among Japanese firms, who compete so aggressively with each other in their domestic market. Thus, once one major foreign competitor is persuaded to invest in production or other facilities abroad, MNEs from the same country tend to follow to prevent the competitor from developing a comparative advantage.[62] That tendency was evident in many cases involving Japanese FDIUS in the 1980s, as every major Japanese auto producer, for example, followed Honda's lead, albeit with some initial reluctance and at MITI's prompting.

The influx of FDIUS was due to many factors, some exogenous and others the result of U.S. Government policy.[63] The collective result was

---

[59] For a discussion, for example, of how this change in exchange rates affected Japanese FDI in the auto industry see "Asian Carmakers: The Sun Also Sets," *The Economist*, May 24, 1986, pp. 66-67.

[60] For details of these measures see Tyson, op. cit., footnote 8; and Ellis S. Krauss and Simon Reich, "Ideology, Interests, and the American Executive: Toward a Theory of Foreign Competition and Manufacturing Trade Policy," *International Organization*, 46, 4, autumn, 1992.

[61] For a detailed discussion of MITI's relationship with the auto firms and illustration of this point regarding the distribution of market shares, see Paul A. Summerville, "The Politics of Self-Restraint: The Japanese State, and the Voluntary Export Restraint of Japanese Passenger Car Exports to the United States in 1981" (Ph.D. Doctoral Thesis, University of Tokyo, 1988).

[62] Frederick T. Knickerbocker, *Oligopolistic Reaction and Multinational Enterprise* (Boston, MA: Harvard University, Graduate School of Business Administration, 1973); and Theodore Moran, "Foreign Expansion as an 'Institutional Necessity' for U.S. Corporate Capitalism: The Search for a Radical Model," *World Politics*, 25, No. 2 (April 1973). For a discussion of this point in application to Japanese investment in the United States, see Tom Roehl, "Firm, Industry and Country Level Influences on Japanese Foreign Investment in the United States," in Vladimir Pucik, ed., *The Internationalization of Japanese Firms* (forthcoming).

[63] For a discussion of a variety of these influences on Japanese investors see Roehl, ibid.

that there were three major changes in the nature of Japanese investment. The first was in the *aggregate amount* of Japanese FDIUS, which grew rapidly, as outlined above. The second was in the *thrust* of this investment, as it shifted from mining, natural resources, and manufacturing to include tertiary industries like finance, insurance, and real estate. The third change was in *the distribution and location of Japanese FDI*, as the North American fraction of all Japanese FDI increased from about a quarter (an average of 26.8 percent between 1951 and 1980) to nearly a half by the middle of the 1980s (46.8 percent in 1986). The increase in Japan's manufacturing investment was more dramatic, rising from an average 19.3 percent of Japanese investment in the United States between 1951 and 1980 to 57.8 percent by the middle of the 1980s.[64]

Changes in the cost of capital and exchange rates in the early 1990s have slowed the growth of FDIUS, particularly from Japan.[65] But it is also possible that increased protectionism may either sustain FDIUS or generate new forms of strategic agreements or alliances among firms, which could affect the structure and competitiveness of the U.S. economy.

∎ Benefits and Disadvantages of Increased FDIUS

Many analysts believe that the increase in foreign investment during the 1980s was influenced both by U.S. presidential policy and congressional politics. The Reagan administration vigorously pursued policies to increase the influx of FDIUS, in order to offset the decline in U.S. competitiveness and the loss of domestic jobs. These efforts by the Reagan and Bush administrations were buttressed by arguments suggesting that the impact of investment by foreign-based MNEs did not differ from that of their domestic counterparts.[66] Congressional proponents of action on behalf of beleaguered domestic industries may also have played a part in promoting the growth of FDIUS, through their advocacy of domestic content legislation.[67] Although the administration disagreed with the domestic content ideas, the congressional efforts often provided the President with a credible basis to suggest that either foreign governments negotiate an informal agreement or face a less sympathetic Congress likely to introduce policy through formal legislation.

The success of this policy, however, has generated policy issues of its own. There have been two responses to the significant expansion of

---

[64] Komiya, op. cit., footnote 57, pp. 122-123.

[65] For a discussion of new limits on and pattern of Japanese overseas direct investment in general, see "Japanese Spoken Here," *The Economist*, Sept. 14, 1991, pp. 67-68. For evidence regarding its reduction in the United States, see "Fewer Deals, Less Investment," *Forbes*, July 20, 1992, p. 290; or the more comprehensive data in Steve D. Bezirganian, "U.S. Affiliates of Foreign Companies: Operations in 1990," in *Survey of Current Business*, May 1992, pp. 45-68; and in Rutter, op. cit., footnote 4.

[66] Notable proponents of the view that foreign and domestic investment is largely undifferentiated in effect include Graham and Krugman, op. cit., footnote 12.

[67] For examples regarding the auto industry, see Hearing before the Subcommittee on Trade, Committee on Ways and Means, *Fair Practices in Automotive Products Act of 1983*, HR 1234, Section 2, later resubmitted as the *Fair Practices in Automotive Products Act of 1983*, HR 5133 (Washington, DC: U.S. Government Printing Office, 1984); Subcommittee on Trade, Committee on Ways and Means, *Domestic Content Legislation and the U.S. Auto Industry: Analyses of HR 5133*, Committee Print, p. 10 and see p. 30; Hearing before the Senate Subcommittee on Economic Stabilization, Committee on Banking, Housing, and Urban Affairs, *The Effect of Expanding Japanese Automobile Imports on the Domestic Economy* (Washington, DC: U.S. Government Printing Office, April 1980). For a discussion of the dynamics of protection in the case of steel see Michael Borrus, "The Politics of Competitive Erosion in the U.S. Steel Industry," John Zysman and Laura Tyson (eds.), *American Industry in International Competition* (Ithaca, NY: Cornell University Press, 1983); Krauss et al., op. cit., footnote 60; Robert S. Walters, "U.S. Negotiation of Voluntary Restraint Agreements in Steel, 1984: Domestic Sources of International Economic Diplomacy" (Pittsburgh, PA: Pew Charitable Trusts/University of Pittsburgh, Graduate School of Public and International Affairs, Pew Case Studies in International Negotiation, no. 107, 1988); Robert W. Crandall, *The U.S. Steel Industry in Recurrent Crisis* (Washington, DC: Brookings Institute, 1981).

FDI in the U.S. economy, one stressing the advantages and the other the disadvantages. These responses are summarized below.

▪ Benefits of FDIUS

Advocates of direct investment by foreign MNEs emphasize four advantages created by FDIUS.[68] The first is the subsidy to levels of investment in the presence of low U.S. savings. This argument cites the stimulating macroeconomic effects of financial infusions to the U.S. economy, regardless of the source, and emphasizes that Americans save less than people in other advanced industrial states. Indeed, U.S. savings and investment growth rates began to diverge in 1983, when the United States began a 5-year period of economic expansion, with the gap between gross saving and investment peaking at $155 billion in 1987.[69]

A second commonly cited advantage is managerial and organizational innovation, especially to manufacturing.[70] Examples are the just-in-time inventory system, the more general system of lean production, and the decentralization of decision-making now being tried by some of America's multinational firms.[71] Consistent with these changes is a shift toward less hierarchical bureaucratic structures, team personnel organization, and a renewed attention to quality that has accompanied foreign manufacturing investment. These, collectively, enhance manufacturing productivity in the United States.[72]

Third, proponents of FDIUS who distinguish between domestic and foreign firms argue that foreign producers in the United States sharpen the competitiveness of U.S. business. They assume that increased competition will encourage domestic firms to enhance their productivity, particularly where they operate under monopolistic or oligopolistic conditions.[73] In this view, FDI is a symptom of a lack of competitiveness, not its cause.[74] Benefits accrue to consumers in the form of lower prices and a wider selection of products.

The fourth benefit of FDIUS is job creation. There are, for example, 10 transplant automakers with plants in the United States, with BMW a proposed eleventh and Daimler-Benz a twelfth. These collectively account for 50,000 jobs in assembly and parts making operations and 16 percent of the 14.8 million vehicle capacity.[75] On a broader scale, as of 1990, British-owned affiliates accounted for over 1 million jobs in the United States, Japan for 617,000, Germany for 513,000, and the Netherlands for 290,000.[76] (See table 3-4.)

---

[68] For examples of work that tend to emphasize the benefits of FDIUS, see Earl H. Fry, *The Politics of International Investment* (New York, NY: McGraw-Hill, 1983) and more recently his "Foreign Direct Investment in the United States: Public Policy Options," a paper prepared for the International Studies Association Conference, April 1990; see also Robert Kudrle, "Good for the Gander," *International Organization*, vol. 45, No. 3, summer 1991, pp. 397-424.

[69] See U.S. Department of Commerce, op. cit., footnote 10, p. 13.

[70] See, for example, Martin Kenney and Richard Florida, "How Japanese Industry is Rebuilding the Rust Belt," *Technology Review*, vol. 94, No. 2, February-March 1991, pp. 25-33.

[71] See, for example, Michael Cusumano, "Manufacturing Innovation: Lessons from the Japanese Auto Industry," *Sloan Management Review 30* (fall 1988) pp. 29-39.

[72] For a discussion of this point see Robert R. Rehder, "What American and Japanese Managers Are Learning from Each Other," *Business Horizons*, 24 (March/April) 1981, pp. 63-70; Kazuhiko Nagato, "The Japan-United States Savings Rate Gap," Daniel Okimoto and Thomas Rohlen, eds., *Inside the Japanese System* (Stanford, CA: Stanford University Press, 1988), pp. 64-70.

[73] For an example of such a claim, see Graham and Krugman, op. cit., footnote 12, pp. 57-59.

[74] Graham, op. cit., footnote 2, p. 1742.

[75] " 'Transplant' Auto Factories Have Redefined the Industry," *New York Times*, July 23, 1992, p. C5.

[76] U.S. Department of Commerce, Bureau of Economic Analysis, *Foreign Direct Investment in the United States: Operations of U.S. Affiliates of Foreign Companies, Preliminary 1990 Estimates*, August, 1992, table A-2.

Table 3-4—Selected Financial Data for U.S. Affiliates of Foreign Companies, 1990

	Japan	United Kingdom	Netherlands	Germany
Number of affiliates	2,142	1,161	346	1,144
Total assets (in $ bil)	370	262	91	101
Sales (in $ mil)	313,138	188,852	72,819	107,521
Net income (in $ mil)	–2,191	2,406	32	219
Number of employees (in thousands)	616.7	1,039.2	290.2	513.3
Average compensation (in $, per employee) ...	37,203	32,036	34,290	34,307
Exports by affiliates (in $ mil)	39,155	7,926	2,829	7,041
Imports to affiliates (in $ mil)	87,712	13,225	6,588	17,858
Ratio of imports to sales	0.28	0.07	0.09	0.17
Ratio of exports to imports	0.45	0.60	0.43	0.39

SOURCE: U.S. Department of Commerce, Bureau of Economic Analysis, *Foreign Direct Investment in the United States: Operations of U.S. Affiliates of Foreign Companies, Preliminary 1990 Estimates*, August 1992, table A-2; U.S. Department of Commerce, Bureau of Economic Analysis, *Foreign Direct Investment in the United States: An Update*, June 1993.

Proponents of FDIUS who emphasize job creation often blur the distinction between foreign and domestic firms and, at the extreme, reject the notion of national firms. Some have argued that a foreign-based MNE with manufacturing facilities in the United States contributes more to the U.S. economy than a U.S.-based MNE that transfers the bulk of its manufacturing to offshore facilities.[77] In this view, U.S. prosperity lies in the skills of the labor force, not necessarily in the success of U.S.-owned firms. The implication is clearly that incentives or regulations should be used to encourage forms of FDIUS that use, and help develop, a skilled labor force for high value-added jobs. Such a theoretical dichotomy between a foreign firm that invests in the United States and a U.S. firm that invests abroad excludes discussion of what many argue is the preferred option—a U.S.-owned firm that invests in plant and labor in America.

■ Disadvantages of FDIUS

Critics of the national treatment approach to FDIUS emphasize four major complications:

harm to competitiveness, unfair employment and hiring practices, financial subsidies, and economic and military security issues relating to technology transfer. All four link multinational corporate responsibility to aspects of U.S. economic and social development.

First, critics stress competitiveness—namely, the potentially adverse economic consequences of unregulated FDI for U.S. manufacturing firms and for the U.S. technology base.[78] In contrast to the argument that direct competition will improve the productivity of U.S. firms, these analysts stress that foreign competitors can destroy domestically based firms because they can compete in an unrestricted U.S. economy from the basis of highly restricted international competition in their own market. As a result, unrestricted competition may benefit consumers in the short term, but both consumers and the national economy will eventually lose.

Along these lines, recent work contrasts the ''trade-creating'' nature of Japanese direct investment abroad (DIA) with the ''trade-destroying''

[77] See, for example, Robert B. Reich, ''Who is Us?,'' *Harvard Business Review*, January-February 1990, pp. 53-64.

[78] See, for example, Martin Tolchin and Susan Tolchin, *Buying into America: How Foreign Money Is Changing the Face of Our Nation* (New York, NY: Times Books, 1988); Pat Choate, ''Political Advantage: Japan's Campaign for America,'' *Harvard Business Review*, 1990: 87-103; Norman Glickman and Douglas Woodward, *The New Competitors: How Foreign Investors Are Changing the U.S. Economy* (New York, NY: Basic Books, 1989); Daniel Burstein, *Yen!: Japan's New Financial Empire and Its Threat to America* (New York, NY: Simon and Schuster, 1988); Thomas Omestad, ''Selling Off America,'' *Foreign Policy*, No. 76 (fall 1989), 119-140.

DIA of the United States.[79] For example, the formation of affiliates of Japanese auto assemblers has been accompanied by the formation of affiliates of some of their supplier keiretsu members. As advocates of the trade-creating view would expect, the U.S. trade deficit with Japan in autoparts has grown as the Japanese assemblers have increased production in the United States.[80]

Table 3-4 examines the import, export, and sales patterns of U.S. affiliates of the four major foreign direct investors. These data seem to support the proposition that Japanese investment is more trade-creating than trade-destroying, with a ratio of imports to sales of .28 (over three times that of Dutch investment, and four times that of British investment). This table also indicates that Japanese-based MNEs tend to use their U.S. affiliates as a conduit for the sale of products made in Japan, rather than as facilities to replace Japanese-made goods with U.S-made goods. A higher proportion of goods sold by Japanese firms seem to be assembled in the United States from components built in Japan, relative to U.S. affiliates of other foreign firms.

What accounts for this pattern, and will it be sustained over time? Proponents of FDI claim that a life cycle pattern exists for FDI, whereby foreign investors initially rely more on imports from their parent organization but increasingly shift to a higher domestic content as they mature. Because Japanese firms have invested in the United States so recently, they would naturally have higher import propensities, but this will change with time.[81]

Critics of this suggestion present two arguments. First, although importing is common among new investors, Japanese-based MNEs tend to transplant suppliers along with production facilities more often than other foreign-based firms. While domestic content might indeed rise, it will not do so because of a heavier reliance on domestic producers. Second, critics stress that vis-à-vis domestic content and use of nontraditional suppliers, the behavior of Japanese firms in the EC differs significantly from that of the same firms in the United States, even when the investment dates from the same period.

What might explain a greater Japanese commitment to domestic content in the EC? One possible answer is the differing rules and regulations that Japanese investors face in Europe and the United States.[82] If this is correct, then responsibility for the decision of Japanese firms to import more or to use their traditional suppliers more in the United States lies partly with the U.S. Government, which has articulated few rules to encourage alternative forms of MNE behavior. Many analysts believe that the U.S. Government cannot fault Japanese firms for playing by the rules as they exist.

The second concern of critics of FDIUS relates to the economic and social effect of FDIUS on domestic employment. This concern has two components. One is about the types and number

---

[79] Robert Gilpin reflects this sentiment in citing the work of Kiyoshi Kojima, a distinguished Japanese economist. Gilpin states that ''[c]ontrasting Japan's foreign direct investment with that of the United States, Kojima argues that Japanese foreign direct investment attempts to be *'trade-creating'*, whereas American foreign direct investment has been *'trade-destroying'*. Japanese foreign direct investment has sought to increase, or at least maintain, Japanese exports; U.S. foreign direct investment, on the other hand, has tended to replace U.S. exports by establishing production facilities abroad to serve the U.S. or world markets. Although Kojima was referring specifically to direct investment by Japanese corporations, his characterization is applicable to almost all Japanese foreign investment.'' The argument offers an explanation why the U.S. trade deficit with Japan ballooned while Japanese FDIUS grew. In Robert Gilpin, ''Where Does Japan Fit In?'' *Millennium: Journal of International Studies*, vol. 18, No. 3, 1989, p. 337.

[80] See, for example, Richard G. Newman, ''The Second Wave Arrives: Japanese Strategy in the Auto Parts Market,'' *Business Horizons*, vol. 23, No. 4, July/August 1990, pp. 24-30; and Andrew Pollack, ''Trade in Auto Parts Favors Japan Despite Gains by U.S.,'' *The New York Times*, July 1, 1993, pp. D1 and D18.

[81] Graham, op. cit., footnote 2, p. 1743.

[82] See Robin Gaster, ''Protectionism With Purpose: Guiding Foreign Investment,'' *Foreign Policy*, fall 1992, No. 88, pp. 96-100; ''The Enemy Within,'' *The Economist*, June 12, 1993, pp. 67-68; Office of Technology Assessment, op. cit., footnote 1, p. 207.

of jobs created by FDIUS, particularly in manufacturing. Critics assert that some transplanted manufacturing facilities are little more than screwdriver plants that assemble high value-added components produced abroad.[83] This practice results in relatively few, and possibly inferior, jobs.

The quality-of-jobs issue is far from clear-cut. Leading analysts assert, for example, that "for manufacturing as a whole, and for individual industries within manufacturing, there is no systematic difference between the foreign and the domestic firms in compensation and value added per employee," and provide aggregate data to support that contention.[84] Yet data drawn from individual industries, such as the auto industry, suggest that this claim is more complex than these analysts assert.[85]

The employment issue is further complicated by assertions that some foreign investors discourage unionization and may employ discriminatory employment practices.[86] This view, critics claim, is buttressed by lawsuits filed against several major Japanese firms. The suits have claimed discrimination against women and against non-Japanese employees in promotion decisions; several companies, including Sumitomo and Honda of America, have settled.[87] Nevertheless, while one position is that the "increased rate of foreign-based multinational investment in the United States raises the specter that discriminatory motives will become substantially more prevalent in plant relocation, site selection, and subcontracting decisions," the same is potentially true of U.S. firms that develop greenfield sites.[88]

The third form of criticism of FDIUS focuses on tax subsidies, infrastructure development, and other incentives that foreign direct investors often receive from State and municipal authorities. The States have repeatedly competed with each other to secure investment by foreign-based MNEs, particularly in the manufacturing sector. Individual States have, in effect, pursued their own industrial policies, offering lucrative tax, infrastructural, and loan incentives to foreign MNEs to

---

[83] Robert B. Reich and Eric D. Mankin, "Joint Ventures With Japan Give Away Our Future," *Harvard Business Review*, vol. 64, No. 2, March-April 1986.

[84] Graham and Krugman, op. cit., footnote 12, p. 70.

[85] For a discussion of how pension plans in transplant facilities are systematically inferior to those at domestic plants, see Candace Howes, "The Benefits of Youth: The Role of Japanese Fringe Benefits Policies in the Restructuring of the U.S. Motor Vehicle Industry," *International Contribution to Labour Studies*, 1, 1991, pp. 113-132; Teresa Ghilarducci, "Pension Costs and Changing Pension Norms: The Case of Japanese Auto Transplants and the U.S. Auto Firms," unpublished paper, University of Notre Dame.

[86] For a variety of arguments that support this point see Timothy J. Bartik, "Business Location Decisions in the United States: Estimates of the Effects of Unionization, Taxes and Other Characteristics of States," *Journal of Business and Economic Statistics*, Jan. 3, 1985, pp. 14-22; John S. McClenahen, "Who Owns U.S. Industry?," *Business Week*, Jan. 7, 1985; and Steven R. Reed, "Japanese in the American South," in Kozo Yamamura, ed., *Japanese Investment in the United States: Should We Be Concerned?* (Seattle, WA: Society for Japanese Studies, 1989), p. 219; Robert E. Cole and Donald Deskins, Jr., "Racial Factors in Site Location and Employment Patterns of Japanese Auto Firms in America," *California Management Review*, fall 1988, pp. 15-18; and Douglas Woodward, "Locational Determinants of Japanese Plants," *Southern Journal of Economics*, vol. 58, January 1992, pp. 690-708.

[87] See Rehder, op. cit., footnote 72, p. 92. Also see Employment and Housing Subcommittee, House Committee on Government Operations, "Employment Discrimination by Japanese-Owned Companies in the United States: Hearings" (Washington, DC: U.S. Government Printing Office, 1992). According to Japanese sources, the following firms have been sued on discrimination charges: Toyota, Nissan, Honda, Mitsubishi Motors, Suzuki, Sony, Matsushita Electric Industrial Co., Hitachi, NEC, Fujitsu, Ricoh, Canon, Toshiba, Kyocera, Dai-Ichi Kangyo Bank, Sanwa Bank, Mitsubishi Bank, C. Itoh & Co., Shiseido, Japan Air Lines, Sanyo Securities, Dentsu Inc., Hakuhodo Inc., and Recruit Corp. See "Companies in U.S. Accused of Discrimination," *Chuo Koron magazine* (Nagami Kishi, September 1992, in FBIS, Sept. 11, 1992), p. 1. However, consistent with the principles of U.S. law, none of these firms should be considered to have transgressed any law until they have been found guilty. For a general discussion of the behavior of Japanese firms see Douglas Woodward, "Locational Determinants of Japanese Plants," *Southern Journal of Economics*, vol. 58, January 1992, pp. 690-708.

[88] For this quotation and a discussion of the issue of discrimination in hiring practices see Marley S. Weiss, "Risky Business: Age and Race Discrimination in Capital Redeployment Decisions," *Maryland Law Review*, vol. 48, pp. 901-1017, especially pp. 917-921.

induce them to locate in their States.[89] Indeed, some critics note that more States maintain economic development offices in Tokyo than in Washington.

The financial incentives offered by competing States have grown dramatically since the mid-1970s. In practice, the incentive package that won the last Japanese factory becomes the opening bid for the next plant. The State of Ohio, for example, paid $16 million in direct incentives to Honda to secure the Marysville plant in 1982; by 1988, Kentucky spent $125 million in incentives convincing Toyota to locate its plant there.[90] Critics question whether State competition for FDIUS is in the nation's interest and whether this competition has reached a stage where the costs of incentives outweigh the benefits even at the local level. Figure 3-7, listing the cost of subsidy per job created, shows how State rivalries have escalated the costs of attracting jobs. Officials of one company that had benefited from such an incentive package told OTA that they would not push as hard for an incentive package if they were to open further facilities in the United States, suggesting that some of these packages may have been too generous, or possibly even unnecessary.

Critics also argue that domestic firms rarely benefit from state incentive packages, even though these packages in principle are equally available to domestic and foreign firms. According to these critics, domestic firms lack the flexibility to shift plant locations because of the costs of moving production and the potential political conflict in replacing urban, unionized plants with nonunionized, rural manufacturing facilities—often in other regions of the country.[91] Officials of domestic firms repeatedly told OTA that they would like to move production to greenfield sites, but were unable to do so for a variety of reasons. Nondiscriminatory state policies have therefore discriminated against domestically owned firms, assisting foreign MNEs more than indigenous ones.

Finally, recent developments have raised the concern that foreign investments in the United States, particularly those made by Japanese multinational firms, may not be permanent. This fear has already been realized. During 1993, the Japanese economy stumbled, and numerous Japanese firms announced plant closings, cutbacks in investment plans, and layoffs in the United States. These firms include Fujitsu, Seiko, Hitachi, Fanuc, Komatsu, Nissan, Daihatsu, Isuzu, and many others in both manufacturing and nonmanufacturing sectors.[92] For example, Fujitsu recently announced plans to close a semiconductor manufacturing facility in California and transfer the production to a plant in Southeast Asia because of currency fluctuations.[93] Consistent with this concern, aggregate data indicates that foreign direct investors in general organized the net transfer of dividends from affiliates to parents in 1990 and

[89] Despite the failure of the Volkswagen venture and the cost to Pennsylvania's taxpayers, State officials subsequently offered an equally lucrative deal to Sony to use Volkswagen's plant for the production of televisions.

[90] T. David Mason and Frank M. Howell, "Japanese Investment in the United States: A Study of Trends and Site Selection Behavior," a paper presented at the Annual Meeting of the International Studies Association, Mar. 30-Apr. 4, 1992, Atlanta, GA, pp. 4-5.

[91] Japanese auto producers often, although not always, locate plants in rural settings. Marysville, OH, home of Honda, had a population of 7,500 prior to the plant's arrival, while Nissan, Diamond Star (jointly owned by Mitsubishi and Chrysler), and Subaru-Isuzu all located in towns of less than 50,000 people. When looking at domestic firms, the most appropriate comparison to draw is between the transplant greenfield sites and that of General Motors' Saturn Plant in Spring Hill, TN, which is unionized. After experimenting with new contractual relations comparable to those found in transplant facilities, Saturn employees chose to return to a more traditionally structured contract. See "Reality Comes to G.M.'s Saturn Plant," *New York Times*, Nov. 14, 1991, p. C5.

[92] "From the Expansion Route to an Emphasis on Profitability" ("Kakucho rosen kara saisansei jushi e"), *Japan Economic Journal* (Nihon Keizai Shimbun), Aug. 26, 1992, p. 3. This raises the question of whether foreign investors have scaled back their operations disproportionately to domestic firms. A critical response would be that the closure of capacity in the United States by MNEs, whether domestic or foreign-owned, is undesirable.

[93] Larry Holyoke, "Who's Afraid of the Big, Bad Yen? Not Japanese Exporters," *Business Week*, Oct. 12, 1992, p. 49.

Figure 3-7—Escalating American State Subsidization to Auto Manufacturers

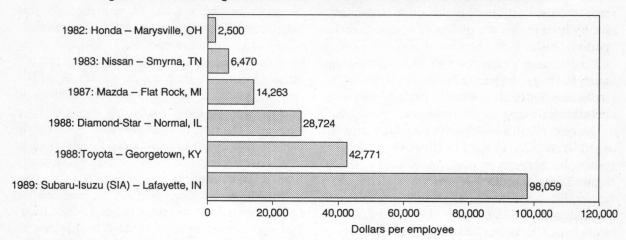

SOURCE: Adapted from Martin Kenney and Richard Florida, "How Japanese Industry is Rebuilding the Rust Belt," *Technology Review*, Feb.-March 1991, p. 30.

1991, even though many of those companies generated negative earnings.[94]

ASYMMETRIES IN NATIONAL POLICY REGIMES

To understand the current state of FDI, it is necessary to review its history. Their have been three distinct periods. The first, from the 1890s to the 1930s, was marked by protectionist trade policies in Europe, Japan, and the United States, complemented by open investment policies. Americans heavily substituted direct investment for portfolio investment in Europe and Japan, particularly in manufacturing production facilities. This preference was reflected in the outward expansion of firms like Singer and Ford.[95]

Japan and France, although later resistant to foreign investment, were at this time receptive to U.S.-based MNE investment.[96] In discussing cultural and structural impediments that confront U.S. firms in Japan, many analysts overlook the rich history of U.S. trade and investment in Japan in the early twentieth century, and their early successes producing and selling in Japan. This raises the question of why U.S.-based MNEs that were successful at providing and selling in Japan in the past should be less able to do so today.

In the second period, from the 1930s to the 1970s, the FDI policies of advanced industrial states diverged systematically. The United States and United Kingdom sustained largely unregulated, enthusiastic national treatment investment policies. Britain became a major recipient of U.S. MNE investment, largely involving the construction of fully integrated manufacturing facilities.

In contrast, in the 1930s, 1940s, and in some cases through the 1970s, Germany, Italy, Japan, and France either completely blocked foreign investment—and sometimes threw U.S. firms out—or took steps to ensure that foreign firms did

---

[94] Graham, op. cit., footnote 2, p. 1740. This tendency was sustained in 1992 according to "Japan Keeps Cash at Home," op. cit., footnote 4, p. 4, with Japanese investors sustaining net losses of $2 billion.

[95] See, for example, Wilkins et al., op. cit., footnote 5; and Mason, op. cit., footnote 5.

[96] For a discussion of Japan in this period, see Michael Cusumano, *The Japanese Automobile Industry* (Cambridge, MA: Council on East Asian Studies, Harvard University Press, 1985); for France see Pariick Fridenson, "French Automobile Marketing, 1890-1970," Akio Okochi and Koichi Shimokawa (eds.), *The Development of Mass Marketing* (Tokyo: University of Tokyo Press, 1981).

not thrive. Of these countries, Japan provides the most consistent example of discriminatory behavior by both the public and private sectors in this period. While the public sector was responsible for Japanese restriction of FDI until the 1970s, analysts have suggested that the private sector introduced effective informal impediments to investment during the 1970s and into the 1980s.[97]

During this period, France and Italy discouraged U.S. FDI altogether. The West German policy was more open and more complex, encouraging FDI while often using subtle impediments to protect domestic firms—thus benefiting from capital inflows and the jobs FDI created, helping to secure an economic base from which to compete effectively in the post-WWII period.[98]

In addition to limiting FDI, these four governments organized the emergence of a series of firms that subsequently became the post-WWII national champions, and ultimately MNEs. Auto industry examples include Nissan and Toyota in Japan, Renault in France, Volkswagen and Daimler-Benz in Germany, and Fiat in Italy. While U.S.-based MNEs penetrated parts of Europe, their success varied greatly by country and sector. In the United Kingdom, they proved to be highly successful, while elsewhere they were less so.

Throughout the third period—the 1970s and 1980s—the United States sustained its policy of national treatment which, as intended, increased the flow of FDIUS. However, this policy, despite attempts by the Organization for Economic Cooperation and Development (OECD) to advance the principal of national treatment, rarely led to reciprocal treatment for U.S.-based MNEs seeking to invest abroad. (See box 3-B.)

The EC's long debate on regulating inward FDI is largely unresolved. Evidence of a convergence in European FDI rules is limited. Agreements on domestic content laws regarding foreign MNEs often appear to be settled in principle, only to be disputed in practice. As one report noted about the provisions of the EC-Japan agreement on Japanese auto imports:

> The agreement may fall apart because it leaves a number of matters open to interpretation—such as whether Japanese cars made in the U.S. will be counted [as imports from Japan]. Even the meaning of the 1999 ceiling on the total Japanese market share of 16.09 percent is not clear. The French and Italians argue that if this ceiling is attained, imports from Japan will have to be cut. Otherwise, they say, what is the point of setting the overall market share to the exactitude of a second decimal point? Not so, says Britain, home to a Nissan factory and soon to a Toyota and Honda one as well. Britain reckons transplant production will not be limited in any way—and that exports should not have to be cut back either . . . Given such different interpretations, the chances of the agreement reaching 1999 intact are remote . . . there is [also] a distinct possibility that the keenest Japan-bashers among EC car makers, like Jacques Calvet of Peugeot (or his successor), will ask for another transition period, delaying real liberalization even longer.[99]

---

[97] See Chalmers Johnson, *MITI and the Japanese Miracle: The Growth of Industrial Policy, 1925-1975* (Stanford, CA: Stanford University Press, 1982); Marie Anchordoguy, "Mastering the Market: Japanese Government Targeting of the Computer Industry," *International Organization*, 42 (summer 1988); T.J. Pempel, "Japanese Foreign Economic Policy: The Domestic Bases for Economic Behavior," in Peter J. Katzenstein, ed., *Between Power and Plenty* (Madison, WI: University of Wisconsin Press, 1978); Hideichiro Nakamura, "Japan, Incorporated and Postwar Economic Growth," *Japanese Economic Studies* 10:3 (spring 1982) pp. 68-109; Isamu Miyazaki, "The Real Reasons for Japan's Success in Economic Growth," *Japanese Economic Studies* 10:3 (spring 1982). For a focus on the shift in investment impediments to the private sector in that decade see Dennis J. Encarnation and Mark Mason, "Neither MITI nor America: The Political Economy of Capital Liberalization in Japan," *International Organization*, winter 1990, pp. 25-54; and Encarnation, op. cit., footnote 56.

[98] Reich, op. cit., footnote 5, pp. 303-328.

[99] "Stalling Japan's Car Makers," *The Economist*, Aug. 3, 1991, pp. 232.

Box 3-B—The OECD Declaration and Decisions on International Investment and Multinational Enterprises

National governments have found it difficult to regulate MNEs. Multilateral regulation may be even more challenging, as demonstrated by the Organization for Economic Cooperation and Development (OECD) efforts to establish rules for MNEs and international investment.

In its 1976 Declaration and Decisions on International Investment and Multinational Enterprises, the OECD established two sets of rules, one governing the practices of MNEs and the other governing FDI.[1] To govern MNEs, the OECD established a voluntary code of corporate conduct that encourages MNEs to give their subsidiaries the autonomy to abide by national laws and to cooperate with local business and labor. The code of conduct advises MNEs to permit labor representation, contribute to technology transfer, and not obstruct competition or harm the environment. To govern FDI, the OECD recommended that all member countries extend national treatment to foreign MNEs. The influence of both sets of rules has been limited primarily because they rely on the good faith of MNEs and member nations.

For example, the code of conduct for MNEs has no quantitative means of measuring effectiveness and commitment. Instead, it promotes good corporate citizenship among MNEs, measured primarily by membership in national business federations that affiliate and consult with the OECD through the Business and Industry Advisory Committee (BIAC).[2] Individual firms have been reluctant to endorse the OECD's rules because of the political and legal implications of explicit commitment, especially in labor and environmental disputes. Moreover, many MNEs reportedly feel that stronger, obligatory rules would be too intrusive.[3] The business community sees asymmetries in policies as the major impediments to foreign investment, and the BIAC has been pressing the OECD to enhance the International Investment and National Treatment portion of the Declaration.[4]

---

[1] Organization for Economic Co-operation and Development, *Declaration on International Investment and Multinational Enterprises*, (Paris: OECD, 1976).

[2] The Business and Industry Advisory Committee to the OECD is based in Paris.

[3] Confidential business federation interviews.

[4] Business and Industry Advisory Committee. *BIAC Statement on a Potential OECD Broader Investment Instrument*, Paris, Dec. 3, 1992.

Examples of successful U.S. investments in Japan are still the exception.[100] OTA interviews with managers of U.S.-based MNEs suggest that the Structural Impediments Initiative has had only limited success in making the Japanese domestic market more receptive to foreign products. Structural, cultural, and governmental limitations on investment practices by U.S. firms still exist.[101] The success of a few U.S. firms in Japan does not indicate widespread application of free trade and open investment practices.[102] U.S.-based MNEs like IBM, Texas Instruments, and Motorola have made commercial inroads often only after exhaustive efforts, and some have been

---

[100] For details concerning the efforts of individual companies in Japan, see Mason, op. cit., footnote 5, pp. 32-96. For a summary of the present situation see Office of the United States Trade Representative, *Second Annual Report of the U.S.-Japan Working Group on the Structural Impediments Initiative*," July 30, 1992, hereafter referred to as 2nd SII report.

[101] Analysis in support of this view comes from a number of sources. See Keidanren report, op. cit., footnote 6; The House Wednesday Group, op. cit., footnote 6; Office of the United States Trade Representative, op. cit., footnote 6, pp. 79-94.

[102] For a list of the limits to free trade and open investment practices in Japan, see Keidanren report, op. cit., footnote 6.

The OECD rules promoting national treatment allow exceptions based on concerns for national security and public order, particularly in regard to the natural resource, energy, and service sectors.[5] Given these exceptions, nations can impose tax obligations and investment controls on foreign controlled enterprises, restrict access to local bank credit and capital markets, and discriminate in government procurement contracts.[6] Concerned with an apparent trend towards excessive restrictions, the OECD recommended a standstill on further exceptions in 1988. In 1991, the OECD encouraged nations to make restrictive measures more transparent and to commit to eliminating them in the future.[7] At the same time, the OECD and the Committee on International Investment and Multinational Enterprises (CIME), which monitors use of the decisions by national governments and MNEs, expressed concern over a number of trends and activities in both private and government policies and practices, including sharp swings in investment flows, trade frictions, conflicting national requirements on MNCs, the marginal contributions of screwdriver assembly plants, preferential treatment in the private sector, the increase in bilateral investment agreements, and the use of reciprocity as a bargaining tool.[8] The OECD fears these conditions undermine the Declaration and Decisions and may impede future multilateral attempts to liberalize foreign investment rules.

In sum, the nonbinding nature of the OECD Declaration and Decisions and their institutionalized deference to national laws and prerogatives leave them inherently weak. Member countries often have different reactions to the effects of asymmetrical investment incentives, and while some wish to strengthen the national treatment decisions, others prefer to include more rights of exception.[9] These different views indicate that real progress towards further liberalization or enforcement of the Declaration and Decisions is unlikely.

---

[5] OECD, *The OECD Declaration and Decisions on International Investment and Multinational Enterprises: 1991 Review*, (Paris: OECD, 1992), pp. 26-32.

[6] OECD, *National Treatment for Foreign-Controlled Enterprises*, (Paris: OECD, 1985), pp. 20-22.

[7] OECD, *The OECD Declaration and Decisions on International Investment and Multinational Enterprises: 1991 Review*, pp. 30-5; "National Treatment: Third Revised Decision of the Council," December 1991, revision of the Declaration by Governments of the OECD Member countries on International Investment and Multinational Enterprises.

[8] OECD, *The OECD Declaration and Decisions on International Investment and Multinational Enterprises: 1991 Review*, pp. 18-20.

[9] Confidential interviews.

---

forced to trade proprietary technology for market access.[103] Many U.S. firms have turned to their government for help in an effort to gain trade or investment access to Japan's market[104] or have simply given up, frustrated by the high costs of market entry.

■ Japan as a Special Case

In some cases, U.S. firms may not have made a realistic effort to gain market access in Japan; accordingly, their claims that the Japanese system is unfair may be inappropriate. On the other hand, charges of Japanese limitations on trade and investment should not be dismissed merely as

---

[103] For a discussion of the experiences of these firms in Japan see Encarnation et al., op. cit., footnote 97, pp. 25-54; Mason, op. cit., footnote 5; and Tyson, op. cit., footnote 8, pp. 53-75.

[104] Peter J. Katzenstein and Yutaka Tsujinaka, "Bullying vs. Buying: U.S.-Japanese Transnational Relations and Domestic Structures," paper delivered at the 1992 Annual Meeting of the American Political Science Association, Chicago, Sept. 3-6, 1992. The U.S. Government has initiated several export-promotion measures such as the "Japan Corporate Program." For details, see the American Chamber of Commerce, *The United States-Japan White Paper 1993* (Tokyo: American Chamber of Commerce in Japan, 1993), p. 2.

complaints by U.S. firms that could not learn to compete effectively.[105] Firms such as Dow Chemical, Motorola, Ford, and Coca Cola have either failed to penetrate the Japanese market or have succeeded only after exhaustive efforts; they have not had comparable difficulties penetrating other foreign markets. Difficulties gaining access to Japan by world-class competitive firms suggest that impediments in Japan are real.[106]

The Trade Expansion Committee of the American Chamber of Commerce in Japan (ACCJ) has identified 34 areas of particular concern for market and investment access, including product and service sector limitations, as well as broader problems relating to distribution, government procurement, investment, and taxation.[107] In a 1993 article, the chairman of the Sony Corp. confirmed the continued discrimination against foreign products in Japan: "It is clear," he wrote, "that many foreign products still have trouble with entry into and distribution in the Japanese market."[108] And even if the cause of failure in many or most cases is lack of effort by individual foreign firms, reports of discrimination from groups such as the ACCJ and prominent Japanese business leaders cannot be dismissed.

There is currently a debate in both the United States and Japan over whether the Japanese Government or Japan's private sector is the primary source for deterrents to U.S. FDI. One view says that the government provides the major roadblocks, while another says that the major constraints on foreign investment have shifted during the last decade from the public to the private sector. The latter view contends that Japan's major firms originally acted as aggressive intermediaries between the Japanese Government and U.S. firms, but have now taken charge of Japan's "strategic investment policy."[109]

During the first three decades of the post-WWII period, the major limitations to U.S. FDI in Japan came from laws initiated and administered by a government intent on protecting its domestic market and encouraging inward technology transfer. The period up to 1950 has been described by one leading analyst as the "closed door" period, and that between 1950 and 1970 as the "screen door" period, when the government carefully filtered foreign investment to maximize technology transfer.[110] A classic example of this pattern was the case of IBM. The Ministry of International Trade and Industry (MITI) made the firm's access to Japan conditional on the licensing of IBM patents to Japanese firms and charging them no more than a 5-percent royalty.[111]

Japanese Government officials gave assurances of liberalization as early as 1969. Nevertheless, the Japanese market is still highly resistant to FDI. Many analysts and managers of U.S.-based MNEs argue that official government restrictions have been supplanted by "private sector impediments" emanating from an "interior layer of business practices."[112] One report recently suggested that access is still limited by ingrained structural factors that "stem from particular features of the Japanese economic

---

[105] For such a critical view of American management, see James Abegglen and George Stalk, Jr., *Kaisha, The Japanese Corporation* (New York, NY: Basic Books, 1985).

[106] It should be noted that some critics contend that the Japanese Government attempts to coopt a few leading U.S. firms for strategic political reasons; for example, see "Chipmakers Call For Easing Burden on Japan," *Wall Street Journal*, June 7, 1993, p. A3.

[107] These are discussed systematically in ACCJ, op. cit., footnote 104, but see, for summary, pp. 2-6.

[108] Akio Morita, "Toward a New World Economic Order," *The Atlantic Monthly*, June 1993, pp. 90 and 96.

[109] Encarnation, op. cit., footnote 56, p. 41.

[110] Mason, op. cit., footnote 5, pp. 209-218.

[111] See comment by Sahashi Sigeru, former deputy director of MITI's Heavy Industries Bureau, quoted in Johnson, op. cit., footnote 97, p. 245.

[112] Ibid., p. 200.

structure, business organizations, and relations between the Japanese private sector and the government."[113]

What factors produce these constraints, and are they amenable to reform? The claim that some are the product of immutable cultural factors and that others stem from an arcane and complex distribution system may have some foundation.[114] Yet some analysts suggest that the constraints created by institutional factors and private and public sector policies are indeed amenable to reform.

In contrast to most countries, new FDI in Japan occurs primarily through greenfield establishments and/or joint ventures.[115] This unusual pattern may be explained by Japanese attitudes toward mergers and acquisitions. Many companies in Japan are hostile to unsolicited takeovers, and the term takeover bid is often used to describe foreign attempts to acquire Japanese companies. Some analysts argue that the private sector in Japan instituted a system of stable shareholders as part of the liberalization of investment rules by the Japanese Government. According to this view, MITI encouraged companies to exchange shares and thus make acquisition by foreign investors more difficult, a practice that began with GM's attempt to purchase shares of Isuzu in 1969:

> MITI finally announced that it would accept up to 35 percent foreign capital participation, on the condition that a substantial portion of the shares be held by stable shareholders. The term was used to indicate shareholders of Japanese nationality who could be counted on to retain their shares, even if the stock declined in market value and favorable prices were offered by foreign interests . . . A feasible means of finding stable shareholders would be for companies in a group or industry to hold each other's shares.[116]

Since then, companies have sought stable shareholders who are not interested in participating in the management of the company and who must obtain approval from the issuing company before selling their stock. The maximum share holding for financial institutions was reduced to 5 percent in 1987, apparently encouraging the wider distribution of company shares. But, in practice, members of the same keiretsu commonly exchange shares, binding their business relationships together more tightly and correspondingly making foreign acquisition of their respective companies more difficult.

It has been suggested that firms such as Toyota, as well as broader business groups such as Mitsubishi, Mitsui, and Sumitomo, consciously pursued stable shareholding acquisitions designed to achieve the "keiretsu-ization" (keiretsuka) of their firms.[117] Keiretsu members and their related companies account for approximately 34 percent of all corporate assets in Japan.[118] In practice, hostile takeovers are rare, and foreign takeovers usually occur only after all domestic possibilities have been exhausted.[119] This view appears consistent with the details concerning a series of

---

[113] Office of the United States Trade Representative, op. cit., footnote 6, p. 143. These constraints are systematically outlined in detail in the 2nd SII report, op. cit., footnote 100.

[114] These are discussed in ibid., p. 144; Internal Memorandum, Department of the Treasury, *Survey of G-7 Laws and Regulations on Foreign Direct Investment* (Washington, DC: Department of the Treasury, Dec. 7, 1988), p. 2; The House Wednesday Group, op. cit., footnote 6, p. 6. See also United Nations Conference on Trade and Development (UNCTAD), Programme on Transnational Corporations, *World Investment Report 1993: Transnational Corporations and Integrated International Production* (New York, NY: United Nations, 1993), pp. 42-43.

[115] Robert Z. Lawrence, "Japan's Low Levels of Inward Investment: The Role of Inhibitions on Acquisitions," *Transnational Corporations*, vol. 1, No. 3, December 1992, p. 47.

[116] Ballon et al., op. cit., footnote 54, pp. 50-51.

[117] Mason, op. cit., footnote 5, pp. 205-206; see also Nakashima Shuzo, *Kabushiki no mochiai to kigyo ho*, p. 46, as cited in Mason, p. 207 no. 16.

[118] Ballon et al., op. cit., footnote 54, p. 42.

[119] Internal memorandum, Department of the Treasury, op. cit., footnote 114, p. 2.

acquisitions of Japanese firms by foreign companies in the early 1990s. Many Japanese companies recently acquired by foreign MNEs were generally described as distressed or unprofitable.[120] The rise in the value of the yen against the dollar in 1993 suggests that even this limited trend towards foreign purchases may be difficult to sustain.

Determined foreign investors may turn to greenfield site construction or licensing. But the high cost of land renders the greenfield option available to only a few companies. This may encourage U.S. firms to settle for licensing agreements, which save them the costs of manufacturing and market entry.[121] Indeed, despite the liberalization of formal Japanese rules regarding inward FDI, in 1990 the $1.2 billion earned by U.S. companies from royalties and licensing fees from Japan accounted for 35 percent of worldwide U.S. receipts from unaffiliated foreigners.[122] This figure of $1.2 billion was 61 percent of the figure for U.S. FDI in Japan in the same year. This proportion of fees to U.S. FDI has grown over the prior 10 years when liberalization of the rules for FDI in Japan suggests that it should have decreased. With liberalization, U.S. firms would expect to invest more and license less. Moreover, this percentage is out of line with the ratio between U.S. licenses and FDI in other countries, and with the ratio between Japanese licenses and FDI in the United States.[123]

These figures suggest that the constraints on mergers and acquisitions, which many believe are caused by keiretsu behavior, push U.S. firms into business arrangements that effectively limit their market access. But more importantly, it limits their capacity to compete in Japan. In joint ventures, U.S. firms often take a minority share. As compared to Europe, U.S. shareholders in Japan are more likely to be the minority partner.[124] At the same time, licensing ensures that Japanese firms gain access to U.S. technology, leading to wide-scale, nonreciprocated technology transfer from the United States to Japan.

As one advocate of this position states,

> . . . the continued dependence on licensing, the heavy reliance on minority-interest ventures and the relatively large investments in majority-owned wholesale trade ventures support the argument that the marketing and distribution of foreign products in Japan is unusually difficult, or that current inflows have been too small to offset the impact of earlier policies.[125]

In contrast to the limited amount of merger and acquisition activity by foreign investors in Japan, such activity among domestic Japanese firms is vibrant and unhindered. Figures provided by Japan's Fair Trade Commission (FTC) for 1990 note that 1,532 mergers and 969 acquisitions occurred.[126] Another source indicates that of 584 mergers and acquisitions involving Japanese firms in 1992, 387 involved Japanese firms acquiring other Japanese firms, and 165 were

---

[120] Jonathan Friedland, "The Urge to Merge," *Far Eastern Economic Review*, Jan. 28, 1993.

[121] Lawrence, op. cit., footnote 115, pp. 47, 51-52, 63.

[122] Ibid. Lawrence notes that Japanese firms earned only $185 million in royalties and license fees from United States firms, p. 50.

[123] Ibid., pp. 52-53.

[124] "In 1990, majority-owned companies accounted for about 78 per cent of the FDI assets of United States firms. By contrast, only 34 per cent of the FDI assets in Japan and only 26 per cent of the assets in manufacturing were in majority-owned companies. Indeed, there is a relationship between countries that have generally discriminated against FDI and the share of majority-owned firms in FDI assets. While in developed countries that ratio averaged 76 per cent, the conspicuous outliers are the Republic of Korea (18 per cent), India (14 per cent) and Japan (34 per cent)." ibid., p. 53.

[125] Lawrence, op. cit., footnote 115, p. 55.

[126] Japan Fair Trade Commission, *Annual Report to the Committee on Competition Law and Policy, OECD, on Developments in Japan* (Tokyo: January-December 1990), p. 32.

Japanese firms acquiring foreign firms. In only 32 cases did foreign firms acquire Japanese firms.[127]

Evidence suggests that the keiretsu system impedes FDI in Japan as well as the capacity of Japanese affiliates of U.S. firms to trade in Japan.[128] The Structural Impediments Initiative stressed the inhibiting role of the keiretsu on market access for U.S. investors in Japan. Consistent with this claim, a recent ACCJ report emphasized the exclusionary business relationships that continually hinder the capacity of its members to trade in Japan. The report noted that the keiretsu arrangements ''have affected the ability of certain American industries, such as the automotive, flat glass, insurance, and semiconductor industries, to take full advantage of market opportunities in Japan, even when the product is highly competitive.''[129]

According to some analysts, a final impediment to FDI instituted by the private sector in Japan is the adoption of articles in company charters that preclude any form of foreign participation in the running of the companies, such as excluding non-Japanese citizens from their boards. Toyota wrote this provision into its charter in the 1960s.[130]

Limitations on new U.S. FDI in Japan are such that during the 1980s the sum of inward FDI in Japan grew primarily through the reinvested earnings of existing firms.[131] The conclusion of many analyses is that the major impediment to investment is the structure of Japan's private sector. The private sector may also create similar obstacles to trade.

Foreign firms able to establish a presence in Japan often face supply and distribution problems when a few firms control the supply of essential products in Japan. For example, efforts by Toys ''R'' Us to establish itself in Japan as a low-cost toy retailer have been undermined by a few supplier firms trying to ensure that other retailers are not damaged by the entry of a new competitor.[132]

The automobile industry provides another example of how the keiretsu system can restrict market access. European auto firms complain about the collusion and exclusivity of the distribution system in Japan.[133]

Automobile companies in Japan have much greater control of their dealership network than do their counterparts in the United States, through both direct ownership and individually negotiated contracts between the independent dealerships and the automobile manufacturers. In the absence of the active encouragement of the auto company that controls the dealership, penetration of the market through dual dealerships is exceptionally difficult. This makes the creation of an effective dealership network in Japan extremely time-consuming and expensive compared to establishing a network in the United States. For example,

---

[127] C. Fred Bergsten and Marcus Noland, *Reconcilable Differences? United States-Japan Economic Conflict* (Washington, DC: Institute for International Economics, 1993), p. 81. The large discrepancy in the total number of mergers and acquisitions between this source and the Japan FTC (cited above) may result from different counting rules. Bergston and Nolan give the following statistics for 1990: total mergers and acquisitions, 801; Japanese firms acquiring Japanese firms, 341; Japanese firms acquiring foreign firms, 450; foreign firms acquiring Japanese firms, 10.

[128] See Michael L. Gerlach, *Alliance Capitalism: The Social Organization of Japanese Business* (Berkeley, CA: University of California Press, 1992), pp. 36-37 and 262-268.

[129] The details of these limits are offered in ACCJ, op. cit., footnote 104, pp. 30-34, 49-50, 64-68, 90-92.

[130] Mason, op. cit., footnote 5, p. 207.

[131] Lawrence, op. cit., footnote 115, p. 70.

[132] For details see Mark Mason, ''United States Direct Investment in Japan: Trends and Prospects,'' *California Management Review*, vol. 35, No. 1, fall 1992, p. 108.

[133] See ''European Auto Industry Proposes 'Joint Sectoral Initiative' With Japan,'' *International Trade Reporter*, May 19, 1993, pp. 830-831. The European Auto Industry also noted the discriminatory effects of unfair taxation, administrative guidance, inadequate protection of intellectual property rights, and the cost of land.

establishing a distribution network in Japan from scratch, with sales outlets equal in number to Mazda or Honda (about 2,500) could be expected to cost more than $1 billion, assuming acceptable locations were available.[134] Training the staff of such a large number of outlets would be time-consuming and expensive, further increasing the costs of creating a competitive dealer network.

Some analysts argue that the Japanese Government has liberalized FDI in order to defuse tension with the United States over its trade surplus.[135] Others contend that, despite the emphasis on capital liberalization, the government pursues policies that effectively constrain FDI. As a 1992 Keidanren report stated:

> Japan has considerably more regulations on business than most other countries, and this undoubtedly obstructs the entry of new firms, both domestic and foreign, into the market. Many foreign firms, which are able to enter other markets, face greater difficulties in entering the Japanese market due to such regulations and administrative guidance.[136]

The solution, according to this report, is a shift towards transparency in government administration. U.S. companies in Japan have made similar claims, suggesting that transparency in the decisionmaking process remains inadequate in Japanese agencies that have denied U.S. firms access to information concerning rules and regulations.[137]

This criticism appears consistent with U.S. claims that Japan's Anti-Monopoly Law is administered "with inadequate penalties, less than vigorous enforcement, and numerous exceptions."[138] Furthermore, the law allows for "exemption cartels" that meet specified legal conditions. These exemption cartels numbered 256 at the end of 1990, and were defined as either "depression cartels" or "rationalization cartels" under The Anti-Monopoly Act.[139] One ACCJ report contends that monopolistic practices still exist in Japan as a result of selective application of the anticompetitive laws by the Japan FTC.[140] Due to these measures, U.S.-based MNEs investing in Japan are often unable to compete directly with their Japanese counterparts in areas where the Japanese firms are least competitive.

Furthermore, Japanese Government proscriptions of investments that threaten national security or public order, affect existing producers, or disrupt the national economy are vague enough to justify government intervention under many different circumstances.[141] The Japanese Government's concern about the effects of disruptive practices may result in a variety of problems for foreign products and firms:

> Foreign air transport companies face difficult and time-consuming obstacles to acquiring airport landing rights and brokerage licenses. Medical equipment companies have experienced both slowing of approvals of new medical technology in which the U.S. has a leadership position, and

---

[134] This estimate is based on a 10-percent share of Autorama, which cost Ford $10 million in 1992. Autorama had 328 sales outlets. Honda and Mazda each had approximately 2,500 sales outlets in 1990. Indirect investments by Mazda (currently 25 percent owned by Ford) to support Autorama, in which it currently has a 41 percent stake, probably exceed $100 million. Source: Ford Motor Co. and Japan Automobile Manufactures Association, Inc., *Automotive Distribution in Japan* (JAMA: Washington, DC: June 1990) p. 3.

[135] See, for example, Julius, op. cit., footnote 9, p. 33.

[136] Keidanren report, op. cit., footnote 6, p. 5.

[137] Examples of the adverse effects of such problems are evident in the case of construction projects, the setting of regulations for solid wood products use, and the procedures for date labeling of certain food products. ACCJ, op. cit., footnote 104, p. 5.

[138] Office of United States Trade Representative, op. cit., footnote 6, p. 144.

[139] For details see Japan Fair Trade Commission, op. cit., footnote 126, pp. 30-31.

[140] ACCJ, op. cit., footnote 104, p. 3.

[141] Internal memorandum, Department of the Treasury, op. cit., footnote 114, table, p. 5. For a list see 2nd SII report, op. cit., footnote 100, pp. 1-63.

funding of Japanese products directly competing with U.S. products. Imported food products face rigid barriers such as unrealistic short delivery deadlines and onerous date-labeling requirements, in addition to being required to meet food safety standards different from those sued in other countries. Restrictions on premium pricing and sales promotions handicap foreign and new-to-market companies, such as travel and tourism agencies and processed food importers.[142]

The definition of a legitimate basis for government intervention to deny foreign investment is therefore far broader in Japan than in the United States.

According to a recent report of the United States Trade Representative (USTR), government measures that are transparent often remain discriminatory. The USTR reported that the Japanese Government retains the authority to restrict investment in specified sectors, including aircraft, space development, agriculture, fishing and forestry, oil and gas, mining, leather and leather product manufacturing, nuclear power, weapons and ordnance manufacturing, and tobacco.[143]

U.S. firms often raise five additional issues. These are:

1. intellectual property and patent rights;
2. Japanese Government and private sector procurement practices;
3. inadequate funding of programs intended to encourage FDI in Japan;
4. the high withholding rate on dividends repatriated to overseas parents;
5. continuing regulation intended to support prices in the property and financial sectors.

The issue of intellectual property rights in Japan is complex, extending both to advanced high-technology sectors such as biotechnology and to more established sectors such as automobiles and textiles. U.S.-based MNEs are concerned that Japanese patent protection rules and the longer duration of patent registration (compared to other nations) has a deleterious effect on the competitiveness of foreign firms.[144] This claim is not new, dating to initial U.S. efforts to re-enter the Japanese market. It has become more acute, however, because of the heightened competitiveness of Japanese firms, the access of Japanese firms to America's best technology, and the importance attached to patent issues at the continuing Uruguay Round of the General Agreement on Tariffs and Trade (GATT). Attempts to address U.S. concerns have not been effective.[145]

The procurement issue focuses on the claim that pervasive " 'Buy Japanese' attitudes and practices persist in such sectors as construction and engineering, radio communications (wireless telecommunications equipment), and semiconductors, for which major 'market-opening' or purchasing agreements exist."[146] The same claim has been advanced about U.S. supercomputers. Despite the clear superiority of U.S.-made supercomputers, the Japanese Government procured only five machines from U.S. companies in the 1980s, preferring to source an additional 46 machines from Japanese firms. This led to agreements between the United States and Japan over supercomputer procurement in 1987 and 1990.[147]

In some cases, specifications for Japanese Government procurement are not made public. But even when they are, critics suggest, they often effectively deny foreign vendors the right to

---

[142] ACCJ, op. cit., footnote 104.

[143] Office of The United States Trade Representative, op. cit. footnote 6, p. 161.

[144] Ibid., pp. 18-20. Recent reforms cut the patent examination period from 37 months in 1988 to 30 months in 1991. 2nd SII report, op. cit., footnote 100, p. 50.

[145] This point is made in ibid., especially pp. 49-50.

[146] Ibid., p. 4. For a listing of procurement limitations in Japan, see pp. 13-17.

[147] For a detailed discussion of this issue, see Office of Technology Assessment, op. cit., footnote 1, pp. 273-78.

participate. The U.S. firms remain unable to penetrate the Japanese market despite transparent, nondiscriminatory procurement standards adopted under a 1990 agreement revised in 1992.[148] MITI officials agree that only limited progress has been made and that "there is a need to do more to improve transparency and avoid discrimination in procurement practices."[149] Progress in reaching an agreement has been made in a number of areas, including software and a variety of chemical treatments.[150]

In addition to restrictions authorized under the Foreign Exchange Control Law, Japan sources cite specific restrictive industry laws in sectors such as air and marine transport, communications, and broadcasting. A 1992 Keidanren report indicated that these individual industry regulations "are actually more responsible for restricting foreign investment than the Foreign Exchange Control Law." Thus "opaque restriction of entry by policies and administrative guidance based on specific industry laws virtually discriminate [against] foreign capital and limit the competition."[151] These laws often complement the industry-, group- or firm-specific private impediments that originated in the 1970s.

U.S. sources support these generalizations with specific examples. An ACCJ report concluded that:

> While deregulation has proceeded to some extent in recent years, many archaic and arbitrary regulations and guidelines remain in effect, serving as impediments to trade. Many building codes preclude the use of certain wood products. Radio communications and telecommunication services and equipment continue to be highly regulated

sectors. These regulations keep prices high and delay access for competitive and high-quality American goods and services. . . . Air transport services suffer from regulations which control the prices they charge and the services they offer. In some cases all that is required is simplification and clarification of regulations (cosmetics), or modification of guidelines for existing "liberalizing" laws (telecommunications services carriers).[152]

Institutions with programs designed to encourage FDI in Japan, such as the Export-Import Bank of Japan's Product Import Promotion Financing Program, lack adequate funding and are consequently limited in effectiveness.

The Japanese Government has also established artificially low ceilings for the financing of projects by foreign corporations through the Japan Development Bank.[153]

Tax policies also discourage FDI. The government has sustained an artificially high withholding tax rate of 10 percent on dividends paid from subsidiaries in Japan, in contravention of the 5 percent OECD model convention. Some analysts suggest that this constitutes discrimination; a Keidenran report separately advocates that the Japanese Government lower its rate to 5 percent, consistent with the multilateral tax convention.[154]

A recent congressional report argues that pervasive government measures continue to regulate land and financial markets, in effect sustaining extremely high prices despite the bursting of the speculative bubble in Japan.[155] Artificially high land prices discourage the establishment of new facilities and the expansion of existing

---

[148] For details see 2nd SII report, op. cit., footnote 100.

[149] Ibid., p. 28.

[150] ACCJ, op. cit., footnote 104, pp. 13-17, 71.

[151] Keidanren report, op. cit., footnote 6, p. 8.

[152] ACCJ, op. cit., footnote 104, p. 4.

[153] Ibid., pp. 8-9.

[154] Ibid., p. 10.

[155] House Wednesday Group, op. cit., footnote 6, p. iii.

operations. Inflated financial markets hinder entry and expansion through acquisitions.

The sources cited above appear to disagree on whether impediments to investors originate in the private or public sector. The Japanese Government claims it is trying to impose liberalization on a recalcitrant private sector, while representatives of the private sector suggest the converse is true. Regardless, both seem to impede FDI in Japan. This conclusion stems from the evidence that Japanese public and private sector officials have often resorted to minor concessions to accommodate foreign pressures for change, while avoiding major changes. Amaya Naohiro, a high-level MITI official, suggested as early as 1969 that this was the thrust of MITI policy.[156]

In interviews conducted by OTA, both U.S. Government officials and business executives echoed these observations. In view of the history of concerted Japanese barriers to inward FDI, several said that those who believe that Japan is liberalizing its FDI policy should provide evidence in the form of concrete results, for many data indicate that this is not the case. In 1990, Japan's level of inward FDI per capita was much lower than other OECD countries such as Germany and the United Kingdom. The U.S. level in 1990 was more than 20 times that of Japan (see figure 1-8 in chapter 1.) Figure 1-4 shows only moderate growth in the overall FDI position in Japan for 1991 and 1992, especially when compared to the growth in Japan's FDI position abroad for the same years.

Japanese figures demonstrate an asymmetry in the comparable position of foreign firms in the United States and foreign firms in Japan. According to MITI, foreign-owned firms employed 0.5 percent of the work force in Japan in 1991, compared to 3.8 percent in the United States. Products of foreign companies came to 1.2 percent of total sales in Japan, compared to 16.5 percent in the United States. Moreover, foreign affiliates controlled only 0.9 percent of total assets in Japan, compared to 20.4 percent in the United States (see figure 1-1 in chapter 1).[157] By the end of the 1980s, U.S. FDI in Japan totaled nearly $20 billion, doubling between 1985 and 1989, and accounting for 9 percent of all U.S. Direct Investment Abroad (USDIA), although that figure remained well behind the leading recipients, Canada (18 percent) and the Britain (16 percent).[158] In 1992, Japanese direct investment abroad reached approximately $250 billion, more that 10 times the amount of FDI in Japan (see figure 1-4 in chapter 1).

The United States and Japan share what many have described as the most important bilateral relationship in the world, a relationship that is critical to the growth of global free trade. At the same time, Japan's export surpluses are a leading cause of the U.S. trade deficit. These two factors help to explain why so many analysts and policymakers focus on policy asymmetries between the United States and Japan and on the structural conditions that shape Japan's private sector.[159]

---

[156] As cited in Mason, op. cit., footnote 5, p. 201.

[157] From Gaishi-Kei Kigyou Koudou Chousa, Houjin Kigyou Toukei, MITI 1991, as cited in House Wednesday Group, op. cit., footnote 6, p. 4: Lawrence, op. cit., footnote 115, p. 48, suggests that all FDI in Japan totals 1 percent.

[158] Encarnation, op. cit., footnote 56, pp. 95-96.

[159] House Wednesday Group, op. cit., footnote 6, p. 26.

Japanese Multinational Enterprises in the United States | 4

This chapter examines some of the major issues regarding the activities of large Japanese-based multinational enterprises (MNEs) in the United States. As the most conspicuous competitors with leading U.S.-based MNEs during the 1980s, Japanese firms' activities here, and the effects of U.S. Government policy on those activities, offer an opportunity to assess how the national policy on foreign-based firms affects our interests.

Throughout the business and academic literature on foreign direct investment (FDI) and U.S. international competitiveness, one theme is constant: the competitive challenge of Japanese corporations. Major manufacturing corporations such as Toyota, NEC, and Mitsubishi have been central to Japan's remarkable postwar economic resurgence. They have also been among the principal players in Japan's late 1980s overseas investment boom.

U.S. firms were among the first to expand production significantly to foreign locations; European firms have made significant international investments, particularly within other European countries. But it is clear at any level of analysis that Japanese firms have greatly expanded their presence in the world economic system and especially within the United States during the last decade. (See figures 1-4 and 3-3.)

Between 1981 and 1991, the number of Japanese firms in the Fortune 500 rose from 78 to 119, with 20 in the top 100 in 1991, twice the number as at the beginning of the decade. As can be seen in table 4-1, Japanese companies increased FDI faster than those from any other nation during the 1980s, accounting for 11

**Table 4-1—Foreign Direct Investment Position
in the U.S., Selected Years**
(In billions of dollars)

Country	1980	1985	1991
All	83.0	184.6	407.8
Developed	72.0	161.2	381.5
EC-12	47.3	107.4	232.0
Japan	4.7	19.3	86.7
Canada	12.2	17.1	30.5

NOTE: Data are based on historical cost and are not adjusted for inflation.

SOURCE: John Rutter, "Recent Trends in Foreign Direct Investment in the United States: The Boom of the 80's Vanishes," U.S. Department of Commerce, International Trade Administration, December 1992, appendix table 2.

percent of FDI by major developed countries[1] and 21.3 percent of cumulative direct investment in the United States by the end of the decade.[2] Japanese direct investment in the United States increased at an average annual rate of 32.5 percent from 1980 to 1985, and continued at a rate of 28.4 percent for the second half of the decade, far outdistancing similar rates for other developed countries.[3]

Although investment leveled off significantly after the 1980s, in 1990 Japanese firms had stakes of 50 percent or more in 1,088 U.S. manufacturing and assembly operations, and smaller stakes in 136 more enterprises. The majority-owned enterprises together operated more than 1,500 factories and employed 284,000 Americans, with another 86,000 jobs at minority Japanese-owned establishments.[4] Despite the decline in Japanese investment in the first 2 years of the 1990s, many analysts suggest that this is only a temporary lull. Indeed, one analyst estimates that by the end of the century, Japan may invest another $700 billion overseas, 40 percent of which can be expected to take the form of direct investment. This would amount to a shift of 15 percent of Japanese production abroad.[5]

By the end of the 1980s, the Japanese presence in the United States was well-established. Japanese direct investment in manufacturing in the United States focused on electric and electronic equipment, primary and fabricated metals, and transportation equipment.[6] Counting both imports into the U.S. and domestic production, Japanese firms accounted for significant market shares in many key industries, reaching 20 percent of the semiconductor market,[7] 29.9 percent of the automobile market,[8] and significant holdings in the steel market.[9]

These changes have stimulated public debate over the competitive challenge from Japanese

---

[1] John M. Stopford and Susan Strange, *Rival States, Rival Firms: Competition for World Market Shares* (Cambridge, England: Cambridge University Press, 1991), p. 17.

[2] Based on book value. John W. Rutter, Department of Commerce, "Recent Trends in Foreign Direct Investment in the United States: The Boom of the '80s Vanishes," December 1992, appendix table 1.

[3] Ibid.

[4] Japan Economic Institute, "Japan's Expanding US Manufacturing Presence, 1990 Update," *JEI Report*, June 1992, pp. 3-4. (The U.S. Government defines a foreign-controlled firm as one with at least 10 percent of its equity held by one foreign owner.)

[5] Kenneth Courtis, Tokyo economist for Deutsche Bank, cited in Robert L. Cutts, "Capitalism in Japan: Cartels and Keiretsu," *Harvard Business Review*, July/August 1992, p. 54.

[6] John W. Rutter, U.S. Department of Commerce, "Trends and Patterns in Foreign Direct Investment in the United States," *Foreign Direct Investment in the United States: Review and Analysis of Current Developments*, August 1991, p. 25.

[7] Semiconductor Industry Association, *Obtaining Access to the Japanese Market: Interim Report on the 1991 US-Japan Semiconductor Agreement* (Washington, DC: May 1993), p. 7.

[8] In 1992; U.S. Department of Commerce, "Motor Vehicles and Parts," *US Industrial Outlook 1993* (Washington, DC: US Government Printing Office, January 1993), p. 35-7.

[9] The Department of Commerce reported that foreign steel makers held substantial positions in almost 25 percent of domestic integrated mills by the late 1980s, with Japanese firms the dominant foreign investors. Ibid., p. 13-3.

corporations and the Japanese economy. Some analysts suggest that the impressive performance of Japanese firms is due primarily to efficient industrial organization and production techniques. Others stress business relationships among Japanese industrial companies along with banks that allow them to obtain capital more cheaply, compete for market share rather than short-term profits, and weather hard economic times. Some argue that government protection and aid to developing industries, and restrictions on foreign sales and investment, are the keys to Japanese success.

Japanese firms have lagged behind their U.S. and European counterparts in the globalization process. This is at least partly due to their latecomer status; the industrial infrastructure of the nation suffered greater destruction during World War II than that of most European nations. But while the physical damage was substantial, much of the structure and operating style of Japanese firms survived from the prewar era. Some aspects of the Japanese system go back to the establishment of the first zaibatsu, or family-based commercial empires, in the 19th century (although parts of the system emerged as early as the 17th century).

Thus, some of the powerful organization evident in modern-day Japanese corporations has developed over time—with influence from governmental planners—as the firms have developed. This may explain the companies' conservatism, their strong identification with Japan, and their reluctance, in many cases, to adapt to what many in the United States consider appropriate forms of corporate behavior and community participation.

Japanese managers tend to view relationships with foreign firms, customers, and governments as opportunities to absorb knowledge and technology. Just as the aristocrats who steered the new Japanese state after the Meiji Restoration of 1868 modeled social and governmental institutions on what they saw as the best of the West, so Japanese corporations have absorbed Western institutions—such as Fordist mass production and the global corporation—and adapted them to Japanese sensibilities and goals. In this view, it may be useful to think of the Japanese firms that loom large in many technology-intensive, high value-added industries as possessing a national ideology of technology absorption.[10]

This chapter addresses factors that have aided the expansion of Japanese firms in the United States, both through exports and direct investment. It discusses the competitive challenge to U.S. industries posed by these firms, and the assistance provided by Japanese Government policies and keiretsu business groupings to the activities of large Japanese enterprises in the United States. The chapter concludes by examining an area of particular concern to Congress: Japan's significant investments in both small and start-up companies in high-technology industries, and in domestic university research. Critics have suggested that such practices result in Japanese firms profiting disproportionately from U.S. strengths in basic sciences and technology research and development (R&D).

CHAPTER FINDINGS

1. The Japanese Government has supported and preserved the competitive position of Japanese firms doing business in the United States, using "administrative guidance" of domestic enterprises and government-to-government activism.

2. Japanese corporate ties, particularly as represented by the keiretsu industrial groupings,

---

[10] For a description of Japan's ideological predisposition toward technology absorption, see David B. Friedman and Richard J. Samuels, "How To Succeed Without Really Flying: The Japanese Aircraft Industry and Japan's Ideology," paper presented for National Bureau of Economic Research Conference, San Diego, CA, Apr. 1-3, 1992.

have helped Japanese firms establish global sales, distribution, and production networks. In the United States, keiretsu-type organization has accompanied the establishment of some Japanese-owned production facilities.

3. Many Japanese producers in the United States are gradually increasing the U.S. content of their domestic production—although they have not reached the levels of domestic content of either their U.S. rivals or other foreign investors—as local suppliers become more qualified and more competitive. This process is in conflict, however, with maintenance of the Japanese producers' keiretsu ties. The issue is further complicated by inconsistent U.S. Government definitions and methods of determining domestic content.

4. Japanese firms look to both U.S. university research in basic and applied sciences, and small, innovative U.S. firms in high-technology areas, as valuable technology resources. They have made extensive efforts to draw on these resources through strategic investments, alliances, and other ties.

Japanese Government Activism

One factor often cited to explain Japan's international commercial success is the skillful intervention of government bureaucrats, particularly the Ministry of International Trade and Industry (MITI). According to numerous examinations of the Japanese system,[11] government officials work closely with industry leaders, strongly influencing firms under the guise of "administrative guidance" in order to foster the development of specific domestic industries and prevent what is often described as "excessive competition." Among the tools at their disposal are government subsidies, loan guarantees, and technology consortia, as well as various measures aimed at restricting the entrance of foreign firms into the domestic market.

Recognizing the difficulties that confront foreign firms, the Japan Export and Trade Organization (JETRO), an agency of MITI, in recent years has encouraged imports to Japan, offering information and introduction services to foreign firms interested in cracking the Japanese market. Similarly, in a program called the "Business Global Partnership Initiative," MITI announced its intention to encourage large domestic firms to increase imports, expand local procurement for overseas production activities, and help foreign firms make direct investments in Japan.[12] Although such plans may invite skeptical responses from foreign observers, they indicate the Japanese Government's sensitivity to outside pressure.

Although financial and economic developments, such as capital liberalization and the rise in value of the yen, were major impetuses during the 1980s for increased Japanese investment in the United States (see ch. 3), the influence of the Japanese Government—in tandem with U.S. actions—was also significant. In the auto industry, for example, the Japanese Government explicitly encouraged firms to invest in the United States and other nations to avoid protectionist measures and threats of further action by the U.S. Government. The intergovernmental relations that led to the bilateral Voluntary Export Restraints of 1981 are a good example of this phenomenon.

The Japanese Government has a history of discriminating against not only foreign firms but

---

[11] Chalmers A. Johnson, *MITI and the Japanese Miracle: the Growth of Industrial Policy, 1925-1975* (Stanford, CA: Stanford University Press, 1982). Alternative interpretations that stress the role of big business and the interplay of different interest groups are provided by Richard Samuels, *The Business of the Japanese State* (Ithaca, NY: Cornell University Press, 1987); and Karel van Wolferen, *The Enigma of Japanese Power: People and Politics in a Stateless Nation* (New York, NY: Vintage Books, 1990).

[12] Ministry of International Trade and Industry, MITI Overseas Public Affairs Office, "Business Global Partnership Initiative," Fact Sheet, November 1991, p. 3.

also certain domestic firms.[13] Those firms that traditionally had been the biggest beneficiaries of government policy in the auto industry were the least enthusiastic about investing in the United States, and were uncharacteristically vocal in articulating their views. They feared that moving production to the United States would reduce their productivity, subject them to unfavorable U.S. regulations over issues such as hiring practices, and affect their ability to maintain close control over the activities of subsidiaries.

Conversely, those firms that previously received fewer benefits from government policies were more receptive to the idea of change; when MITI officials approached all the auto manufacturers in late 1979 with the idea of building U.S. facilities, Honda alone announced that the company would build a U.S. plant in Ohio in January of 1980. Honda apparently implemented an overseas investment strategy that won favor with Japanese Government officials while reducing their influence on the company.

Both Nissan and Toyota in contrast, announced that they would not build U.S. plants.[14] Their continued resistance provoked strong and public criticism from MITI.[15] The two firms subsequently responded rather differently: Nissan capitulated, announcing that it would build a U.S. plant, while Toyota balked.

In the United States, the United Auto Workers (UAW) and Ford filed petitions with the U.S. International Trade Commission (ITC) under Section 301 of the Trade Act, requesting protection on the grounds that imports were the primary cause of the auto industry's distress. MITI officials met with U.S. Trade Representative (USTR) officials in June 1980, promising them that Japanese firms would exercise restraint in imports, and MITI's head publicly criticized the companies for their lack of cooperation, particularly Toyota.

What had hitherto only been hints that U.S. protection was a possibility then became more explicitly stated, if not formalized, in September 1980, with a request for a Voluntary Export Restraint (VER) order transmitted by the U.S. ambassador in Tokyo. Tokyo agreed, but the major Japanese auto producers reneged. MITI officials encouraged U.S. officials to demand Japanese responsiveness.[16]

The U.S. Justice Department declared that a VER would not violate U.S. antitrust law if it was administered by the Japanese state. Further negotiations between U.S. and Japanese Government officials then settled on a VER of between 1.5 and 1.8 million automobiles per year. MITI thus reasserted its authority to supervise the allocation process and thereby exercise significant leverage over the domestic firms. Within a week, MITI and USTR officials agreed on a figure of 1.68 million units for 3 years.

By limiting exports, the two governments created an incentive for direct investment by the Japanese firms to sustain market share. Toyota and Nissan both resisted moving production to the United States but their loss of market share to Honda[17] motivated them to invest in the United States.

---

[13] For a discussion of this point, see Simon Reich, *The Fruits of Fascism: Postwar Prosperity in Historical Perspective* (Ithaca, NY: Cornell University Press, 1990).

[14] Paul A. Summerville, ''The Politics of Self-Restraint: The Japanese State, and the Voluntary Export Restraint of Japanese Passenger Car Exports to the United States in 1981'' (unpublished doctoral dissertation, University of Tokyo, 1988), p. 322.

[15] Noboru Fujii: ''The Road to the U.S.-Japan Auto Crash,'' *U.S.-Japan Relations: New Attitudes for a New Era, Annual Review 1983-1984* (Cambridge, MA: The Program on U.S.-Japan Relations, Center for International Affairs, Harvard University, 1984), p. 41.

[16] Summerville, op. cit., footnote 14, pp. 326, 356.

[17] Honda increased its share of Japanese companies' automobile sales in the United States from 21 to 26 percent between 1981 and 1985. Ibid., p. 395.

Foreign direct investment in the United States (FDIUS) did have advantages for Japanese firms. It allowed them to insulate themselves from further export cutbacks and the effects of currency variations, to compete with U.S. firms directly in their home market, and to reduce the influence of both the Japanese and U.S. Governments. The Japanese Government lost influence over these firms by encouraging the globalization of production, while the U.S. Government lost influence because it could no longer threaten protectionist restraints. The United States instead had to deal with transplants that were able to develop domestic political strength by signing agreements with State governments regarding job, investment, and production levels.

The new transplants were able to compete effectively against their domestic counterparts by locating plants with cheaper labor costs, and by transplanting their efficient production systems. They did this in part by encouraging or coercing Japanese subcontractors and suppliers to move production capacity to the United States, thus to a large extent reproducing the domestic system of industrial groupings, or ''keiretsu,'' in this country, as the following section describes.

KEIRETSU

There is increasing evidence that the structure of the Japanese business groups known as keiretsu gives them an advantage against U.S. firms. The keiretsu, a general term for horizontally or vertically organized networks of companies, provide member firms with preferential procurement by group members, low-cost capital, stable shareholding, and support in hard economic times. There has been extensive academic and media examination of the keiretsu, as well as government attention, both in bilateral trade negotiations and in domestic antitrust actions. This section examines the relevance of the keiretsu to the activities of large Japanese firms in the United States, and whether there are grounds for congressional concern.

Many keiretsu relationships have been transplanted to this country as part of the highly efficient production systems of the large Japanese manufacturing firms. Examination of the geographical dispersion of Japanese manufacturing facilities demonstrates quite clearly that supplier firms have established production facilities in the United States to service their important customers.[18] This transplantation is based at least partly on cultural preferences for doing business with other Japanese companies, but it can also be seen as a rational economic decision to maintain established, reliable supplier relationships. As Japanese producers form relationships with domestic suppliers and customers, however, the keiretsu relationships may weaken. U.S. Government demands and media attention appear to speed this process.

Many Japanese firms producing in the United States apparently prefer to do business with Japanese suppliers that have established their own U.S. manufacturing affiliates, thus denying business to U.S. companies. When such practices have been challenged, Japanese manufacturers typically respond that they have been unable to find U.S. suppliers capable of meeting their high quality standards at acceptable prices.[19] Toyota, for example, claimed in 1990 that the average defect rate of parts it bought from U.S. suppliers

---

[18] Michael L. Gerlach, ''Twilight of the Keiretsu? A Critical Assessment,'' *Journal of Japanese Studies*, 18:1, winter 1992, pp. 112-115.

[19] Martin Kenney and Richard Florida, ''How Japanese Industry is Rebuilding the Rust Belt,'' *Technology Review*, February/March 1991, p. 28.

[20] Lindsay Chappell, ''Double-Edged Sword,'' *Automotive News*, Mar. 4, 1991, p. 1. At the Toyota plant in Georgetown, KY, Japanese-made parts are reportedly kept on hand as emergency inventory in case the U.S.-made parts that are delivered are unacceptable. Alex Taylor, ''Japan's New U.S. Car Strategy,'' *Fortune*, Sept. 10, 1990, p. 68.

was 100 times that of parts from Japanese suppliers.[20]

There is some evidence that more business is now going to U.S. parts suppliers: total sales of U.S.-made parts and accessories to Japanese automakers (for their operations in both Japan and the United States) increased from $1.7 billion in 1985 to $10.5 billion in 1990.[21] This could, however, be due to political considerations. A Nissan representative was quoted as saying that his company bought U.S.-made parts for its U.S. production even when they were 20 percent more expensive than Japanese products, and that Nissan was willing to push that margin up to 50 percent.[22]

Japanese keiretsu have been the focus of significant U.S. Government interest in two important areas. The first was the 1989 U.S.-Japan Structural Impediments Initiative, which identified the Japanese business groups as a barrier to U.S. firms' access to Japanese markets, and as an unfair advantage for Japanese firms in international competition. Although various Japanese Government officials and commissions, as well as private-sector groups, have agreed that the keiretsu do give member firms an unfair advantage,[23] little change appears to have occurred.[24]

The U.S. Government has also attempted to moderate the potency of the keiretsu through new policies encouraging Justice Department enforcement of antitrust provisions against Japanese firms or their U.S. subsidiaries, on the grounds that the Japanese keiretsu structure amounts to monopolistic or anticompetitive activity. A 1992 change in the Justice Department's policy on prosecution of antitrust violations by foreign enterprises indicated a new dedication, by at least some parts of the U.S. Government, to protecting domestic firms against bigger and richer foreign competitors, particularly Japanese firms.[25] The new policies abandoned a prior interpretation of U.S. antitrust law that required proof that corporate collusion harmed U.S. consumers. Rather, the Justice Department argued in 1992, antitrust laws could also be used to aid U.S. firms seeking access to foreign markets.[26] Although the Justice Department emphasized that the new policy was not aimed at specific foreign markets, the implication was clear that there were special grounds for complaint against Japanese organizational structures.[27]

WHAT ARE THE KEIRETSU?

The Japanese word "keiretsu" means system, lineage, or linkage. The vagueness of that definition is appropriate, because the term is used to cover a broad variety of relationships among companies. In its most fundamental definition, the word describes the cooperative arrangements formed by Japanese companies to reduce the risks of commercial activity.

There are two major types of keiretsu: horizontal, or "bank-centered," and vertical, or producer-centered, which include chains of suppliers extending upstream from a principal manufacturing company and chains of distributors downstream.

---

[21] U.S. Department of Commerce, "Motor Vehicles and Parts," *U.S. Industrial Outlook 1993* (Washington, DC: U.S. Government Printing Office, January 1992), p. 35-21. This figure does not distinguish between U.S.-owned firms and U.S. affiliates or subsidiaries of Japanese auto parts makers.

[22] Nobuyuki Oishi, "Auto Parts Makers Fear Fallout from 'Buy American,'" *Nikkei Weekly*, Mar. 7, 1992, p. 19.

[23] Keidanren (Federation of Economic Organizations), Ad-Hoc Committee on Foreign Direct Investment in Japan, "Improvement of the Investment Climate and Promotion of Foreign Direct Investment into Japan," Oct. 27, 1992, p. 13.

[24] Chalmers Johnson, "Japan's Lesson: Start With A Plan," *The New York Times*, Jan. 12, 1992, section 4, p. 19.

[25] Janice E. Rubin and Dick Nanto, "Japan's Keiretsu and U.S. Antitrust Laws," *CRS Review*, Sept. 1992, p. 31.

[26] "US Moving to Strengthen Its Antitrust Powers in Trade," *The New York Times*, Apr. 4, 1992, p. 43.

[27] John S. Magney, "U.S. Extends Reach of Antitrust Enforcement," *International Financial Law Review*, June 1992, p. 18.

The two types of keiretsu function differently in helping Japanese MNEs compete in high-technology areas.

Although the term keiretsu has become fashionable in U.S. business journalism, the practice of companies cooperating to provide capital and spread out risk has its roots in the prewar zaibatsu, the great industrial combines run by aristocratic families. In fact, the oldest of the zaibatsu, the Mitsui group, was founded in 1616 by Sokubei Takatoshi, a samurai who abandoned his class' traditional contempt for the world of business with the proclamation, "No more shall we have to live by the sword. I have seen that great profit can be made honorably. I shall brew sake and soy sauce, and we shall prosper."[28]

The zaibatsu, organized around holding companies controlled by the founding families, expanded into many different areas of commerce, although they tended to specialize in certain segments.[29] Because their manufacturing ability was crucial to the Japanese war effort during World War II, they were identified as a major target of the Allied program to demilitarize Japan during the Occupation. The holding companies and practices such as cross-shareholding were outlawed, and the zaibatsu were broken up.[30] However, as part of the 1949 Allied Occupation policy change known as the "reverse course," when Japan was recognized as a vital ally of the West against Communist expansion, zaibatsu dissolution was ended. After regaining autonomy in 1951, the Japanese Government amended the Anti-Monopoly Law imposed by the Allies to allow cross-stockholding and interlocking directorates. Those two practices, along with regular private meetings of executives known as "presidents' clubs," are the three most conspicuous structural elements of modern horizontal keiretsu affiliation.

■ The Horizontal Keiretsu

The structure of horizontal keiretsu is roughly similar to that of the zaibatsu, except that the coordinating role of the holding company is split among the main bank, the general trading company, and the presidents' council of the group. In fact, three of the current eight major horizontal groups—Mitsui, Mitsubishi, and Sumitomo—are continuations of traditional zaibatsu.[31] Most analyst classify three more "new" groups—Fuyo, DKB (Dai-Ichi Kangyo Bank), and Sanwa—with the first three as major horizontal keiretsu. There are two more "medium-sized" keiretsu, the Tokai Group and the group based on the Industrial Bank of Japan.

Horizontal keiretsu usually include a major bank, a trust bank, a major insurance company, and a trading company, with members in most if not all major areas of industrial production: electronic equipment, autos, construction, metals, mining, chemicals, textiles, heavy equipment, financial services, real estate, and transportation. The government encouraged this diversity to stimulate competition and to concentrate resources in critical industries.[32] The practice is known as "one-set-ism," (wan setto-shugi) since each group has a complete "set" of companies spanning the spectrum of major industries.[33]

---

[28] Terutomo Ozawa, "Japan's Industrial Groups" *MSU Business Topics*, autumn 1980, p. 34.

[29] Ibid., p. 34.

[30] Ibid., p. 35.

[31] Dodwell Marketing Consultants, *Industrial Groupings in Japan 1988-89* (Tokyo: Dodwell Marketing Consultants, 1988), p. 3. This is the most commonly cited reference for statistical information on the keiretsu. The cited edition identifies 8 horizontal keiretsu and 39 vertical ones. However, these numbers vary not only with time—since companies leave and join keiretsu increasingly frequently—but among sources.

[32] Marie Anchordoguy, "A Brief History of Japan's Keiretsu," *Harvard Business Review*, July-August 1990, p. 58.

[33] Ozawa, op. cit., footnote 28, p. 40.

All together, these eight groups accounted for more than a fifth of the total paid-in capital of Japanese firms and nearly 13 percent of total corporate profits in the nation in 1987.[34] The six major horizontal groups are estimated to have accounted for about a quarter of Japanese gross national product (GNP) since World War II.[35] Furthermore, over two-thirds of Japan's imports pass through the hands of the large trading companies affiliated with the major keiretsu.[36]

The practice of stable mutual shareholding protects companies against U.S.-style pressures for short-term profits or high dividends, as well as outside takeover attempts.[37] Typically, the "main bank" at the center of a keiretsu will hold 5 to 10 percent of member companies' stock, while other keiretsu members may hold 2 to 5 percent of the stock each;[38] this often amounts to as much of a quarter of the company's stock held within the keiretsu.[39] In addition to creating symbolic bonds among companies, keiretsu members implicitly agree not to trade the stock they hold.[40] Financial ties among companies are further strengthened by intragroup loans, usually but not exclusively from the central bank; at one point in 1989, for example, more than 46 percent of Mitsubishi Corp.'s outstanding loans were held by Mitsubishi group banks.[41] Companies within a group reportedly tend to give business to each other, as well as financial support; although a Japanese Government commission estimated that mutual transactions within keiretsu accounted for 30 percent of members' total business, academic estimates describe that figure as extremely low.[42]

The above characteristics vary among and within groups. Companies may leave, or join, a keiretsu; there are various affiliations across keiretsu; and there are suggestions that keiretsu dynamics are changing. Some observers see the system dissolving as the importance of banks as a source of capital declines,[43] while others see some keiretsu strengthening their group identity by increased leadership from the central corpora-

---

[34] Dodwell, op. cit., footnote 31, pp. 36, 38.

[35] Carla Rapoport, "Why Japan Keeps On Winning," *Fortune*, July 15, 1991, p. 80.

[36] Michael S. Gerlach, *Alliance Capitalism: The Social Organization of Japanese Business* (Berkeley, CA: University of California Press, 1992), p. xviii.

[37] Kozo Yamamura, "Will Japan's Economic Structure Change? Confessions of a Former Optimist," K. Yamamura, ed., *Japan's Economic Structure: Should It Change?* (Seattle, WA: Society for Japanese Studies, 1990), p. 30.

[38] Anchordoguy, op. cit., footnote 32, p. 59.

[39] Yoshinari Maruyama, "The Big Six Horizontal Keiretsu," *Japan Quarterly*, April-June 1992, p. 192.

[40] The practice goes back to the postwar period when Japanese companies felt vulnerable to takeover attempts through equity purchases by foreign firms. Ozawa, op. cit., footnote 28, p. 37.

[41] Maruyama, op. cit., footnote 39, p. 193.

[42] Ibid., p. 194.

[43] As Gary Saxonhouse observes, "with the growth of equity financing and with the equalizing of the terms of access to capital between keiretsu and non-keiretsu firms, one of the main props of the keiretsu system is coming undone. An acceleration of keiretsu hopping and disaffiliation can be expected in the future." (Comment on Robert Z. Lawrence, "Efficient or Exclusionist?: the Import Behavior of Japanese Corporate Groups," *Brookings Papers on Economic Activity*, No. 1, 1991, p. 334); also Hugh Levinson, "Keiretsu relations changing," *Japan Times Weekly Intl. Edition*, Aug. 10-16, 1992, p. 18, and W. Carl Kester, *Japanese Takeovers: The Global Contest for Corporate Control*, (Boston, MA: HBS Press, 1991), p. 206.

tion and mergers of key entities.[44] The appreciation of the yen and increasing global competition have forced companies to tie up with "the most powerful partners"—not necessarily those in the company's keiretsu—in particularly expensive and/or risky business areas such as telecommunications, shipbuilding and ocean transportation, and chemicals.[45] This would include ventures such as the developing cooperation of Mitsubishi with Germany's Daimler-Benz.[46]

During the first 2 years of the 1990s, the economic contraction that severely affected the activities of many Japanese corporations brought to media attention the capacity of keiretsu networks to aid struggling members. There have been several spectacular rescues of overextended Japanese companies by their keiretsu partners. Although such events can demonstrate the costs of keiretsu membership, they may ultimately result in even closer relationships, as the beneficiaries of such help are obligated both financially and psychologically to their main banks and other principal keiretsu members. Itoman Corp., for example, was acquired by another member of the Sumitomo keiretsu after it could not repay extensive debts to Sumitomo Bank.[47]

To the extent that keiretsu relationships are undermined, Japanese firms could be expected to source in a manner more like that of their U.S. and European counterparts, while suppliers could expect prices that include an independent equity profit. One convincing analysis of the state of the keiretsu in the early 1990s suggests that if anything, the keiretsu are restructuring rather than collapsing.[48] Given their historical role in the Japanese industrial system, it seems reasonable to place the burden of proof on those who argue that the keiretsu are breaking down.

■ Vertical Keiretsu

The other major type of keiretsu, the vertical group, may have more relevance to the activities of Japanese companies in this country. The vertical keiretsu is essentially a supplier chain leading to a major manufacturer of automobiles, electronics, or other complex products. There are probably 30 to 40 vertical keiretsu of significant size.[49] The multiple levels of suppliers descending from the apex of a Toyota or a Matsushita can extend into extraordinary numbers: Toyota reportedly contracts with 175 primary suppliers and 4,000 secondary ones.[50] One researcher cites an automaker with not only 168 primary subcontractors and 4,700 secondary ones, but 31,600 tertiary suppliers.[51] The relationships in the supplier pyramid are intended to be long term, but are not guaranteed sales for the supplier. The manufacturer will often maintain relationships with sev-

---

[44] See Gerlach, op. cit., footnote 18; James R. Lincoln, Peggy Takahashi, and Michael L. Gerlach, "Keiretsu Networks in the Japanese Economy: a Dyad Analysis of Intercorporate Ties," *American Sociological Review*, October 1992, pp. 561-585. Lincoln, Takahashi, and Gerlach state that because banks have increased their provision of capital to affiliated companies via the purchase of stocks and bonds (rather than loans), and because supplier relationships are even more important in technology-intensive industries, "it is premature to assume that the keiretsu is an obsolete organizational form."

[45] Dodwell, op. cit., footnote 31, p. 21.

[46] Charles Smith, "Two's Company," *Far Eastern Economic Review*, May 24, 1990, p. 67.

[47] Jonathan Friedland, "Systematic Solution: Itoman's Problems Will Be Spirited Away," *Far Eastern Economic Review*, Oct. 1, 1992, pp. 86-7; Robert Neff, "For Bankrupt Companies, Happiness is a Warm Keiretsu," *Business Week*, Oct. 26, 1992, pp. 48-9.

[48] Gerlach, "Twilight of the Keiretsu?," op. cit., footnote 18.

[49] Yamamura, op. cit., footnote 37, p. 30.

[50] Rapoport, op. cit., footnote 35, p. 77.

[51] Helou Angelina, "The Nature and Competitiveness of Japan's Keiretsu," *Journal of World Trade*, June 1991, p. 103, footnote 18.

eral suppliers for each component, to ensure competition as well as steady supplies.[52]

The vertical keiretsu is an efficient means of sharing information, contributing to efficiency and vertical integration. It is also an efficient mechanism for exploiting lower tiers, enabling the top tier firm to extract prices that take advantage of lower wage rates and do not include an arms-length equity profit for the supplier. This aspect of the keiretsu system helps explain why Japanese firms operating abroad may be less likely to source from domestic suppliers.

The term vertical keiretsu also describes the chain extending from major manufacturers through levels of distributors down to the retail level, particularly in consumer goods; this is far less a matter of cooperation among firms than of coercion by powerful suppliers to prevent price reductions and competition from other (especially foreign) brands in the same shop.[53] The manufacturer controls distributors by providing capital and offering rebates. Many Japanese retailers of electronics goods, for example, sell only one brand; Matsushita Electric Industrial Co. has 24,000 exclusive retailers, Toshiba has 11,000, Hitachi has 9,000, and so on.[54] Even where allowed by law, this type of distribution system requires large investments in retail outlets.

In the agreement resulting from the bilateral Structural Impediments Initiative negotiations of 1989-90, the United States noted that "economic rationality of keiretsu relationships notwithstanding, there is a view that certain aspects of keiretsu relationships also promote preferential group

trade, negatively affect foreign direct investment in Japan, and may give rise to anticompetitive business practices."[55] This ambivalence affects much of the debate on keiretsu, since it appears that many characteristics of the groupings help Japanese firms at the same time that they hurt foreign ones. Highly efficient Japanese MNEs derive much of their advantage from superior management and process technology rather than product technology. Much management skill is embedded in their traditional service, component, and equipment supplier base. Introducing new suppliers to replace existing ones could be highly disadvantageous.[56] In a similar vein, some defenders of keiretsu suggest that the keiretsu structure is simply a natural result of Japanese cultural values. As one journalist notes, "an attack on [the keiretsu system] runs the risk of being construed as an attack on Japanese culture."[57]

■ Keiretsu: Influence on Market Access and Competition

In an analysis of the effect of keiretsu on Japanese imports and exports, one authority concluded that vertical keiretsu are more defensible from the Japanese perspective than horizontal keiretsu, since they appear to improve efficiency in exports while the horizontal groupings do not.[58] When appraising their effect on activities of Japanese firms in the United States, the vertical keiretsu are of more immediate concern. The apparent preservation of keiretsu ties among major Japanese auto producers and component

---

[52] Anchordoguy, "Brief History," op. cit., footnote 32, p. 59. Alan S. Blinder notes that the companies can vary the "market share" of each supplier for reward and punishment. "A Japanese Buddy System That Could Benefit U.S. Business," *Business Week*, Oct. 14, 1991, p. 32.

[53] Chalmers A. Johnson, "Keiretsu: An Outsider's View," *Economic Insights*, September/October 1990, p. 16.

[54] Dick Nanto, "Japan's Industrial Groups: The Keiretsu," *CRS Report*, Nov. 5, 1990, p. 14.

[55] Quoted in Lawrence, op. cit., footnote 43, p. 311.

[56] See Gerlach, op. cit., footnote 18, especially pp. 92-93.

[57] Charles Smith, "Keiretsu: Reform Runs into Resistance," *Far Eastern Economic Review*, June 21, 1990, pp. 50-54.

[58] Lawrence, op. cit., footnote 43, p. 322. He notes, however, that both types of keiretsu appear to stifle imports significantly.

suppliers with production facilities here could exclude and harm U.S. parts suppliers.

The horizontal keiretsu in theory benefits all member companies by guaranteeing stable shareholding, information-sharing, access to financing, and cooperation in areas where the costs of development of a technology, for example, can be spread out among several members of a group. The keiretsu may provide some security in hard economic times. Members of the Sumitomo keiretsu, for example, helped bail out Mazda, its automaker, in the early 1970s: "The Sumitomo bank extended loans to Mazda; other keiretsu members agreed to employ Mazda employees temporarily until the company was out of trouble; and all members of the keiretsu purchased only Mazda cars."[59] In addition, Sumitomo bank helped arrange for Ford to purchase a 25 percent share in Mazda.[60] Some analysts have also suggested that horizontal keiretsu ties tend to reduce imports in relevant industries;[61] one reason for this might be collusion among the major players in an oligopolistic market, which would result in exclusion of all newcomers, whether domestic or foreign.

The vertical groupings, however, principally benefit the central manufacturer, and often work against the interests of suppliers in the chain who depend on keiretsu business, but suffer from demands for continuous rationalization and/or price reductions. Distributors' freedom to sell other companies' products or compete on price with local rivals is also constrained, but they benefit through guaranteed high profit margins.

Despite the disadvantages of the keiretsu voiced by some suppliers, the flexibility of the Japanese system is impressive, especially in the production of automobiles, which combines thousands of components that can be produced by outside suppliers. The two extremes of almost total in-house production of components and almost total market procurement both appear inefficient, observes one U.S. analyst: "The American approach has been either to do it in-house (GM) or to buy a large fraction of parts in the marketplace (Chrysler). Neither approach seems to work as well as the group system of Japanese competitors such as Toyota."[62] As a result GM, Ford, and Chrysler have begun to modify their sourcing and procurement strategies.

U.S. automakers are criticized for creating a system in which "costs have been shifted from higher to lower levels of the production system."[63] Ironically, this is one of the major factors in the Japanese producers' ability to weather the significant increases in the value of the yen since 1985. The system allows the manufacturers to employ highly skilled workers who perform very high value-added work, pushing the lower value work down to subcontractors, who are forced to cut prices to ease the pain of economic adjustment for the parent company.[64]

Nippondenso, the world's largest auto-parts manufacturer, with 11 plants in North America, 4 in Europe, and 12 in Asia,[65] is an example of the growing complexity of the supplier relationship, especially as supplier companies grow into large corporations capable of exploiting scale econo-

---

[59] "The Mighty Keiretsu," *Industry Week*, Jan. 20, 1992, p. 53.

[60] Mark Mason, *American Multinationals and Japan: The Political Economy of Japanese Capital Controls, 1899-1980* (Cambridge, MA: Harvard University Press, 1992), pp. 239-40.

[61] Lawrence, op. cit., footnote 43, p. 328.

[62] James P. Womack, statement before the Joint Economic Committee, Dec. 10, 1991, p. 3.

[63] Ibid., p. 3.

[64] Yamamura, op. cit., footnote 37, p. 32.

[65] Louise Do Rosario, "Riding the Slipstream," *Far Eastern Economic Review*, Dec. 26, 1991, pp. 72-73.

mies themselves. Although Nippondenso is a member of the Toyota keiretsu, with the manufacturer holding nearly a quarter of its stock, it also produces components for Honda, Mazda, and Mitsubishi,[66] and has begun supplying parts to U.S. manufacturers. Yet it retains close ties with Toyota.

Keiretsu can aid companies in R&D and advanced manufacturing by coordinating "pre-competitive" research in new technologies, and by easing access to capital for high-tech ventures that are extremely expensive to start up and have short production-life spans. An example of the latter is a semiconductor fabrication facility that may cost $500 million and be at the leading edge of technology for only 4 years or less.[67]

Supplier relationships are the most obvious manifestation of keiretsu activity in the United States. Along with 11 Japanese auto manufacturing facilities in North America have come 66 steelworks, 20 rubber/tire facilities, and more than 270 auto parts suppliers.[68] Japanese firms initially defended this practice on the grounds that local producers were not immediately capable of meeting the demanding standards of Japanese production techniques.[69] There may also be elements of cultural preference in the choice: as one anonymous Japanese auto executive told a U.S. reporter, in selection of suppliers for his company's transplants, "First choice is a keiretsu company, second is a Japanese supplier, third is a local company."[70] This pattern prompted the Federal Trade Commission to investigate Japanese transplant sourcing practices.[71]

Japanese keiretsu, whether horizontal or vertical, are probably more likely to offer U.S. firms limited amounts of business in contested areas than to welcome them as full members of the group. Nissan allowed 2 U.S. companies into its network of 192 primary suppliers,[72] and Toyota has formed an organization of local suppliers called the "Bluegrass Automotive Manufacturers Association."[73] But there are numerous examples of how Japanese firms favor familiar suppliers. For example, in 1988 less than 30 percent of the electronics content and 1 percent of the semiconductors of Japanese-branded televisions assembled in the United States came from U.S. suppliers. Similarly, less than 3 percent of the electronics content of VCRs assembled in the United States by Japanese firms came from U.S. suppliers.[74] Of products assembled in this country by Sony Corp., for example, only about 20 percent of the company's $8 billion worth of U.S. sales were manufactured domestically.[75]

Rather than retaliation or protection, various analysts have urged a U.S. attempt to emulate the system in some way. Such emulation could take two forms: entry by U.S. firms into Japanese keiretsu, or the formation of U.S. keiretsu-like organizations. Other analysts suggest that U.S. companies can and should try to adopt certain

---

[66] Ibid., p. 72.

[67] Charles H. Ferguson, "Computers and the Coming of the U.S. Keiretsu," *Harvard Business Review*, July-August 1990, p. 57.

[68] Kenney and Florida, op. cit., footnote 19, p. 25.

[69] Ibid., p. 28.

[70] Rapoport, op. cit., footnote 35, p. 80.

[71] Bill Powell, "Japan: All in the Family," *Newsweek*, June 10, 1991, p. 38.

[72] Ibid.

[73] Kenney and Florida, op. cit., footnote 19, p. 32.

[74] John Eckhouse, "How U.S. Could Learn from Europe," *San Francisco Chronicle*, Oct. 1, 1990, p. C1.

[75] Sheldon Weinig, Vice Chairman, Sony Engineering and Manufacturing of America, "Globalization's Impact on Corporate Technological Competitiveness," paper presented to the American Association for the Advancement of Science, AAAS 93, Boston, MA, Feb. 14, 1993, p. 4.

keiretsu practices. One, for example, calls for a network of U.S.-European linkups for development, production, and marketing—a straightforward bulwark against further Japanese expansion.[76]

According to media reports, many U.S. firms have attempted to mimic Japanese-style corporate ties, "recasting their investment practices to form cooperative links both vertically, down their supply lines, and horizontally, with universities, research labs, and their peers."[77] Less stringent enforcement of antitrust regulation by the Bush administration may have encouraged intra-industry collaboration, both bilateral and in consortia.[78] The Big Three automakers are collaborating on electric car technology, and IBM has begun tie-ups of varying levels of formality with Apple, Siemens, and other electronics firms.[79]

It is important to make the distinction, though, between productive government-sponsored consortia and policy actions that stifle the positive aspects of vigorous competition. As one analyst observes: "The strength of Japanese industry in world competition involves the combination of extremely intense competition between firms in the same sector coupled with long-term shared destiny with financial organizations and firms in other sectors."[80]

DOMESTIC CONTENT OF JAPANESE-OWNED U.S. PRODUCTION

A major issue of contention in the debate over foreign, and particularly Japanese, investment is the question of how much value a foreign-owned production facility adds to the local and national economy. One way of determining this is to evaluate how much of the product of such a facility is "domestic content," and how much is imported. A foreign-owned assembly facility located in the United States might use local workers to do little more than assemble kits of components designed, engineered, and produced in the firm's home country, thus avoiding political pressures associated with the trade deficit, while contributing little to the host nation. Alternatively, such a facility might be a stand-alone plant containing the entire production chain, from research and development to marketing staff.

Determining the level of domestic content, however, can be tricky. One reason is that different parts of the U.S. Government define a North American product differently. For the purposes of levying import duties under the Canadian Free Trade Agreement (CFTA) or the North American Free Trade Agreement (NAFTA), the U.S. Customs Service (USCS) defines a domestic product differently than the Environmental Protection Agency (EPA) does when it evaluates gasoline mileage of automakers' domestic and imported fleets under the Corporate Average Fuel Economy (CAFE) standards.[81] Actual domestic content, on a components basis, could be less than 50 percent, even when for EPA purposes it reaches a 75 percent level.[82]

There are problems associated with domestic content requirements, on both technical and

---

[76] Ferguson, op. cit., footnote 67, p. 68.

[77] Kevin Kelly and Otis Port, "Learning from Japan," *Business Week*, Jan. 27, 1992, p. 52.

[78] Ibid., p. 52.

[79] Ibid., p. 55.

[80] Womack, op. cit., footnote 62.

[81] Under the CFTA, USCS does not allow the practice of "roll-up" of domestic content when evaluating assemblies of numerous components. (Samuel Banks, Assistant Commissioner for Commercial Operations, U.S. Customs Service, press briefing, Mar. 2, 1992).

[82] For a detailed discussion of how roll-up can allow very small actual levels of domestic components and assembly to qualify much larger imported content as domestic content see U.S. International Trade Commission, "Rules of Origin Issues Related to NAFTA and the North American Automotive Industry," USITC Publication 2460, November 1991.

political grounds. On the technical side, it can be difficult to assess the actual amount of value added to a given industrial product, since this requires looking at each step of the industrial process, assessing whether the producer is correctly justifying each material and labor component and accurately representing its source.

In some formulations, such as the CFTA rules, elements such as depreciation on capital equipment or debt interest can account for significant amounts of the "domestic content" a producer calculates. For example, the largest domestic-content item claimed by Honda in 1990 for engines produced at its Anna, Ohio, plant was depreciation on machinery, much of which was imported from Japan.[83] One U.S. official associated with a 1989-90 Customs Service audit of Honda estimated that the real value added domestically to the cars assembled by Honda in North America was probably no more than 25 to 30 percent of the total value of the final product.[84] (See box 4-A.) An analysis conducted by the University of Michigan, however, found a 1989 Honda automobile produced in Marysville, Ohio, to have 62 percent North American content, and 38 percent import content, including parts of foreign (Japanese) origin purchased from suppliers located in North America.[85] A General Accounting Office (GAO) analysis, meanwhile, found Japanese auto transplants had 50.5 percent domestic content on average in 1989, compared to 38 percent in 1988. A significant part of this increase was accounted for by increased purchases of parts from domestic suppliers.[86]

Evaluation of domestic content is further muddied by the presence of foreign-owned suppliers. In the Honda audit, the USCS evaluated parts purchased from the U.S. subsidiary of a Japanese firm as U.S. products.[87] Critics claim that this may be misleading; according to one U.S. official: "It is easy to set up a sham 'domestic supplier' who is actually the subsidiary of a Japanese company doing minimal assembly on a Japanese-designed component."[88]

An additional problem in determining domestic content is the practice of "roll-up," in which, for example, a part that is made of 51 percent domestic inputs (including labor) and 49 percent foreign inputs is counted as 100 percent domestic product at the next stage of assembly. By skillfully manipulating this process, according to a U.S. Customs Service official, it would be possible to qualify a product with a very high percentage of foreign content as North-American made.[89] (See box 4-A.)

On the political side, domestic content requirements can have complex ramifications. Most obviously, they are a barrier that conflicts with the free trade approach the United States has traditionally espoused. While many exceptions to the principle of free trade can be found in practice, domestic content requirements are one of the clearest examples of a government-imposed market distortion.

---

[83] Paul Magnusson and James B. Treece, "Honda: Is It an American Car?" *Business Week*, Nov. 18, 1991, p. 106.

[84] OTA interview, Oct. 21, 1992.

[85] University of Michigan Transportation Research Institute, *The US-Japan Automotive Bilateral 1994 Trade Deficit* (Ann Arbor, MI: UMTRI, May 1991), p. 67.

[86] U.S. Congress, General Accounting Office, *Foreign Investment: Japanese-Affiliated Automakers' 1989 US Production's Impact on Jobs*, GAO/NSIAD-91-52 (Washington, DC: October 1990), p. 3.

[87] Keith Bradsher, "Honda's Nationality Proves Troublesome for Free-Trade Pact," *The New York Times*, Oct. 9, 1992, p. A1.

[88] J. Michael Farren, Under Secretary of Commerce for International Affairs, quoted in David E. Sanger, "Is 'Local Content' the Smartest Way to Judge Imports?" *The New York Times*, Mar. 8, 1992, section 4, p. 3.

[89] Banks, op. cit., footnote 81. Banks indicated that this practice of roll-up accounting of domestic content in order for products to be classified as North American would not be allowed, p. 15.

Box 4-A—Honda: The Sourcing Behavior of a Leading Japanese Transplant

Honda was the first Japanese automobile company to produce vehicles in the United States. Claiming that Honda's U.S. affiliate should be treated like a U.S. automaker, one executive argued, "Whether a company is beneficial to the United States is not a function of the capital that created the company."[1] The company should be judged on the basis of the contribution it makes to the U.S. economy. On that basis, the time when Honda's contribution to the U.S. economy and technology base is fully equal to that of the leading U.S. firms remains on the horizon.

The Big Three—GM, Ford, and Chrysler—conduct the bulk of their R&D in the United States, where they also design and engineer most of the vehicles they manufacture and sell in the United States, Mexico, and Canada. Most of their supplier base is located within the United States, and much of the rest within the NAFTA region. They report their average domestic content on a component basis for vehicles sold in the United States at 88 percent. U.S. automakers who compete with Honda estimate that the average local content of all Japanese transplant assemblers would be about 50 percent.[2]

Honda, like other Japanese transplant assemblers, retains its key competencies in its Japanese operations. Research, development, engineering, design, and the bulk of their assembly capacity and supplier base remain centered in Japan. Typically, high value-added activities are the last to be moved abroad.

The vehicles that Honda assembles here have an excellent reputation. Its assembly facility is judged to be productive and its workforce well-trained and well-compensated. Although wages and benefits in Honda's assembly operations are comparable to the Big 3, actual costs are lower due to the much younger average age of the workforce. By locating in Ohio, Honda and its keiretsu-related suppliers located in the U.S. avoid many of the social costs associated with workers being displaced from the Big 3 and their traditional supplier base.[3]

Most experts believe that Honda has made more progress in domestic sourcing for its U.S. operations than the other transplant assembly operations. Honda has an estimated EPA domestic content (which allows roll-up) for vehicles assembled in the United States of about 70 percent. One published study estimated that its actual domestic content, including assembly, was 62 percent.[4]

---

[1] Charles M. Thomas, "Honda Considers Itself American Despite Heritage" *Automotive News*, Jan. 18, 1993, p. 33.

[2] Statement of Ronald R. Boltz, Vice President, Product Strategy and Regulatory Affairs, Chrysler Corporation, Before the Joint Economic Committee, Dec. 10, 1991, chart 13; Personal communication, Dean Harlow, General Motors Corp., June 1, 1993.

[3] For a discussion of the worker-age advantages the transplants enjoy, see: Candace Howes, testimony before the Joint Economic Committee hearing on The Future Of U.S. Manufacturing: Auto Assemblers and Suppliers, Dec. 10, 1991 p. 12.; and Candace Howes, "The Benefits of Youth: The Role of Japanese Fringe Benefit Policies in the Restructuring of the U.S. Motor Vehicle Industry," *International Contributions to Labour Studies*, vol. 1, 1991, pp. 113-132.

[4] Sean P. McAlinden, David J. Andrea, Michael S. Flynn and Brett C. Smith, *The U.S. Japan Automotive Bilateral 1994 Trade Deficit*, Report Number UMTRI 91-20 (Ann Arbor, MI: Transportation Research Institute, May 1991). Honda disputes these figures. Also see, Paul Magnusson, James B. Treece, and William C. Symonds, "Honda: Is It An American Car?" *Business Week*, Nov. 18, 1991, pp. 105-112.

In a U.S. Customs Service audit of Honda cars produced in Canada in 1989-90, conducted under the terms of the Canadian Free Trade Agreement, the use of domestic components to roll up imported components was not allowed.[5] The Customs Service concluded that domestic content was 38 to 46 percent, not the 50 percent being claimed.[6] They also found that the single largest item of local content for the Anna, Ohio, engine plant, as defined for customs purposes, and counted as domestic content, consisted of depreciation on facilities and equipment sourced from Japanese suppliers.[7] This would suggest that Honda's investments have had a relatively small positive effect on the local manufacturing equipment supplier and tool and die industries.

Qualifying new suppliers is both time consuming and expensive,[8] and economies of scale and capacity utilization are critical to profitability in auto production. These factors have led Honda and its suppliers to source less of their vehicles' content from the U.S. manufacturing sector than do the Big Three. One would expect technology transfer to the U.S. supplier base to be gradual, and this appears to have been the case, although there is considerable anecdotal evidence that certain facilities have benefited greatly. Honda now produces more than half the cars it sells here in this country, which gives it the incentive to continue to shift technical and design functions to the United States as long as production volumes warrant such a shift.[9] Currently, however, just over 20 percent of the company's production is done in this country,[10] indicating that its key competencies are still, logically, in its home base. For the foreseeable future, Honda and its keiretsu suppliers[11] can be expected to conduct less research and development and source fewer components in the United States or North America than the Big Three.

---

[5] This discussion is based on a briefing provided by the U.S. Customs Service to OTA in October 1992. If roll-up had been allowed under the terms of the CFTA, the Honda cars probably would have qualified as North American products. Also see John Daly, "A Collision Course," *Maclean's*, July 1, 1991, pp. 84-5.; and William C. Symonds, Paul Magnusson, and John Pearson, "Gunfight at the Customs Corral," *Business Week*, Mar. 2, 1992, p. 54.

[6] Honda North America Inc., Comments on OTA draft, July 2, 1993, p. 8.

[7] Magnusson, Treece, and Symonds, op. cit., footnote 4, p. 106.

[8] A recent study conducted by a U.S. consulting firm for the Japan Auto Manufacturers Association describes the difficulties that an auto parts supplier would face in being qualified by any major automaker, U.S. or Japanese. The study suggests that resistance on the part of the Japanese transplants to purchase parts from domestic suppliers, while significant during the early 1980s, has decreased "substantially." Boston Consulting Group, "Context of U.S.-Japan Automotive Issues and Competitiveness of Automobile-Parts Suppliers" (Tokyo: Boston Consulting Group, March 1993), p. 19.

[9] Honda North America Inc., op. cit., footnote 6, p. 11.

[10] Honda's U.S. production in 1992 was 475,718 (Dean Harlow, op. cit., footnote 2). Total global production of the company in 1991 was 1,975,000 vehicles. (Automotive News, "Top 12 Global Vehicle Producers—4 Years," 1992 Market Data Book, May 27, 1992, p. 3.)

[11] Honda Motor, Japan's third-largest automaker, heads a vertical keiretsu estimated at over 300 subsidiaries and affiliates. Dodwell Marketing Consultants, *Industrial Groupings in Japan, 1988-89* (Tokyo: Dodwell Marketing Consultants, 1988), p. 259.

In addition, domestic content requirements may affect the competitiveness of U.S.-based MNEs. Corporations with manufacturing and sourcing operations in several countries take advantage of shifting supply and demand and resource availability to minimize production and shipping costs. Although many U.S. producers in major industries tend to have higher average levels of domestic content than foreign-based competitors, OTA interviews suggest that they might still resent government-imposed restrictions that could limit their freedom to source globally.

In response to criticism that they are not adding significant value to the production process in the United States, many U.S. affiliates of foreign-based MNEs contend that it is unfair to compare a new investment with a complete industrial operation producing in its home country. Transferring production abroad can be a gradual process, with the value added increasing as overseas employees gain in skills and sophistication, and establish a local supplier base.

All the major Japanese automakers and many of their Japanese suppliers have established styling, engineering, and design facilities in this country, some as integral parts of manufacturing affiliates and some as separate operations.[90] Most of the automakers claim that significant portions of recent models of automobiles built here (e.g., the 1992 Nissan Stanza[91] and the 1992 Toyota Camry),[92] were styled, designed and/or engineered here, although basic research may have been conducted in Japan. At Honda's Marysville, Ohio, plant, the first Japanese transplant in this country, the design and engineering not only of cars but of robots, machine tools, and other production equipment was reportedly being performed domestically in 1988, the sixth year of the plant's operation.[93]

The subject of domestic content—which typically includes labor costs and other related expenses of car production—has become a legal issue between the U.S. Government and Japanese automakers in two contexts. The first case concerns Honda Civics manufactured in Canada and imported to the United States duty-free under the terms of the U.S.-Canada Free Trade Agreement. The USCS has determined that about 90,000 1989 and 1990 model year Civics do not qualify as North American-produced vehicles, and has imposed an additional $17 million duty on Honda.[94] The USCS and Honda differ over the amount of value added in the machining of the engine block of the cars in question; Honda claims the USCS decision stems from political motivations. One Honda executive stated that the Honda case "has been aimed at hitting Japanese enterprises" in the United States.[95]

The NAFTA currently requires 50 percent North American content to qualify for preferential treatment under the agreement; that threshold is to rise gradually to 62.5 percent by 2002.[96] A customs official knowledgeable about the audit suggested that Honda, after revising its produc-

---

[90] Kenney and Florida, op. cit., footnote 19, p. 46-47.

[91] Richard Rescigno, "Yen for the Fast Lane: Japanese Auto Makers Step on the Gas," *Barron's*, Feb. 12, 1990, p. 16.

[92] Gary S. Vasilish "Competing With the World From Kentucky," *Production*, December 1991, p. 61.

[93] Robert R. Rehder, "Japanese Transplants: a New Model for Detroit," *Business Horizons*, January-February 1988, p. 53.

[94] "Japanese Automakers Respond to Local Content Issue—Ripples Caused by Civic Case," *Asahi Shimbun*, Apr. 20, 1992 (morning edition), p. 7, from FBIS.

[95] Nobuyuki Oishi, "Managed Trade Gaining Favor with Carmakers," *Nikkei Weekly*, Mar. 3, 1992, p. 1.

[96] Keith Bradsher, "Nationality of Autos Big Trade Issue," *The New York Times*, Oct. 9, 1992, p. D2.

[97] OTA interview, Oct. 21, 1992.

tion and sourcing procedures, may qualify under the NAFTA standard.[97] (See box 4-A.)

In relation to cars produced by Japanese affiliates in the United States, another domestic content issue has to do with the CAFE level of some Japanese automakers' products. The EPA sets minimum CAFE levels for automakers' foreign and domestically made cars. Since the EPA sets the minimum domestic content of a U.S. car at 75 percent, an automaker can determine which cars to produce in the U.S. and which to import, in order to keep its domestic CAFE level down.[98] This can be as simple a matter as changing the sourcing of a few high value-added components, an issue relevant to U.S. automakers as well. In one case, for example, Ford reportedly switched from a domestic to a foreign supplier for certain components of one particular low-mileage car model in order to transfer it from its domestic fleet to its imported fleet.[99]

JAPANESE INVESTMENT IN SMALL U.S. HIGH-TECH FIRMS

Since the late 1980s, there has been widespread speculation in Congress and the media that Japanese firms were investing in small, innovative U.S. high-tech companies in order to obtain technology at relatively low cost. Some analysts have described a Japanese strategy to gain the edge in an area where the United States still clearly dominates: state-of-the-art technology in R&D-intensive industries such as computers, semiconductors, and biotechnology. The computer industry trade press, in particular, has taken the position that the Japanese are even funding U.S. innovation.[100] It is often argued that difficulty in obtaining start-up capital forces companies to trade their cutting-edge technology for Japanese money or both.

Although data are inconsistent on the subject, OTA research suggests that of all U.S. high-tech start-ups, perhaps as few as 5 percent have received Japanese financing. For example, in 1989, a peak year for Japanese investment in the United States,[101] there were 1,500 high-tech start-ups in this country.[102] Yet in that year the most comprehensive source of data on Japanese mergers and acquisitions in the United States reported only 46 Japanese investments in or acquisitions of U.S. firms in the areas of computer equipment, telecommunications, and electric and electric components.[103] Although not conclusive, these figures indicate the relative scale of these phenomena. The Japanese were not financing the development of advanced technology in Silicon Valley.

However, within more specific industry segments, even small numbers of acquisitions could afford Japanese firms significant control of key technologies. A telling example is in the photomask industry, in which there are effectively no U.S. merchant mask makers without Japanese

---

[98] Chappell, op. cit., footnote 20.

[99] Alex Taylor, "Do You Know Where Your Car Was Made?," *Fortune*, June 17, 1991, p. 52.

[100] Valerie Rice, "Losing the High-Tech Lead," *Infoworld*, Sept. 23, 1991, p. 40. Other representative headlines in national magazines and newspapers included: "American Technology at Fire-Sale Prices," *Forbes*, Jan. 22, 1990, pp. 60-64; "A Shopping Spree in the US: Japan Still Has a Voracious Appetite for Technology Invented Overseas," *Business Week*, June 15, 1990, pp. 86-87; and "Is the U.S. Selling Its High-Tech Soul to Japan?" *Business Week*, June 26, 1989, pp. 117-118.

[101] Emily Thornton, "How Japan Got Burned in the USA," *Fortune*, June 15, 1992, p. 115; 1989 marks the beginning of the downturn, according to the Japan Economic Institute, *JEI Report* No. 46A, Dec. 13, 1991, p. 3.

[102] C. Gordon Bell, *High-Tech Ventures; The Guide for Entrepreneurial Success* (New York, NY: Addison-Wesley, 1991), p. 4.

[103] *Japan M&A Reporter*, Ulmer Brothers Research Institute, Jan. 1990, p. 7. Another widely cited database reported Japanese investments in 399 of the 608 foreign investment deals found in U.S. high-tech industries in 1988-92. ("High Technology Acquisitions," compiled by Linda M. Spencer, Economic Strategy Institute, Washington, DC.) OTA used the ESI database as one of its initial sources to identify Japanese acquisitions.

affiliations. Figure 4-1 shows that, according to a widely cited source, of 141 deals reported from 1987 to 1991 the highest percentage of Japanese acquisitions in computer-related industries (42 percent) were in the semiconductor and semiconductor manufacturing areas.

Since 1992, equity investments by Japanese firms have declined along with Japanese investment in the United States in general,[104] but industry observers suggest that the formation of nonequity strategic alliances between Japanese and U.S. firms remains steady.[105] This could indicate a number of things, including a thriftier approach to technology acquisition, a stage of equilibrium as major firms pause to evaluate their acquisitions and how best to use them,[106] or a shift toward technology partnerships with larger U.S. firms, as in recently announced alliances among Intel and Sharp, Toshiba and IBM, and Fujitsu and AMD.[107]

Another form of Japanese investment into small high-tech firms, difficult to measure but potentially significant, is the funding of start-ups and young firms through local or Japanese-directed venture capital funds. Industry sources estimate that Japanese investors have provided roughly half of foreign investment in U.S.-based venture capital funds. International investors may have provided as much as 23 percent of the capital raised by the U.S. venture capital industry in certain years.[108] Some venture-funding relationships, especially within the context of funds specializing in a particular technology area, allow

Figure 4-1—Japanese Acquisitions in the U.S. Computer-Related Industries, 1987-1991

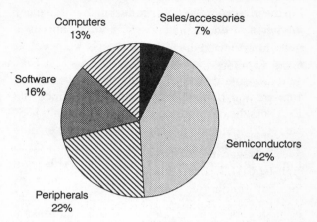

SOURCE: "Japanese Acquisitions in the U.S. Computer and Related Industries, 1987-1Q 1991," Ulmer Bros. Research Institute, July 1991, p. 1, table A.

investors access to the firm's products and researchers, which could amount to an inexpensive and discreet window on developing technology. Several industry sources described Japanese corporate investments as typically aimed at obtaining access to emerging technology.

Although industry sources suggest to OTA that Japanese companies have been a significant source of venture capital to young firms in various technology areas, without more authoritative data it is impossible to evaluate this trend. Such an approach, however, would be consistent with the direct equity investments examined in OTA's Silicon Valley interviews and other research.

---

104 "Japanese Acquisitions Keep Slowing," *Japan M&A Reporter*, Ulmer Bros., Inc., July/August 1992, pp. 1-3; Michael R. Sesit, "Japanese Are Shying Away From Investments in U.S.," *Asian Wall Street Journal*, Feb. 1, 1993, p. 26. Some analysts put the end of the Japanese investment boom even earlier; see Susan MacKnight, "Japan's Expanding U.S. Manufacturing Presence: 1990 Update," *JEI Report*, No. 46A, Japan Economic Institute, Dec. 13, 1991, pp. 1-5.

105 Junko Matsubara, "Company Analysis," *Dataquest Perspective*, May 25, 1992, p. 17.

106 Japan Economic Institute, *JEI Report*, No. 46A, p. 3.

107 "Cost Explosion Fuels Continued Rush by Chip Companies To Find Partners," *Asian Wall Street Journal Weekly*, July 20, 1992, p. 8.

108 The average annual foreign share of total capital committed from 1980 to 1991 was slightly over 12 percent. Venture Economics, fig. 2.0, "Capital Commitments by Limited Partners to Institutionally-Funded Independent Private Venture Capital Funds," *1991 Yearbook* (New York, NY: Venture Economics, Inc., 1991), p. 24.

The recent decline of Japanese investments also demonstrates another salient point about Japanese corporate behavior: there is a strong follow-the-leader tendency. Many of the executives interviewed by OTA believed the investment in their companies was at least partly motivated by a perceived need by the Japanese firm to match the investments of its Japanese rivals.

Interviews with companies[109] and other research suggests that the basic reason small high-tech U.S. firms obtain Japanese (or other foreign) funding is because the money is not available from domestic sources. Although virtually all the industry sources interviewed agreed that technology acquisition was a principal goal of most of the investments by Japanese firms in small U.S. high-tech start-ups, the relationships tended to include more aspects than a simple cash infusion in exchange for technology. Although the total number of high-tech start-ups that have received Japanese funding is relatively small, the phenomenon should be viewed as a significant means of technology absorption, consistent with support of U.S. university research and other technology-absorbing activities described in this report.[110]

■ Sources of Investment

Seed money and initial venture funding in the computer industry comes primarily from venture capital firms, or, less frequently, from larger firms in the industry. These investors are concerned with making a profit on their investment. Industry interviews indicate that large Japanese companies that invest in small U.S. high-tech firms typically do not primarily seek a risk-adjusted financial return on their investment, but are more interested either in obtaining technology, marketing rights, or access to the U.S. market. If this is the case, then the question of whether a given high-tech start-up can succeed with a certain product may be irrelevant; what matters most to the (Japanese) investor is whether it can obtain what it seeks.

Industry representatives clearly indicated to OTA that there is a lack of incentive for U.S. venture capital investors to develop a long-term perspective and to provide resources beyond a limited time scale. Indeed, many of the interviewees described a similar scenario: high-technology firms generally run out of financial resources at a stage when they are on the verge of making technological and commercial breakthroughs. It is then, when U.S. start-ups are most vulnerable, that Japanese corporations may prove to be the only viable source of capital—often, although not always, making contractual demands that involve

---

[109] OTA interviewed 18 firms in 5 technology areas: computers and computer equipment, semiconductors, semiconductor manufacturing equipment, advanced materials, and biotechnology. These five areas were chosen as industries that meet generally agreed-on characteristics of "high technology": a high proportion of costs goes into research and development; the technology is generally regarded as critical to an industrialized nation's technology base; and the technology is constantly developing.

The firms were chosen from lists of Japanese investments in U.S. high-tech firms compiled by the Department of Commerce, the Japan Economic Institute (a private research organization funded by the Japanese Government), and the Economic Strategy Institute, a private policy research organization, as well as from articles in general interest, business, and trade periodicals. Firms were selected from the lists based on their location, their principal area of business, and their size (less than 500 employees, the threshold used by the Small Business Innovation Research (SBIR) program).

The fact that all the firms interviewed are in California, is indicative of the geographic distribution of high-tech start-ups in the United States. Commerce Department studies, as well as interviews with industry sources in Silicon Valley, Boston's Route 128, and North Carolina's Research Triangle Park—three areas commonly cited as high-tech centers in the United States—indicate that a significant majority of small start-ups that have received Japanese funding are in California, mostly in the Silicon Valley area, which extends from San Francisco to San Jose.

[110] Because of issues unique to the industry, technology transfer in the biotechnology industry is quite different from other high-tech areas, and presents somewhat different policy concerns. It is discussed below.

the transfer of technology patent rights, and often production, to Japan.

The firms interviewed frequently complained that U.S. venture capitalists' horizons are too short, and that they need more patient capital than is available from U.S. investors. Venture capitalists, according to industry sources, typically seek a return on their investment within 3 years. This does not mean, of course, that the venture capitalists are short-sighted. Having experience with the market and the Silicon Valley environment, such investors are in fact likely to judge a company's prospects more accurately than its founders. Even if a company has good technology, the business climate or other factors such as poor management can cause it to fail. The market is extremely competitive and moves very quickly.

Timing of financing is key to what a Japanese investor can obtain from a business relationship. One company executive observed that it is often more difficult for a company to get "bridge financing" after several rounds of venture capital than to attract the initial seed money. The late entrant Japanese investor may thus be able to get significant technology/marketing rights if the target firm is in sufficiently dire straits.

Many company officials suggested that large U.S. firms' reluctance to invest in small domestic start-ups has important consequences for the nation's technology base, and claimed that they would prefer to deal with U.S. firms rather than with foreign investors. But in many cases, these large corporations either demonstrate little interest in the development capacity of start-ups, or are "too interested" and want to acquire them. The large firms are therefore generally not inclined to make equity investments, and when they do, tend to adopt a more "adversarial" posture than their Japanese counterparts. This further encourages small U.S. firms to seek Japanese investment partners.

Representatives of several large U.S.-based technology firms told OTA that their firms were interested in obtaining technology from U.S. start-ups, but that they received many more queries from such firms than they could fund. Clearly, this issue is a matter of point of view; the question of whether large U.S. companies are taking full advantage of the technology resources of the start-up community cannot be answered without more empirical research.

Virtually all the industry sources OTA interviewed agreed that technology acquisition was a principal goal of most of the Japanese investments in small U.S. high-tech start-ups. In only a few of the firms interviewed did the U.S. executives believe that the Japanese investor was interested even partially in return on their investment. Most assumed that the firm considered the investment the price of the technology/market access. Other industry sources confirmed this view.

When the U.S. firms had a unique technology, they often appeared to have a much greater control over the terms of Japanese investment. Executives of several companies believed they had successfully limited their investors' access to technology, control over the location of manufacturing process, or sales rights. Nevertheless, this might change should additional investment capital be required.

Marketing rights, as opposed to simply a presence in or access to the U.S. market, appear to be a close second to technology acquisition as a motive for investment by large Japanese firms. High technology, and in particular information technology, has become a global market; a firm can no longer be successful if it sells only in its own domestic market. Further, in industries such as semiconductor equipment, both R&D and marketing (including service) are so expensive that a firm must be present in all significant markets in order to compete. With such noncommodity products, manufacturing economies of scale are small, so while a small company can compete in terms of manufacturing, it must still market its products.

Industry sources also noted that the "status" of being associated with a high-tech company or with a glamorous Silicon Valley name was often an attraction for Japanese investors: Canon's $100 million investment in Steve Jobs' Next Computer Corp. may be an example of this. In the same vein, several companies described examples of equity purchased at a very generous valuation, with little apparent financial return as of yet.

Japanese companies' ideology of technology acquisition resonates with the history of Japanese industrial development since the Meiji Restoration (1868), which has included a strong strand of government-encouraged technology absorption from the West. Since World War II in particular, government agencies such as MITI have structured policies to stimulate the influx of technology, such as requirements that foreign companies investing in Japan make technology licenses available to domestic firms.[111] (See ch. 3.)

∎ Types of Relationships

In addition to straightforward cash for equity exchanges between Japanese investors and U.S. firms, relationships often include marketing agreements, joint ventures, funding for R&D, codevelopment projects, supplier relationships, and personnel exchange. These aspects of the relationship are not always clearly in the Japanese investor's favor; although technology transfer from Japan to the United States is generally minimal, Japanese investors can sometimes extend certain kinds of technical support to the U.S. firms. More importantly, several companies reported that their Japanese investors had introduced them to Japanese customers, or provided access to low-cost capital from Japanese banks. In one case, a Japanese bank made capital available to the U.S. firm at 1 1/2 percent below the U.S. prime rate.[112]

Cases where the U.S. company supplies a component to its Japanese investor appear to have the most immediate chance for productive interaction, since any benefits to the U.S. firm's technology result in a direct benefit to the investor. This does not mean that the U.S. supplier, however, is protected against losing its customer later if the Japanese firm gains enough know-how to produce the components itself. Similarly, the extent to which the connection with a Japanese investor opens markets in Japan could vary. In the case of one semiconductor manufacturer, for example, there seemed to be little market-opening until the 1986 Semiconductor Trade Agreement (STA) forced Japanese firms to make an effort to source in the United States. Ironically, one executive suggested, its Japanese investor could conceivably count purchases of chips from its own fabrication facility as U.S. imports for purposes of fulfilling the STA quota.[113]

Amicable relationships do not automatically preclude the Japanese firms from obtaining technology that they could potentially use to compete with their U.S. partners. In the case of several companies, the terms of the deals—often evolving through repeated requests from the U.S. partner for money—allow the Japanese firm at some point to use the U.S. firm's own technology to compete with it. One company president admitted that this was a strategic error that could have significant negative consequences for his firm.

---

[111] See Johnson, op. cit., footnote 11; and Marie Anchordoguy, *Computers Inc.: Japan's Challenge to IBM* (Cambridge, MA: Harvard East Asian Monographs, 1989).

[112] OTA interview, July 1992.

[113] He suggested that this might take place by shipping the chips to the United States and then reimporting them, or even by conducting a paper transfer without moving the product at all. (OTA interview, July 1992.)

It would be inaccurate to conclude, of course, that Japanese firms are always astute, strategic investors. OTA interviews—including some with representatives of the Japanese investors themselves—revealed instances of inept Japanese investment decisions and unsuccessful attempts at integration of U.S. affiliates, as well as of mutual exchange of information. The benefits to a Japanese investor in terms of technology transfer and generation of profits depend on the circumstances.

Predatory investment behavior is most apparent in cases where Japanese corporations invest in U.S. firms with related technologies. In many cases, however, a firm from a sunset industry such as steel is looking to diversify, to give itself a ''high-tech'' image, or simply to make a profitable equity investment. Or the investment might be from a trading company whose only interest is in marketing a finished product in Japanese or third-country markets. In such investment relationships, the effect on the development of the independent U.S. firm is believed to be generally neutral at worst, at best highly beneficial.

With the exception of the biotechnology industry, OTA teams found that the Japanese sunset industry firms accounted for the majority of investments in U.S. start-ups from 1988-1992, and often seemed as interested in learning about a new technology area on a relatively basic level as in obtaining state-of-the-art technology. As one scholar put it, ''the chances of Kubota exploiting an area of U.S. technology are a lot less than of NEC doing it.''[114]

In contrast, predatory investment strategies are designed eventually to own the U.S. firm outright, or simply to absorb the technology and/or manufacturing rights of the start-up's product, or more likely to be associated with investors from the same sector with closely allied products. Such investors can benefit through directly integrating the technology that the U.S. firm is developing into their own production process. Respondents in interviews repeatedly voiced their support for legislative measures designed to limit technology transfer in these cases, citing European and Japanese practices that constrain the free flow of technology.

■ Japanese Investment in Biotechnology

Because of country-specific regulatory regimes, technology transfer in the biotechnology pharmaceutical industry is fundamentally different from other high-tech areas, and presents somewhat different policy concerns. Since the costs of getting a drug or medical product approved in a particular country can be astronomical, involving extensive clinical testing and documentation, and knowledge of the specific national regulatory system is essential, it is standard practice for companies to license products across borders. In the case of small start-ups, which not only need large amounts of cash to keep their research and approval applications going but also generally lack sales forces abroad, the logic of licensing products to pharmaceutical companies in other countries prior to regulatory approval is even more obvious.

For this reason, the relationships between Japanese and other foreign investors and U.S. biotechnology start-ups seem to follow a simpler pattern, presenting unique challenges and threats to the U.S. technology base. Although further study would be valuable, there was little indication from the OTA interviews that Japanese pharmaceutical companies behaved much differently than other foreign or U.S. firms. The unique phenomenon, rather, is the existence of the U.S. biotechnology start-up environment, which draws on the availability of venture capital and the strength of U.S. research institutions, as well as

---

[114] Michael Borrus, University of California, Berkeley, personal communication, Sept. 9, 1992.

extensive government funding, primarily through the National Institutes of Health (NIH).

Efforts to nurture biotechnology in Japan have not had the impressive success that many other targeting ventures have, although the Japanese Government has declared biotechnology a "strategic" industry.[115] Japanese companies are improving at biotechnology, but are still clearly behind U.S. (and some European) companies' technology in most aspects of the business. A major possible explanation for this is in the activities of NIH, which has conducted or sponsored a broad variety of research initiatives in biotechnology. The bulk of the outside research NIH has sponsored has been at U.S. universities. OTA was told in nearly every interview that the Japanese university system has not produced the quality or quantity of biotechnology research or researchers that the U.S. university system has. This suggests that one reason for the scientific success of U.S. biotechnology companies is publicly funded research from which foreign companies are now beginning to profit.

OTA found no instance in which a U.S. biotechnology company received substantial technical assistance from either their Japanese investors or their Japanese contacts. Most of the Japanese investors are far larger than the U.S. firms, and when they seek a U.S. firm to assist with clinical trials and FDA approvals, they typically choose more established U.S. firms that are better equipped to perform those duties.

The biotechnology industry is young, with its oldest firms little more than a decade old. It fits the model of high-technology industry in that it requires advanced scientific and technological knowledge, and it has lofty barriers to entry. The success of a firm depends heavily on its human capital, and there is a great deal of personnel movement among firms. R&D costs are extremely high, with the added burden of clinical trials and FDA approvals. The industry is made up of many small firms working in radically new areas of technology, all competing for funding. They offer payoff as much as 5 to 10 years down the road, with the strong possibility that returns on investment might disappear at any step in the process.

The youth of the industry also means that the stock market, an important source of capital, turns on small events. Not many products invented or produced with biotechnology have been proposed for FDA approval; the regulatory fate of the few that have been submitted has significantly influenced the stock prices of biotech firms. Approval of one experimental drug, for example, caused a boom in biotechnology stocks, while another drug's failure to obtain approval caused a sharp decline in the market.[116] This volatility, in turn, affects the ability of new firms to issue initial public offerings.

OTA interviews gleaned little quantitative evidence on the extent of foreign investment in the industry, but it appears to be common. There are several reasons for foreign, especially Japanese, interest in the industry. First, alliances with foreign companies are standard practice in the pharmaceutical and medical-devices business because of the difficulties of dealing with the heavy regulation of these products in the various nations that account for the biggest markets—the United States, Japan, and the member states of the European Community (EC). Even big companies typically form partnerships with foreign companies to get their drugs through clinical trials and regulatory processes overseas. For many small

---

[115] Kevin W. O'Connor, "Biotechnology: An International Survey," *Biotechnology Development: Expanding the Capacity to Produce Food*, United Nations Department of Economic and Social Development, Advanced Technology Assessment System, Issue 9, winter 1992, p. 133.

[116] OTA interview, August 1992; Gina Kolata, "Halted at the Market's Door: How A $1 Billion Drug Failed," *The New York Times*, Feb. 12, 1993, p. A1.

companies, investment from a Japanese company represents the best opportunity to expand the market for their products to Japan or other East Asian nations. The necessity of having a Japanese investor to sell in Japan is especially great since Japan's regulatory process is particularly stringent and requires that clinical trials be done on Japanese nationals.

The primary reason the biotechnology companies interviewed wanted Japanese investment, however, was not only to expand their eventual markets (most of them had only one or two products on the market, some had none), but to obtain funding for further research and clinical development in the United States. Corporate investors were deemed preferable to venture capitalists, being more likely to be patient and provide capital on better terms. Venture capitalists' only hope of getting a return on investment lies in the company succeeding financially; if the company fails, they get nothing. The other, strategic type of investor would seek different types of benefits, such as learning about technology, getting marketing rights or licenses, and establishing relationships with firms for possible future benefits. In short, strategic investors have many more ways of obtaining a good return on investment than appreciation of their stake in the company. As a consequence, they are reportedly willing to accept a smaller equity stake for a given investment than are venture capitalists.

It appears likely that without foreign capital, fewer small biotech start-ups would make it to market with an approved product. At the same time, venture capital, although valuable, is not a substitute for strategic investment. This implies not that there is a failure in the venture capital market, but that venture capital cannot provide the amount of capital that many technology-intensive start-ups need. Strategic investors, then, can play a vital role in nurturing companies and technologies.

The strategic investors are clearly getting technology. Japanese companies that have invested in small biotech firms all have been trying to learn about biotechnology. Although there have been few instances of Japanese firms sending their scientists to do long-term research at the U.S. firms, Japanese investors all have been expected to do clinical trials in Japan, which could provide a thorough grounding in many of the technologies. The licenses that many of these investors are getting through or in addition to their investments also transfer technology, since in many instances the licenses are for process as well as product patents.

Japanese investment in U.S. biotechnology firms may present a greater threat to the U.S. industry than similar investment in information technology, since the Japanese firms have more to learn in the biotechnology area. The question to be answered here regards the linearity of the development of biotechnology products; that is, would one key technology acquisition then provide a step for a Japanese company on which to base future product development? A successful drug can make a small company's fortune, but the major international pharmaceutical companies tend to produce products in many different therapeutic and diagnostic areas. Typically, the companies OTA visited did have a base technology on which a product family was produced, but a deeper examination of the biotechnology industry might produce further insights as to how this would position a company for future growth.

JAPANESE MNEs AND U.S. UNIVERSITY RESEARCH

During the late 1980s, Congress and the media gave increased attention to the transfer of U.S. technology to foreign MNEs that might have resulted from their relationships with U.S. universities and research institutions. As the number of such relationships—particularly those involving Japanese firms—grew, congressional and media attention correspondingly focused on the fear that we were "selling our science."[117] Some analysts argued that foreign corporations had achieved excessive access to advanced research that had been funded by U.S. taxpayers.

In recent years inquiries by members of Congress have resulted in several studies by GAO, in congressional hearings, and in investigations by the NIH.[118] Although reliable figures are not available, OTA estimates that the share of all U.S. university research funded by Japanese or other foreign-based firms remains small. It is, nevertheless, possible that a foreign company could strategically sponsor research or license university-developed technology to obtain significant returns. If that technology was originally funded with government support, there might be reason for U.S. taxpayers to be concerned. Furthermore, since the Government is a significant consumer of health care through Medicare, Medicaid, and military/veterans' insurance programs, it has an interest in how government-sponsored medical research ultimately benefits consumers.[119] Con-

cern about the issue, then, is not unreasonable, and the U.S. Government would do well to expect universities to cooperate fully in keeping the American public informed about these concerns.[120]

Major research institutions maintain consistent standards for such corporate funding to retain academic freedom to publish, and to safeguard the institutions' financial interests. As standard practice, all the top-tier research institutions that OTA interviewed retain patents and other ownership rights to any research performed by university investigators. Universities report that the law regulating such relationships, the Bayh-Dole amendment (see below), is effective and relatively easy to comply with, and that corporate sponsors of research or firms that seek to license university-developed technology are unlikely to request exceptions to these standards.[121]

The discussion of corporate-university relationships that follows is primarily intended to respond to congressional concerns. The relationships, especially those involving Japanese firms,

---

117 Martin and Susan J. Tolchin, *Selling Our Security: The Erosion of America's Assets* (New York, NY: Alfred A. Knopf, 1992), p. 217.

118 These studies include: U.S. Congress, House Committee on Government Operations, Subcommittee on Human Resources and Intergovernmental Relations, *Is Science For Sale? Conflicts of Interest vs. the Public Interest*, June 13, 1989; U.S. Congress, House Committee on Science, Space and Technology, Subcommittee on International Scientific Cooperation, *International Technology Transfer: Who is Minding the Store?* July 19, 1989; U.S. Congress General Accounting Office, *Engineering Research Centers: NSF Program Management and Industry Sponsorship*, GAO/RCED-88-177 (Gaithersburg, MD: 1988); U.S. Congress General Accounting Office, *R&D Funding: Foreign Sponsorship of US University Research* GAO/RCED-88-89BR (Gaithersburg, MD: U.S. Congress Government Printing Office, 1988); U.S. Congress General Accounting Office, *University Research: Controlling Inappropriate Access to Federally Funded Research Results*, GAO/RCED-92-104 (Gaithersburg, MD: 1992).

In February 1993, an amendment to NIH's funding bill was introduced to limit advance access to U.S. government-funded research by foreign corporations. The amendment was withdrawn, but further hearings on the subject are reportedly planned. (*Congressional Record*, Feb. 17, 1993, S1701.) In the spring of 1993, the National Institutes of Health were conducting a survey of more than 100 major U.S. research institutions, all of which receive federal funding, to examine their relationships with foreign corporations. The NIH has not yet announced when it will release findings of its survey.

119 See U.S. Congress, Office of Technology Assessment, *Pharmaceutical R&D: Costs, Risks, and Rewards*, OTA-H-522 (Washington, DC: U.S. Government Printing Office, February 1993).

120 The primary vehicle for technology transfer remains, as it has been, students who take their knowledge and research skills to a private company. While the number of foreign graduate students in U.S. science and engineering programs is significant, rising from 20 percent of all science, engineering, and health-field graduate students in 1983 to 31 percent in 1991 (National Science Foundation, *Foreign Participation in U.S. Academic and Engineering: 1991* (NSF 93-302), cited in "In Print," *Science and Government Report* (Washington, DC: Science and Government Report, Inc., July 1, 1993, p. 8), that mode of technology transfer is not the focus of this study.

121 Susan Wray, University of Florida, speech at National Institutes of Health/Pharmaceutical Manufacturers of America Technology Transfer Conference, Washington, DC, May 5, 1993.

are of interest as an example of how foreign firms may tap into the U.S. technology base, and how Japanese firms in particular have been able to take advantage of such resources.

It is important to note that in general, reciprocity would be difficult to obtain in regard to these issues. Observers agree that advanced research in the sciences is far more likely to be done within company laboratories in Japan than in university facilities. Research conducted in Japanese universities does not compare in quality or scope with the work done at academic institutions in the United States; thus neither U.S. firms nor U.S. graduate students are lining up for access to Japanese university research laboratories.

■ Extent of Corporate Funding of U.S. Academic Research

Academic research comprises a large component of the total U.S. research effort. Academic institutions conducted about $17.2 billion in basic and applied research in 1991,[122] increasing from a 12-percent share of total U.S. research spending in 1985 to a 15-percent share in 1991. During the 1980s, academic R&D expenditures rose at an even faster pace than total U.S. spending, increasing more than 180 percent from 1980 to 1991, while total national spending increased about 140 percent.[123] The top 100 educational institutions

accounted for about 70 percent, or nearly $12 billion. From 1980 to 1990, industry's share of total funding of academic R&D rose from 4 to 7 percent, or about $1.16 billion.[124]

Estimates of how much money foreign corporations spend at U.S. universities vary widely. Many analysts believe that foreign and especially Japanese funding of U.S. universities escalated rapidly in the late 1980s, but this was an increase on a very low base, and remains low in comparison with total funding from domestic firms. In 1986, the National Science Foundation (NSF) polled 1,270 Japanese enterprises, and found that a total of 56 firms had funded a total of about $3.6 million in U.S. academic research in 1983, that 71 had funded a total of $5 million worth in 1984, and that 98 had funded a total of $9 million worth in 1985. In a more complete study, conducted in 1988, GAO put total foreign corporate funding of academic R&D at $27.6 million for fiscal year 1986, or about one-third of 1 percent of the total R&D expenditures of the 107 universities reporting foreign funds (27 reported no foreign funds).[125] This represented about 5 percent of total industry funding of academic R&D.[126]

Meanwhile, foreign governments and other nonbusiness sources spent another $46.8 million at U.S. universities, with one-third of that total going to an international ocean-drilling program

---

[122] National Science Foundation, op. cit., footnote 120, p. 306, table 4-2. This did not include about $5 billion, or $3.5 billion in constant 1982 dollars, at federally funded research and development centers (FFRDCs), which conduct R&D almost exclusively for use by the Federal Government. One problem in estimating these numbers is defining a "university" or "academic institution." The NSF prefers a broad definition, including university-affiliated research centers, experimental stations, and medical centers as well as traditional departments. National Science Foundation, Division of Science Resources Studies, *The Science and Technology Resources of Japan: A Comparison with the United States*, NSF 88-318 (Washington, DC: 1988), p. 23.

[123] Ibid.

[124] National Science Foundation, Division of Science Resources Studies, *Academic Science and Engineering: R&D Expenditures, Fiscal Year 1990*, NSF 92-321, detailed statistical tables (Washington, DC: 1992), table B-1, p. 19.

[125] These numbers tend to minimize the extent of foreign funding, however, as they ignore industrial liaison program (ILP) membership fees and endowments and gifts for research programs. GAO did not attempt to estimate how much money university ILPs received from foreign sources, although it stated that the amount of support was "not extensive" (GAO, *R&D Funding*, op. cit., footnote 118, p. 18). Foreign sources (not just corporations) accounted for $27.3 million in gifts and endowments for research programs in FY 1986 (Ibid., p. 21).

[126] Ibid., p. 8.

[127] Ibid., p. 8.

at Texas A&M University.[127] MIT received $5.3 million, or 2 percent, of its research budget from ties with foreign corporations; Japan accounted for roughly half of that. The GAO found 13 foreign corporation-university agreements worth $500,000 or more.[128] These arrangements, which varied in length from 3 to 20 years, provided $127 million to the universities over time.[129] Finally, GAO found that most foreign corporate funding was not in areas identified by the Department of Commerce as critical technologies for future U.S. economic growth.[130]

OTA's research suggests that a conservative estimate of Japanese corporate funding of U.S. university research (including endowments to research programs) would be about $50 million per year, with total foreign corporate funding at about $75 million. That would make the foreign corporate contribution to university research about two-thirds of 1 percent of the top 100 universities' research spending, with Japanese corporations by far the main foreign corporate funders of U.S. university research.

■ Legislative Grounding of Corporate-University Relationships

America's universities have long served as the country's primary centers of basic research activity. U.S. universities' role in promoting national economic competitiveness has been largely "precompetitive"—building the country's human capital and knowledge base, rather than producing marketable products. The Federal Government has thus funded research at U.S. universities primarily as part of a national commitment to basic science, rather than as an attempt to achieve specific goals. With the major exception of defense-related research, the United States has not conditioned its research funding of universi-

ties on the generation of concrete results or a certain return on investment. It has generally supported the peer review process for Federal grants to ensure standards of scientific merit as defined by the research community.

However, in the 1970s, amid deepening concerns about the trajectory of the U.S. economy, Congress began to examine ways to encourage a more active university role in promoting the country's well-being. One of the outcomes of this debate, which continues vigorously, was a focus on Federal patent policy. Congress was concerned that U.S. patent rules had allowed foreign firms to gain ground on domestic ones in global markets. At the time, the Federal Government claimed title to all wholly or partially federally funded patents developed by universities. Since the government did not actively promote licensing of those patents to the private sector, and since it did not grant exclusive licenses, Congress feared that much commercializable research was not reaching the U.S. private sector. The result was PL 96-517, the University and Small Business Patent Policy Act (also known as the Bayh-Dole Act). Under the Bayh-Dole Act, the universities and other research performers could receive title to patents resulting from federally funded research. Thus they could now profit from granting exclusive or nonexclusive licenses to federally funded innovations.

For U.S. universities, a majority of whose research funding came from the Federal Government, the act promised to be a major financial windfall. Not only would they collect licensing fees on their innovations, but they would also be able to use the licensing "carrot" to convince corporations to fund projects already partially underwritten by the Federal Government. For U.S. corporations, it promised to be an innovation

---

[128] Ibid., p. 5.

[129] Ibid., p. 36.

[130] Ibid., pp. 10-11.

windfall, giving them a clear advantage over competitors from foreign countries, whose university research could not compare with America's in quantity or quality.

From both these points of view, Bayh-Dole appears to have been a qualified success thus far. Universities are always pleased to receive corporate funding, especially as Federal research funds decrease or fail to keep pace with rising costs. University officials and researchers have told OTA that they prefer on the whole to work with domestic firms, both for reasons of patriotism and practicality. Indeed, because of linguistic and cultural understanding, they found U.S. firms more convenient than foreign sponsors, and wished U.S. corporations were more aggressive in sponsoring research and licensing university-developed technologies.

Representatives of corporations, on the other hand, expressed more skepticism about the value of such research. They typically felt that immediate returns on such investments are unlikely, and that any technology coming out of a university lab is likely to be far from commercialization. Corporate interviewees often said that the cost of licensing a technology from a university was likely to amount to only a fraction of the cost of commercializing such research. Rather, they suggested, their biggest benefits from relationships with universities are likely to be in recruitment opportunities and in keeping in touch with the advanced work conducted in university research facilities.[131]

■ Types of Corporate-University Relationships

Foreign corporate tie-ups with U.S. universities take many different forms, none of them

unique to foreign companies. The most significant include:

- sponsored research at universities,
- licensing university-controlled patents,
- membership in university industrial liaison programs (ILPs),
- corporate philanthropy, and
- location of facilities in university-related research parks.

This discussion will focus on the first three of these, which have been the subject of most congressional concern and media scrutiny.

■ Sponsored Research and Technology Licensing

Sponsored research involves the most intimate interaction and therefore the largest amount of potential knowledge transfer between universities and foreign firms. This is especially true when, as is typical, research tie-ups offer the possibility of a technology licensing arrangement at the end of the project. Corporations cannot dictate the specific nature of a project or direct the progress of research; they can only opt to support a research project that an investigator proposes. Major research universities, such as MIT, Harvard, and Princeton, will not negotiate conditions of sponsored research relating to ownership of intellectual property or restrictions on what results of the research may be published, although some may agree to give sponsoring corporations access to results and article manuscripts a certain number of days, typically 30, before publication.

Some university officials suggested that smaller or less well-established universities may be willing to accept more direction on the nature of research, or even to perform what one university scientist described as "product-testing," but no

---

[131] OTA interviewed officers of university technology licensing offices, offices of sponsored research, and industrial liaison programs, as well as researchers from MIT, Princeton, Harvard (including Massachusetts General Hospital, a teaching hospital of the Harvard Medical School), the University of California at Irvine, and the Scripps Research Institute.

interviewee would cite specific institutions where these compromises might take place. It is likely, however, that the larger and more prestigious research institutions have less incentive to accede to corporate pressures to withhold publication or to cater to specific corporate research purposes.

Contract research is usually limited to a precise objective, and the firm often has the right to an exclusive license to research results. In this category, the firm may or may not participate in the performance of the research, but it usually has rights to observe the research in progress, which may be partially based on proprietary information provided by the company. Sponsored research and contract research can culminate in a license, either exclusive or nonexclusive, for a university-held patent. If the original sponsor chooses not to license a particular invention or technology, the research institution may also license third parties not originally involved.

Industry-university research centers and consortia involve firms paying an annual fee to observe and help direct the center or consortium's research projects, which are generally at a precompetitive stage. They may also pay an additional fee for projects in which they are actively involved. Patentable research results are often licensed on a nonexclusive basis to any and all members of the consortium. One unique facet of industry-university consortia is that they can span several disciplines, bringing together not only employees from different firms but also university researchers from different departments. The MIT Media Lab, which has been cited as receiving a large amount of support from Japanese corporations, is perhaps the premier example of the university-industry research consortium.[132]

While some European companies are active in the Media Lab, the much larger Japanese presence often amounts to a fifth of the Lab's funding.[133] The director of the Media Lab, noting the sensitivity of such disclosures, has suggested that the Lab should reduce its fundraising efforts from Japanese corporate sources to avoid unfavorable domestic opinion.[134]

■ Industrial Liaison Programs

Foreign corporate membership in university-sponsored ILPs has drawn considerable media and congressional attention in recent years, but typically offers companies a less intimate relationship with university researchers than sponsored research projects. These programs, which blossomed in the 1980s and are now quite common at major research universities, generally charge a fee (rarely more than $100,000) in exchange for providing "facilitated access" to research in fields of interest to the corporate member. In practice, facilitated access usually means invitations to conferences and subscriptions to publications summarizing the activities of university researchers, the possibility of reviewing papers and research results before official publication dates, and special incentives to faculty to cooperate with ILP members.

Liaison programs take two basic forms: general-purpose (university-wide) liaison programs and focused liaison programs that specialize in a particular technology area or academic field. Liaison programs offer more limited access to university research than research consortia or research centers. A 1992 GAO survey of 35 important research universities found that of the 30 offering ILPs, 24 had foreign members, with

---

[132] In 1992, the lab performed contract research with such Japanese corporations as NHK, Nintendo, Toshiba, Yamaha, NEC, Honda, Sharp, Sony, Sony Industrial Products, Hitachi, Mitsubishi Electric, Seiko Epson, and Toshiba in different specialized consortia, and had received major building gifts and endowments from Asahi Broadcasting Corporation, Asahi Shimbun Publishing Company, Fukutake Publishing, Hitachi, Matsushita, MCA, NEC, Nintendo, Sony, and Toshiba.

[133] MIT Media Lab, press release, 1992; Stewart Brand, *The Media Lab: Inventing the Future at MIT* (New York, NY: Viking, 1987).

[134] Brand, ibid., p. 167.

499 foreign companies participating.[135] At MIT's program, by far the largest of these, Japanese firms accounted for more than a fifth of the corporate membership.[136]

MIT officials suggested, however, and U.S. corporate members of MIT's ILP confirmed, that while membership in a liaison program may be more beneficial to a foreign firm than to a domestic one, it may not afford the foreign firm privileged access. The reason for this apparent anomaly is that liaison programs provide entree into networks of scientists and researchers with which U.S. firms are already likely to be familiar. It may well be of more benefit for a Japanese firm to be updated on current research activities at MIT than a domestic firm whose scientists may have come from that university and have more opportunity to obtain information informally.

■ Corporate Philanthropy

Not surprisingly, corporate gifts are the preferred form of sponsorship from the universities' point of view, since they typically have the fewest strings attached. If a corporation wishes to learn about research activities at a university, philanthropy is not the most cost-effective means of achieving its goal, compared to sponsorship of research or even membership in an ILP. Overall, corporations gave $2.17 billion to higher education in the academic year 1989-90, up 11.5 percent from the previous year.[137] Although the total amount of foreign corporate giving is unclear, of the approximately $260 million listed as "large corporate gifts" for 1990, about $46 million (18 percent) came from foreign corpora-

tions. Japanese gifts accounted for about $18 million, or about 7 percent of the total.[138]

The benefits corporate donors receive for their gifts vary, ranging from "mix and mingle opportunities" with faculty (and other corporate donors) to low-cost executive training programs that business schools tailor to the corporation's needs, among other modest benefits. Endowing a chair for a researcher at a university of the rank of MIT or Harvard typically costs about $1.5 million, for which a corporation may receive research reports or copies of papers published by the holder of the chair, but rarely any closer access to university research. Japanese firms may view philanthropy as a gesture of goodwill that could indirectly induce the university to view the firm in a positive light if opportunities to expand the relationship were to arise.

■ University-Related Research Parks

The popularity of university-related research parks has increased rapidly since 1983. As of 1992, there were 128 such parks in the United States, 80 percent of which had been established since 1983. In addition, a large number of new parks were planned.[139] Research parks are real estate development projects undertaken by a university, usually in cooperation with a private developer. They also often include "business incubators" for start-up companies; these start-ups may closely involve university faculty in their operations. The key difference between university-related and private industrial parks is that companies can draw on the resources of facilities, researchers, and libraries available at the participating universities. The university gets revenue

---

[135] GAO, 1992, op. cit., footnote 118, p. 17.

[136] Massachusetts Institute of Technology, "The International Relationships of MIT in a Technologically Competitive World; Report by the Faculty Study Group on the International Relations of MIT" (Cambridge, MA: Massachusetts Institute of Technology, 1991), p. 5.

[137] AAFRC Trust for Philanthropy, "Giving USA 1991" (Washington, DC: AAFRC, 1991), p. 111.

[138] Ibid., pp. 97-99.

[139] American Association of University-Related Research Parks, "Research Park Statistics" (Tempe, AZ: AAURRP, 1991), p. 3.

and the possibility of performing joint research with industry. Industry gets access to university libraries and other resources (which often include an office for technology transfer to research park occupants), plus the unquantifiable advantage of being situated in a highly intellectual, cutting-edge environment.

Foreign firms have usually been welcome in research parks. Although figures are not available on the percentage of foreign corporate occupancy at research parks, there is certainly a sizable presence. A spokesman for the Association of University-Related Research Parks noted that there are:

> . . . no nationalistic policies at research parks. They probably like international companies to

locate there. If you're the type of company doing the activities parks allow, it doesn't matter where you're from.[140]

Foreign investment in university-related research parks is welcomed by municipal and State governments, because it provides them with high-skill, high-wage, high-tech employment, together with potential spillover effects from research. Although companies may see various advantages in locating close to universities, the real benefit may lie more in image and atmosphere than in direct technology transfer.

---

[140] Chris Boetcher, President, American Association of University-Related Research Parks, personal communication, July 1992.

International Strategic Alliances 5

Large numbers of international strategic alliances (ISAs) among multinational enterprises (MNEs) emerged during the 1980s in response to the pressures of rapid technological change and the increased internationalization of capital, production, and knowledge. ISAs constitute a significant tool for MNEs to meet the challenges of increased competition and globalization. They enable MNEs to spread the costs and risks of research and new product development, while providing greater flexibility and speed for commercialization.

ISAs are introducing a range of new factors into the relationships among nations and multinational enterprises. Because they have increased dramatically in number and scale in recent years, they are likely to further obscure the nationality of MNEs. In the future, international competitiveness may be defined less in terms of competing firms based in different nations, and more in terms of shifting, competing coalitions of MNEs engaged in international strategic alliances. At the same time, ISAs are causing profound shifts in the long-term competitiveness of U.S. industry; their full impact has yet to be understood.

International strategic alliances have created both competition and interdependence between rival states and multinational firms, rendering corporate planning and U.S. policymaking more difficult and uncertain. National economic sovereignty may become increasingly illusive as the United States grapples with increased dependence on key economic and technological assets controlled by MNEs involved in ISAs. International strategic alliances are also blurring the national identity of U.S.-based MNEs, further weakening the link between their activities and the competitiveness of the U.S. economy as a whole.

This chapter analyzes the recent growth of international strategic alliances. It discusses the complex motivations, patterns, and varying impact of ISAs across U.S. manufacturing industries. The chapter also assesses the policy implications stemming from the involvement of U.S. companies in such international alliances.

CHAPTER FINDINGS

1. The causes underlying the recent growth and extensive development of strategic alliances between MNEs are primarily economic and technological. The rise of ISAs can be attributed to various factors, including increased foreign competition in key manufacturing industries, rapidly escalating costs of R&D, and growing technological convergence among some industries. Nevertheless, governments play a critical role in influencing the formation, structure, and content of ISAs.

2. Asymmetries between different foreign governments' trade, investment, industrial, and technology policies, particularly those that affect market access, may impede the ability of U.S.-based MNEs to use strategic alliances competitively. For instance, some foreign governments will restrict market access unless U.S.-based MNEs supply critical technologies, manufacturing capabilities, and distribution rights to their foreign alliance partners. At issue for U.S. policymakers is how to address such asymmetries in foreign governments' policies. Should the U.S. Government provide support for its domestically based MNEs via industrial technology and other policies? Should the United States pressure multilateral institutions to secure the harmonization of policies across borders?

3. The impact of ISAs has distinct and perhaps conflicting implications for U.S. firms and for policymakers. On the one hand, international strategic alliances are a response by MNEs to the competitive pressures associated with the transition to a more global economy. On the other hand, ISAs raise tough new issues for U.S. policymakers concerned about preserving the competitiveness of U.S. manufacturing industry, and its high-wage, highly skilled employment base.

4. On the domestic front, ISAs challenge directly the presumption that the competitiveness of U.S.-owned MNEs is the same as U.S. competitiveness. Since ISAs involve coalitions of U.S. and foreign MNEs, defining an American company and devising national treatment policies becomes extraordinarily complex. At the international level, U.S. policymakers must anticipate the antitrust implications in industries where ISAs are likely to lead to further global concentration. While U.S. antitrust concerns have remained largely a domestic affair, pressure may build for the United States to collaborate with foreign authorities and to impose conditions on ISAs that are likely to harm consumers.

5. These concerns arise because ISAs may present the potential for cartelization and even collusion among alliance partners, particularly in industries characterized by high barriers to entry and oligopolistic competition. There is concern that combining technology, manufacturing, marketing networks, and other assets of competing firms into ISAs may concentrate too much market power in the hands of too few firms.

6. In a number of industries, ISAs have enhanced the international competitiveness and productivity of U.S. firms, workers, and the economy as a whole. ISAs have pressured U.S. firms to change and to learn by requiring them to develop, adopt, and disseminate new technologies, while encouraging them to become more open and flexible to new managerial and manufacturing methods. International strategic alliances have also increased U.S. companies' awareness of and access to new international

markets. In effect, U.S.-based MNEs are becoming better at learning from and thus mastering ISAs.

WHAT ARE INTERNATIONAL STRATEGIC ALLIANCES?

No single definition exists for international strategic alliances. In general, strategic alliances involve long-term arrangements that focus on several issues of mutual concern to different corporations. This chapter focuses on ISAs that involve the collaborative development and sharing of R&D, manufacturing, marketing, and distribution.

Strategic alliances move beyond simple arms-length transactions. Rather, they seek to improve the competitive position of the partners and reflect the long-term objectives of each corporate partner. They usually involve substantial commitments of capital, technology, and/or other assets.[1] Alliances designed to pursue short-term market opportunities are called "tactical," and do not necessarily reflect the broader strategies of the firms involved. ISAs have become so important that some firms consider them to be intrinsically desirable; as a position statement issued by one large corporation suggested, "the alliance itself is a goal."[2]

The institutional forms that international strategic alliances take are both numerous and complex. They include precompetitive R&D consortia, a variety of technological cooperation and production agreements, and exchanges of marketing and distribution networks.[3] In fact, international strategic alliances usually encompass several of these interrelated activities. ISAs may involve equity sharing, or the formation of a new company managed jointly by participating firms, or they may be based on looser, less institutionalized forms of cooperation.

Compared to internal development, mergers, or acquisitions, strategic alliances enable MNEs to reconfigure rapidly to meet new market conditions and technological challenges. As one authority notes, "the time required to build expertise or gain market share internally is likely to exceed the time required with a coalition."[4] Additionally, ISAs offer greater flexibility because they are easier to dissolve than either mergers or acquisitions; their sunk costs are lower and commitments less irreversible.[5]

RECENT TRENDS IN INTERNATIONAL STRATEGIC ALLIANCES

In the 1980s, internationalization brought on by advances in telecommunications and transportation, coupled with increasingly open markets, effectively heightened competition among multinational firms. Companies must now view their markets from a regional and/or global, rather than national perspective. For these reasons, among others, corporate managers have recognized the benefits of ISAs, and as a consequence, the number of such alliances has increased dramatically.

This section provides an overview of the recent trends in international strategic alliances. Based on a number of statistical studies conducted in the

---

[1] David C. Mowery (ed.), *International Collaborative Ventures in U.S. Manufacturing* (Cambridge, MA: Ballinger Press, 1988); and Lynn K. Mytelka (ed.), *Strategic Partnerships and the World Economy* (London: Fairleigh Dickinson University Press for Frances Pinter Ltd., 1991) provide extensive treatment on the definitional aspects of international strategic alliances.

[2] Toyota White Paper presented to the Office of Technology Assessment, Feb. 24, 1993.

[3] Licensing agreements are not considered to be strategic alliances for the purposes of this report.

[4] Michael E. Porter and Mark B. Fuller, "Coalitions and Global Strategy," Michael E. Porter (ed.), *Competition in Global Industries* (Boston, MA: Harvard Business School Press, 1986), p. 328.

[5] Claudio Ciborra makes this important point. See his chapter, "Alliances as Learning Experiments: Competition and Change in High-Tech Industries," in Mytelka (ed.), op. cit., footnote 1.

Figure 5-1—Trends in International Strategic Alliances by Regional Partnerships, 1979-1985

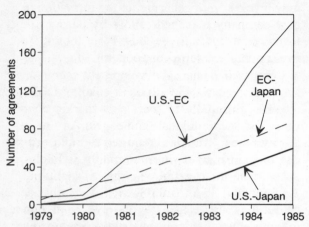

SOURCE: Adapted from Michael Hergert and Deigan Morris, "Trends in International Collaboration Agreements," Farok J. Contractor and Peter Lorange (eds.), *Cooperative Strategies in International Business* (Lexington, MA: Lexington Books, 1988), p. 101.

United States, Europe, and Japan, it assesses the rate of growth in ISAs in the 1980s and 1990s, and analyzes the patterns as well as the modes of international collaboration by country, industry, and motivation.[6]

■ The Increase in ISAs

Various studies demonstrate that the number of ISAs has increased significantly since 1980.[7] Figure 5-1 indicates a steady increase in the number of ISAs from 1979 to 1985, particularly between U.S. and European firms. Examination

of international strategic alliances from 1980 to 1989 in three major core technologies—biotechnology, information technology, and new materials—confirms the sharp, upward trend in ISA formation throughout the decade. As shown in figure 5-2, in all three core technologies about 90 percent of the agreements were established during the 1980s: "In new materials over 62 percent of the alliances were made since 1985; in biotechnology and information technologies these shares reach about 60 percent and 54.5 percent respectively."[8]

According to *Pharmaceutical Strategic Alliances*, a database directory that tracks alliances in the pharmaceutical and biotechnology industries, there has been a tremendous surge in strategic alliances, especially between U.S. firms and European corporations. During the first half of 1992, 90 strategic alliances involving biotechnology were signed, up sharply from 58 in the same period of 1991.[9] According to a U.S. medical industry publication, "there are more alliances going on now than there have ever been. It's the hottest period of deal-making in biotech that has ever been seen."[10]

■ Distribution of International Strategic Alliances

The critical role that strategic alliances play in the global strategies of companies is reflected in the distribution of ISAs over the past decade. Due

---

[6] For empirical studies of international strategic alliances see John Hagedoorn and Jos Schakenraad, "Inter-firm Partnerships and Co-operative Strategies in Core Technologies," C. Freeman & L. Soete (eds.), *New Explorations in the Economics of Technical Change* (London: Pinter Publishers, 1990); and their more recent study, "Strategic Technology Partnering and International Corporate Strategies," K. Hughes (ed.), *European Competitiveness* (Cambridge, MA: Cambridge University Press, (forthcoming)). Refer also to a chapter by Michael Hergert and Deigan Morris, "Trends in International Collaborative Agreements," Farok J. Contractor and Peter Lorange (eds.) *Cooperative Strategies in International Business* (Lexington, MA: Lexington Books, 1988); P. Mariti and R. H. Smiley, "Co-operation Agreements and the Organization of Industry," *The Journal of Industrial Economics* vol. 31, No. 4, 1983, pp. 437-451; K.J. Hladik, *International Joint Ventures: An Economic Analysis of U.S. Foreign Business Partnerships* (Lexington, MA: Lexington Books, 1985).

[7] Hergert et al., Ibid.

[8] Hagedoorn et al., "Inter-firm Partnerships and Cooperative Strategies in Core Technologies," op. cit., footnote 6, p. 5.

[9] This information was attributed to Roger Longman, editor of *In Vivo*, cited in Sandra Sugawara, "Biotech Firms Forming More Strategic Links," *The Washington Post*, Oct. 19, 1992, pp. H1, H14. *Pharmaceutical Strategic Alliances* is published by Windhover Information Inc.

[10] Ibid.

Figure 5-2—Trends in International Strategic Alliances by Selected Industries, 1970-1989

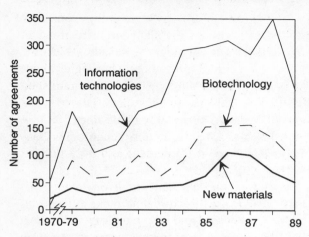

SOURCE: John Hagedoorn and Jos Schrakenraad, "Inter-firm Partnerships and Cooperative Strategies in Core Technologies," C. Freeman and L. Poete (eds.), *New Explorations in the Economics of Technical Change* (London: Pinter Publishers, 1990), p. 5.

to differences in research methodology, a lack of uniform definitions, and inconsistent data collection methods, various studies reach differing conclusions as to the predominant international pattern of strategic alliance partnerships. Nevertheless, all studies emphasize the dominance of the so-called Triad—Europe, Japan, and the United States.

For example, one study published in 1988 found that the majority of strategic alliances are formed between companies within the European Community (EC) (31 percent) or between U.S. and EC firms (26 percent), followed at some distance by EC-Japan (10 percent), and U.S.-Japan (8 percent).[11] However, a more recent study indicates that during the same time period (1980s), intra-U.S. cooperation consisted of the largest share of strategic alliance partnering (25 percent), followed closely by U.S.-EC alliances (22 percent), intra-EC (20 percent), and U.S.-Japan (14 percent).[12] Technology alliances between Europe and Japan, intra-Japanese cooperation, and non-Triad partnering take an average share of between 5 and 10 percent.[13]

Most studies conclude that over 90 percent of all agreements are made between companies from the United States, Western Europe, and Japan. Intrabloc partnering, e.g., intra-U.S., intra-European Community, intra-Japanese alliances, has continued to increase its portion of alliance formation since the second half of the 1980s.[14]

■ ISA Formation by Industry and Industry/Country

Although international strategic alliances have been employed with increasing frequency, they are concentrated in relatively few industries.[15] As figure 5-3 illustrates, international strategic alliances involving U.S. firms occur in a range of manufacturing industries—from mature industries such as automobiles, to embryonic ones such as biotechnology, and include technology-intensive sectors in aerospace, information technology, and new materials.

A number of other trends can be deciphered from this figure. First, in terms of absolute numbers and percentages, international strategic alliance formation leads by a vast margin in the information technology field (41 percent of ISAs), followed by biotechnology (19 percent), chemi-

---

[11] Hergert et al., op. cit., footnote 6, p. 102.

[12] Hagedoorn et al., "Strategic Technology Partnering and International Corporate Strategies," op. cit., footnote 6, p. 13.

[13] Ibid.

[14] Hagedoorn and Schrakenraad in their chapter "Inter-firm Partnerships," op. cit., footnote 6, p. 9, find that in all three core technologies, intra-U.S. collaboration takes the largest share of agreements, in particular in biotechnology, where over 35 percent of the agreements refer to intra-U.S. alliances.

[15] Hergert et al., op. cit., footnote 6, p. 105; and Andrew Pollack, "Technology Transcends Borders Raising Tough Questions," *The New York Times*, Jan. 1, 1992, pp. 1, 20-21; as taken from the Maastricht Economic Research Institute on Innovation and Technology.

Figure 5-3—New International Strategic Alliances Among U.S., European, and Japanese Firms by Selected Industries (1980-1989)

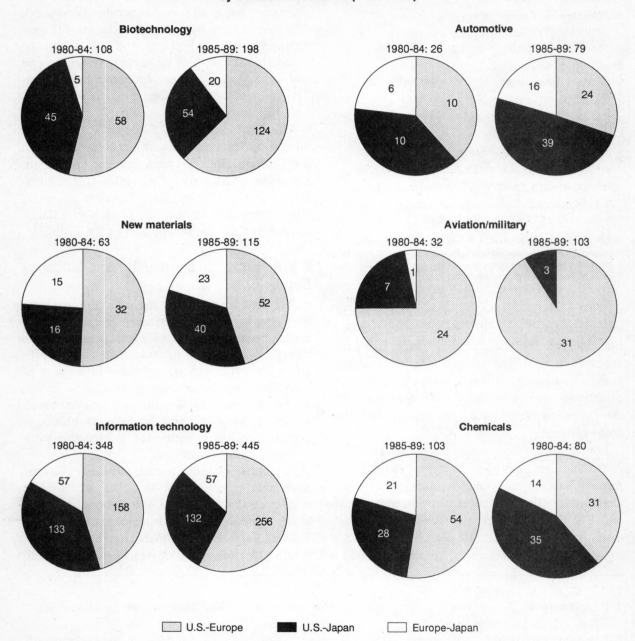

Biotechnology

1980-84: 108   1985-89: 198

5   45   58   20   54   124

Automotive

1980-84: 26   1985-89: 79

6   10   10   16   24   39

New materials

1980-84: 63   1985-89: 115

15   16   32   23   40   52

Aviation/military

1980-84: 32   1985-89: 103

1   7   24   3   31

Information technology

1980-84: 348   1985-89: 445

57   133   158   57   132   256

Chemicals

1985-89: 103   1980-84: 80

21   28   54   14   35   31

☐ U.S.-Europe   ■ U.S.-Japan   ☐ Europe-Japan

NOTE: The total number of new alliances in an industry within the specific period is listed after the range of years.

SOURCE: Adapted from Andrew Pollack, "Technology Transcends Borders Raising Tough Questions in the U.S.," *The New York Times*, Jan. 1, 1992, pp. A1, A20-21; as taken from the Maastricht Economic Research Institute on Innovation and Technology.

cals (11 percent), new materials (11 percent), automotive (6 percent), and military aerospace (4 percent). Second, with respect to U.S.-European multinational corporate technology alliances, the areas of growing collaboration are in the biotechnology, information technology, and chemical sectors. U.S.-Japan strategic alliances have expanded rapidly in recent years in the information technology, automotive, and new materials industries. Far fewer are the number of alliances formed between European and Japanese multinationals. They are concentrated largely in the information technology industries, followed at some distance in new materials, chemicals, and biotechnology.

TYPE OF COLLABORATION BY REGION

Table 5-1 indicates by region the most frequently cited reasons firms give for entering into strategic alliances. As can be seen, the purposes for international collaboration vary across international trading blocs.

Clearly an important determinant in both U.S. and European international strategic alliances is access to Japanese manufacturing technology, rather than straightforward market access. In terms of EC-U.S. international collaborative agreements, shared research and product development are notable reasons for alliance behavior.

WHY INTERNATIONAL STRATEGIC ALLIANCES ARE ON THE RISE

A number of overlapping economic and technological developments are shaping the environment of MNEs, encouraging and conditioning the formation of international strategic alliances. These developments include: technological leveling across countries; converging product markets; slow economic growth; excess capacity; shorter product life cycles; escalating R&D costs; and increasingly complex product and production process technologies.

U.S.-based MNEs dominated the international economy of the 1950s and 1960s. Since then, their market share in many industries has declined as foreign MNEs have achieved technological parity. The ability of foreign MNEs to absorb, exploit, and develop advanced technologies makes them attractive partners in ISAs. In some industries, such as automobiles, foreign MNEs ''are either the technological equals of U.S. firms, and therefore able to contribute managerial or technological expertise . . . or are more advanced.''[16]

Demand for many products is becoming more homogeneous throughout the global market. Firms that can exploit this convergence may achieve economies of scale and scope, which frequently enhance profitability. As a consequence, securing access to the United States as well as to foreign markets has become crucial to MNEs' development, production, and marketing strategies. While in many manufacturing industries market access is becoming increasingly open, in a number of defense and other high-technology industries, market access still remains restricted by U.S. and foreign government nontariff trade barriers and industrial policies.

A final economic factor is the combined impact of slow growth associated with the recession in the late 1980s and global surplus capacity in many manufacturing industries. Key strategic industries, such as automobiles, semiconductors, and aerospace, face enormous pressures for consolidation and rationalization. International strategic alliances enable companies to achieve and exploit greater product specialization with the necessary economies of scale. In mature and

---

[16] David C. Mowery, ''Collaborative Ventures Between U.S. and Foreign Manufacturing Firms,'' *Research Policy*, vol. 18, No. 1, February 1989, p. 24.

Table 5-1—Reasons Firms Give for Establishing International Strategic Alliances, by Regional Partnership

Region	Development (percent)	Marketing (percent)	Production (percent)	Number of agreements
EC-Japan	40	28	72	50
EC-U.S.	57	12	31	117
U.S.-Japan	24	30	46	33

SOURCE: Adapted from Michael Hergert and Deigan Morris,"Trends in International Collaboration Agreements," Farok J. Contractor and Peter Lorange (eds.), *Cooperative Strategies in International Business* (Lexington, MA: Lexington Books, 1988), p. 108.

consolidating industries, ISAs can reduce excess capacity, and thus enhance market discipline.[17]

Across a wide array of technology-intensive manufacturing industries, product life cycles have shortened considerably; indeed, in some cases they barely exceed the length of time required to secure U.S. patent protection. Shrinking product cycles have made it more difficult for companies to justify the high fixed capital costs required for each new product generation. In the telecommunications sector, for example, industry analysts report:

> The pace of technical change in microelectronics and computer technology has shortened life cycles of switching products while increasing their costs of development. Electronic switches for public carrier central offices can cost from $500 million to $1 billion to develop and become obsolete within five years of introduction.[18]

Skyrocketing fixed development costs, together with reduced recoupment cycles, have increased the pressure on firms to market on a global scale and to achieve product development and market access at lower costs.

Second, as product cycles shorten, many companies must increase R&D spending to remain at the frontier of technology. Referring again to the telecommunications industry, one industry expert cites that in 1986 the top 10 firms spent $753 million (7.5 percent of turnover) on R&D, which represented an increase of 9.3 percent over the previous year.[19] With margins under pressure from excess capacity and slow economic growth, firms are under pressure to deploy R&D spending more effectively, reduce capital expenditures and operating costs, and seek additional cost savings through economies of scale and scope. As the president of Texas Instrument's Japanese subsidiary acknowledged, "technology advances require a huge cost, both in human resources and equipment to develop semiconductors, so it is becoming necessary to share as much as possible."[20]

While soaring R&D costs have motivated MNEs to form international strategic alliances, other technological factors play an equally influential role. Many broad-based manufacturing sectors, such as the aerospace and automotive industries, must rely on a diverse array of emerging technologies—new materials, optoelectronics, robotics—that are outside their core competencies. For example, microprocessors are now a key component in automobiles, household durables, and computers; manufacturing and designing them requires advanced manufacturing capabilities and access to the latest developments

---

[17] The same point has been made with regard to joint ventures. See Kathryn Rudie Harrigan, *Managing for Joint Venture Success* (Lexington, MA: Lexington Books, 1986), p. 19.

[18] Gary P. Pisano, Michael V. Russo, and David J. Teece, "Joint Ventures and Collaborative Arrangements in the Telecommunications Equipment Industry," in Mowery (ed.), op. cit., footnote 1, p. 38.

[19] Data provided by Mytelka (ed.), "Crisis, Technological Change and the Strategic Alliance," op. cit., footnote 1, p. 19.

[20] The comment was made by Sachiaki Nagae, cited by Jacob Schlesinger, "Texas Instruments and Hitachi: Enter Pact to Expand Alliance in Chip Making," *The Wall Street Journal*, Nov. 21, 1991, p. B3.

in a variety of scientific disciplines.[21] To many firms, ISAs represent a cost-effective way to acquire these competencies.

In addition, industries such as telecommunications, computers, pharmaceuticals, and biotechnology are being transformed by the convergence of overlapping and underlying technologies. Computer and telecommunications firms, for example, often form strategic alliances to ensure compatibility between various network systems, such as private branch exchanges (PBXs) and local area networks (LANs). The merging of technologies from these two industries has also spurred innovation in the telecommunications equipment, software, and integrated circuits industries.[22]

The impact of this technological revolution, particularly at the component level, has made it more difficult and inefficient for many companies to track all the relevant technological fronts themselves. Unable to develop new technologies on their own, many MNEs seek ISAs to augment and complement their existing technological portfolios. In essence, MNEs are harnessing ISAs to reduce the gap between the corporations' technological competence and the technological complexity of their environment caused by continuous and rapid technological change. ISAs enable firms to reduce costs, risks, and uncertainty in their environment, and enhance simultaneously their internal technological and manufacturing capabilities.

WHY MNEs ENTER INTO STRATEGIC ALLIANCES

The previous section outlined the broad economic and technological developments that condition the formation of international strategic alliances. This section analyzes specific, firm-level factors that motivate MNEs to pursue international strategic alliances. MNEs seek strategic alliances for at least six principal reasons:

1. cost and risk sharing,
2. generation of economies of scale and scope,
3. asset pooling,
4. market access,
5. speed, and
6. competitive positioning.

■ Cost and Risk Sharing

One frequently offered motivation behind ISAs is the ability of firms to spread the costs and risks associated with R&D activities as well as new product development and commercialization. As discussed earlier, technology-related factors have exerted a broad, compelling influence on the external environment of MNEs. In the aerospace industry, for example, the costs of developing a new commercial passenger aircraft are estimated to be well over $4 billion. Such costs, in conjunction with the risks of an uncertain market, are difficult, if not impossible, for one corporation to finance alone. International strategic alliances, such as Airbus and the one recently contemplated by McDonnell-Douglas and Taiwan Aerospace, are notable examples. In the fall of 1991, McDonnell-Douglas sought $2 billion from Taiwan Aerospace in return for a 40-percent equity stake for the development and commercialization of the MD-12 passenger aircraft—a key product if McDonnell-Douglas is to survive against Boeing and Airbus. The company's chairman asserted that "without this alliance and international risk-sharing partners, we will be unable to grow as a commercial aircraft company."[23]

---

[21] Michael Delapierre and Jean-Benoit Zimmerman develop this argument in their chapter, "Towards a New Europeanism: French Firms and Strategic Partnerships," Mytelka (ed.), op. cit., footnote 1, p. 102.

[22] Pisano et al., op. cit., footnote 18.

[23] Cited in Richard W. Stevenson, "Gain for McDonnell-Douglas Raises Fears of U.S. Loss," *The New York Times*, Nov. 20, 1991, pp. D1 and D4.

The U.S. computer industry has been similarly motivated to enter into strategic alliances because of the need to reduce and spread costs and risks associated with a company's strategy of product diversification. Apple has formed strategic alliances with two Japanese MNEs. It has teamed with Toshiba to manufacture a CD-ROM player, and with Sharp to manufacture personal digital assistants (PDAs). According to Apple's CEO, "We cannot afford to fund these projects by ourselves. These alliances give us a chance to be players in an important growth area."[24] Apparently Apple is contributing software know-how and product design in exchange for Japanese manufacturing expertise and key components such as flat panel displays.

▌ Economies of Scale and Scope

Steadily increasing minimum economies of scale and scope often raise investment costs and limit the number of firms that can independently underwrite the costs of efficient-sized facilities. Many MNEs are negotiating alliances to mobilize additional financial resources. For example, in July 1992, U.S.-based Advanced Micro Devices (AMD) and Japan's Fujitsu began collaborating on flash memory chip development. To generate the economies of scale necessary to price the chips competitively, a plant costing an estimated $700 million would be required. AMD had annual sales of $1 billion at the time. As AMD's chief financial officer admitted, " . . . it was an enormous nut for us to swallow alone."[25] International strategic alliances have long occurred in the aircraft industry, where enormous costs of new

product development, combined with low volumes, require a company to sell anywhere from 350 to 400 commercial aircraft within the first 10 years and at least 600 overall in order to achieve profitability. Approximately 30 basic types of aircraft have been introduced during the jet age; about 8 have sold at least 600 units, although several more may yet do so.[26] To date, the industry as a whole has lost significant amounts of money, which has further intensified interest in strategic alliances to share costs, control risk, and enhance market access.

▌ Asset Pooling

International strategic alliances are a means of pooling other, nonfinancial, firm-specific assets that are not easily licensed, such as proprietary technology, manufacturing know-how, marketing, and distribution channels. For instance, several alliances in the pharmaceutical and biotechnology industries have been formed in order to pool the complimentary technologies of the partners. In April 1992, 15 U.S. and European multinational pharmaceutical companies announced collaboration in AIDS drug research.[27]

The emphasis on asset complementarity and pooling is also evident in the telecommunications industry. In the AT&T-Philips alliance, AT&T provided most of the underlying technology and technical know-how used in developing the next generation of digital switching equipment. Philips contributed its superior production technology, European identity, and familiarity with the tightly controlled and regulated European telecommunications markets.[28]

---

[24] Edward W. Desmond, "Byting Japan," *Time*, Oct. 5, 1992, p. 69.

[25] John Burgess, "Ventures Share Cutting Edge with Japan," *The Washington Post*, Sept. 6, 1992, p. F1.

[26] See U.S. Congress, Office of Technology Assessment, *Competing Economies: America, Europe, and the Pacific Rim*, OTA-ITE-498 (Washington, DC: U.S. Government Printing Office, October 1991). Personal communication with Wolfgang Demisch, Managing Director, UBS Securities, July 26, 1993.

[27] Peter Coy, "Two Cheers for Corporate Collaboration," *Business Week*, May 3, 1993, p. 34.

[28] Karen J. Hladik, "R&D and International Joint Ventures," Contractor et al., (eds.), op. cit., footnote 6, pp. 190-191.

Market Access

As indicated, market access is a critical motivation for firms to establish ISAs. Access to some markets, most notably Japan, remains restricted by government trade and industrial policies as well as informal barriers to entry and FDI (see Chapter 3). Strategic partnerships with foreign companies are central to overcoming this key barrier to entry. Coalitions based on international market access can "achieve access to local know-how, local legitimacy, government blessing, and strong local market positions gained through first-mover effects."[29]

Speed

As competition in international markets has intensified, product life cycles have been reduced. If profitability is to be maintained, MNEs must reduce the time necessary for R&D, product development, commercialization, production, and marketing. ISAs can offer MNEs opportunities to accelerate all these activities. This is especially important, for example, in the biotechnology industry, where the recent wave of U.S. strategic alliances with foreign companies is aimed at shortening the time required for commercialization. Indeed, pressure on biotechnology firms to get their products into global markets faster is one reason why small U.S. biotechnology firms are forming strategic alliances with both domestic and foreign pharmaceutical giants.

Competitive Positioning

As indicated earlier, MNEs may establish international strategic alliances to strengthen their current and future competitive positions.

There are three important competitive uses of ISAs for multinational enterprises.[30]

First, ISAs enable companies to monitor (and in some cases acquire) the technological developments of competitors and potential future rivals. This strategic rationale is especially apparent in a number of automotive industry ISAs involving U.S. and Japanese MNEs—example, NUMMI (General Motors and Toyota) and Ford-Mazda.

Second, ISAs can influence the evolution and the structure of an industry by creating new entry barriers, such as affecting the industry's cost structure or ensuring that competitors employ a certain technology. In this respect, ISAs are frequently initiated at the precompetitive R&D stages, when enterprises can develop common technical standards. While forming a barrier to entry, technological standardization can also ensure a greater degree of product line compatibility.

The role of ISAs to secure common technical standards is critical to the computer and telecommunications industries. For example, one of the motivating factors for the now dissolved AT&T-Olivetti alliance was to sell AT&T's UNIX operating system in Europe. The adoption of UNIX in 1986 by five of Europe's major computer producers, including Philips and Siemens, was perceived as a successful move and a challenge to IBM's position in Europe.[31] More recently, Sun, DEC, and Hewlett-Packard have formed alliances to increase the likelihood that their particular RISC-chip standard will dominate that segment of the semiconductor market.

Third, international strategic alliances can shape the competition in an industry by attempting to deter and/or preempt rival firms. In the

---

[29] Porter et al., op. cit., footnote 4, p. 334.

[30] On the competitive uses of international strategic alliances, see Porter et al. (eds.), op. cit., footnote 4; Harrigan, op. cit., footnote 17; Gary Hamel, Yves L. Doz, and C.K. Prahalad, "Collaborate with Your Competitors—and Win," *Harvard Business Review*, January-February 1989, pp. 133-139. For a critique of this approach refer to Claudio Ciborra, "Alliances as Learning Experiments," Mytelka (ed.), op. cit., footnote 1.

[31] Pisano et al., op. cit., footnote 18, p. 48.

computer industry, ISAs are often used by an aggressive partner to fight proxy battles against a dominant competitor, "as in the use of Amdhal, ICL, Bull, and Siemens as frontline troops by Fujitsu and NEC in their assault on IBM."[32] ISAs can also serve as defensive or preemptive measures. Boeing, for instance, has formed deeper alliances with its Japanese suppliers in part because it hopes to prevent these firms from developing links with its European rival, Airbus.[33]

As ISAs solidify into long-term partnerships, they may be used by allied MNEs in anticompetitive ways. New oligopolies could be formed by MNE alliances through the very process of sharing technology and controlling market distribution. For example, the recently proposed alliance between Boeing and members of the Airbus consortium to develop jointly a super jumbo aircraft could preclude meaningful competition in this market segment. If fully realized, the alliance could also lead to greater market discipline in other market segments.[34]

HOW GOVERNMENTS SHAPE THE FORMATION AND CONTENT OF ISAs

Previous sections have delineated the firm-level, internal, and competitive motivating factors for MNE strategic partnering. However, the government plays a critical role in constructing policy environments and in influencing the market forces that inform MNEs' decisions and choices regarding ISA activity. In particular, trade, industrial, and regulatory policies help shape the formation, structure, and content of international strategic alliances.

▮ Trade and Investment Policies

Government control over market access, via trade and investment policies, has tremendously encouraged international strategic alliances among multinational enterprises.

First, governmental moves to nontariff barriers have created strong incentives for international corporate alliances. One scholar argues that tariffs tend to encourage foreign direct investment and joint production arrangements as a means of market penetration, "nontariff barriers favor the use of collaborative ventures that incorporate product research, development and marketing as well as manufacture."[35] Nontariff import and export restrictions, such as those permeating the automotive and semiconductor industries, have led to increased collaboration between U.S. and foreign firms for reciprocal market access. One prominent analyst links the escalation in strategic alliances in the 1980s between U.S. and Japanese automakers to Japanese concern over future U.S. trade barriers.[36]

Second, continued Japanese and, to a lesser extent, European government restrictions on foreign direct investment— especially in high technology and defense-related industries—have encouraged firms to enter into ISAs. (As discussed in chapter 3, U.S. restrictions on FDI primarily apply to defense-related activities.) U.S.-European and U.S.-Japanese alliance activity in

---

[32] Ciborra, "Alliances as Learning Experiments," op. cit., footnote 5, p. 53.

[33] Airbus has expressed interest in including Japanese companies allied with Boeing (like Mitsubishi Heavy Industries, Fuji Heavy Industries, and Kawasaki Heavy Industries) in a proposed consortium to develop and produce a 600-seat passenger aircraft. See Jacob M. Schlesinger, "Airbus Industries Said to be Seeking Japanese Alliance," *The Wall Street Journal*, Nov. 19, 1991, p. A16; and John Holusha, "The Global Lab: Aerospace; International Flights, Indeed," *The New York Times*, Jan. 1, 1992, p. A49.

[34] "Boeing and Airbus Work on Super Jumbo," *Financial Times*, June 11, 1993, p. 3.

[35] Mowery, op. cit., footnote 16, p. 24.

[36] Robert B. Reich and Eric D. Mankin, "Joint Ventures with Japan Give Away Our Future," *Harvard Business Review*, vol. 86, No. 2, March-April 1986, p. 83.

key strategic sectors, such as aircraft and telecommunications, are obvious cases.

Finally, because government procurement practices often restrict domestic market access, they encourage ISAs. In Europe and Japan, especially, the prominent and continued role of government ministries as both purchasers and regulators of their telecommunications industries means that U.S. firms must establish alliances with foreign partners, who can then provide them with a national "cloak" in order to gain market access.

■ Industrial Policies

Though intended to stimulate the international competitiveness of national industry, European and Japanese governments' provisions of R&D funding, risk capital, and state purchasing have spurred U.S. MNE alliance activity abroad.

In Japan, for example, the government through its various ministries—Ministry of International Trade and Industry, Ministry of Finance, and the Ministry of Post and Telecommunications—has played a central role in the successful development of the country's computer-related industries. Through measures such as the promotion of interfirm collaboration, R&D funding, procurement, and leasing programs, Japanese computer and semiconductor MNEs have challenged IBM's global position.[37] In Europe as well, various governments have pursued national champion strategies in high-technology industries to combat the growing competition and market penetration by U.S. and Japanese MNEs. However, rising R&D costs, shorter product cycles, and econo-

mies of scale are making national champion strategies anachronistic. Accordingly, some Triad governments have begun to support ISA formation. For example, the EC has established a number of strategic alliance programs in the information technology-related industries. These include the European Strategic Program for R&D in Information Technologies (ESPRIT), and the Joint European Submicron Silicon Initiative (JESSI). The U.S. semiconductor industry, in conjunction with the U.S. Government, has formed the pre-competitive R&D consortia, SEMATECH.

For U.S.-based MNEs, the combination of industrial policies (particularly those that provide access to risk capital) with the high cost of new product development has enhanced the appeal of strategic alliances with European and Japanese firms. For example, IBM and NEC both have equity stakes in Bull, and IBM has participated in EC-sponsored programs such as JESSI.[38]

■ Regulatory Policies

The regulatory policies of governments have an underlying though pronounced effect on international strategic alliance formation. Three areas for review include antitrust policies, deregulation, and technical standards.

With regard to antitrust issues, many analysts argue that because U.S. antitrust laws are far tougher than those in Europe or Japan, U.S. MNEs are at a comparative disadvantage domestically, and are thus more likely to form strategic alliances with foreign companies. The debate

---

[37] For an excellent discussion of the role of the Japanese Government in promoting its computer industry see Kenneth Flamm *Targeting the Computer* (Washington, DC: The Brookings Institution, 1987); *Competing Economies*, op. cit., footnote 26, chapter 7, pp. 237-291; and Jonah D. Levy and Richard J. Samuels, "Institutions and Innovation: Research Collaboration as Technology Strategy in Japan," in Mytelka (ed.), op. cit., footnote 1. For Japanese policies towards high-technology industries in general, refer to Daniel Okimoto, *Between MITI and the Market: Japanese Industrial Policy for High Technology* (Stanford, CA: Stanford University Press, 1990).

[38] *Competing Economies*, op. cit., footnote 26, p. 222; and Richard L. Hudson, "Bull Weighs Expanding Ties to Other Firms," *The Wall Street Journal*, May 28, 1993, p. A5.

surrounding the impact of U.S. antitrust laws on ISAs, however, is especially contentious.[39]

In 1984, in response to pressures from the U.S. semiconductor industry, the U.S. Congress passed the National Cooperative Research Act (NCRA) on the basis that domestic alliances in precompetitive research would improve U.S. international competitiveness in high-technology industries. The Japanese, by contrast, tend to view R&D and commercialization as less distinct, and thus have long permitted domestic strategic alliances involving joint product development and manufacturing.

Despite the NCRA's passage, various U.S. corporations have maintained that the threat of U.S. antitrust action still poses a chilling effect on domestic alliance formation. Citing the antitrust suit filed against Microsoft, Intel, and Open Software Foundation, many U.S. computer firm managers say it is simpler and less risky to team with foreign partners.[40]

One area where U.S. antitrust and regulatory policies have played an indisputable role in ISA formation is the dramatic restructuring of the U.S. telecommunications industry during the late 1970s and early 1980s. Deregulation of the U.S. telecommunications equipment and services markets— the world's largest—and the 1984 divestiture of AT&T, arising from U.S. antitrust litigation, stimulated numerous international strategic alliances.

Another consequence of U.S. regulatory changes in the telecommunications industry was that AT&T was freed to compete in new domestic markets, such as computers, and in previously prohibited foreign equipment and services markets.[41] This regulatory change led to the proliferation of strategic alliances initiated by AT&T to diversify and expand its product lines (AT&T-Olivetti) and to gain market access, especially in Europe (AT&T-Philips).

A third area where government regulatory policies influence international corporate alliance formation is in the setting and adoption of technical standards. Standards can both open and close domestic markets to foreign firms. On the one hand, by adopting a different standard for its domestic market, a government can create a barrier to entry for foreign competitors. On the other hand, as in the case of Europe, where national markets are too small and fragmented, the lack of a common standard hurts domestic companies because they cannot develop sufficient economies of scale. Recognizing the importance of EC-wide standards for global competitiveness in high-technology industries, intra-EC alliances have emerged, such as RACE (Research for Advanced Communications in Europe), which was established to define standards for integrated broadband communication (voice, text, data, and visual).

Another example of the importance of standard setting for ISAs is the international race to develop and commercialize high-definition television technology (HDTV). The U.S. Federal Communications Commission's 1991 decision to adopt a digital standard shifted various member-

---

[39] Thomas M. Jorde and David J. Teece, "Innovation and Cooperation: Implications for Competition and Antitrust," *Journal of Economic Perspectives*, vol. 4, No. 3, summer 1990, pp. 75-96; Joseph Brodley, "Antitrust Law & Innovation Cooperation," *Journal of Economic Perspectives*, vol. 4, No. 3, summer 1990, pp. 97-112; Carl Shapiro and Robert D. Willig, "On the Antitrust Treatment of Production Joint Ventures," *Journal of Economic Perspectives*, vol. 4, No. 3, summer 1990, pp. 113-30; and Gene M. Grossman and Carl Shapiro, "Research Joint Ventures: An Antitrust Analysis," *Journal of Law, Economics and Organization*, vol. 2, fall 1986, pp. 315-337.

[40] Andrew Pollack, "Technology; Antitrust Actions on the Rise Again," *The New York Times*, Nov. 10, 1991, section 3, p. 12.

[41] For examples of strategic alliances between U.S. and overseas service providers, see Martin Dickson, "MCI Gains More Firepower in Telecoms War," *Financial Times*, June 17, 1993, p. 13; Bart Ziegler, Mark Lewyn, and Paula Dwyer, "Who's Afraid of AT&T?," *Business Week*, June 14, 1993, pp. 32-33; and "Company News: AT&T in International Services Alliance," *The New York Times*, May 26, 1993, p. D3.

ships in rival strategic alliances.[42] Initially involved in European-supported, analog-based 95 HDTV project, both Philips and Thompson have now joined with NBC, the Sarnoff Research Center, and Comparison Labs, Inc. to win the U.S. digital competition.[43] Advances in digital technology provide U.S. partners with an important competitive advantage, while France's Thompson and the Netherlands' Philips contribute their expertise in analog and camera development. In May 1993, all three consortia agreed to develop a single digital standard for HDTV.

To summarize, governments shape international strategic alliances in a number of ways. First, differences in trade, industrial, and regulatory policies have created a market for the exchange of strategic assets among multinational firms. To compete internationally, U.S., European, and Japanese MNEs are using international strategic alliances to transform and alter their portfolios of strategic competencies and assets.

Second, governments can also alter the parameters of ISAs by influencing firms' partnering decisions. For example, one consequence of the pervasive involvement by governments in various EC collaborative programs—RACE, ESPRIT, JESSI—has been to transform European firms from competitors to attractive alliance partners. In interviews with European high-technology MNEs involved in ISAs, one analyst reports that European company executives "repeatedly stressed that they could not hope for balanced corporate alliances unless they were perceived as technologically and industrially attractive partners."[44] Indeed, European MNEs point to IBM's participation in JESSI as a noteworthy demonstration of their argument.

In general, such asymmetries between government policies, particularly in terms of market access, can significantly influence the ability of U.S.-based firms to initiate and control the terms of ISAs.

HOW SUCCESSFUL ARE INTERNATIONAL STRATEGIC ALLIANCES?

The conditions that motivate the creation of these ISAs often contribute to their termination. Indeed, despite the frequency with which they are employed by MNEs, many ISAs are very short-lived, averaging perhaps only 5 or 6 years.[45] All MNEs have experienced various difficulties in forming as well as continuing their strategic alliances. In many cases, problems arise because firms fail to realize and/or anticipate the many cultural, managerial and other obstacles they are likely to confront. Furthermore, simultaneous competition and cooperation between companies engaged in an international strategic alliance requires a balancing act that some MNEs are unable to manage. Some analysts are concerned that ISAs pose considerable risk to U.S.-based MNEs, because U.S. firms appear less able to absorb new technologies and skills rather than many of their strategic partners.[46]

This section examines some of the common obstacles confronting ISAs, drawing on case

---

[42] By 1991, the HDTV competition involved three alliances: General Instrument Corp. and MIT; Zenith and AT&T; and Philips Electronics, Thomson Consumer Electronics, NBC, and the David Sarnoff Research Center.

[43] Elizabeth Mily, "The HDTV Alliance: U.S. and European Industrial Policy Approaches," Masters research paper submitted for a class in "International Strategic Alliances," the School of Foreign Service, Georgetown University, Washington, DC, May 1993.

[44] Wayne Sandholtz, *High-Tech Europe: The Politics of International Cooperation* (Berkeley, CA: University of California Press, 1992), p. 314.

[45] Bruce Kogut, "Joint Ventures: Theoretical and Imperial Perspectives," *Strategic Management Journal*, vol. 9, 1988, pp. 319-332; and "A Study of the Life Cycle of Joint Ventures," Contractor et al., op. cit., footnote 6.

[46] David Lei and John W. Slocum, Jr., "Global Strategy, Competence-Building and Strategic Alliances," California Management Review, Fall 1992, pp. 81-82.

studies primarily from the experiences of U.S.-based companies. In some of the cases, MNEs failed either to establish the strategic alliance in the first place, or intercorporate differences led to the eventual termination of the alliance. In other examples, U.S.-based MNEs successfully resolved differences with their foreign partners.

▪ Overeagerness

As AT&T learned, overeagerness is a mistake when seeking foreign partners. With the break-up of AT&T in the mid-1980s and the lifting of restrictions on international equipment sales, AT&T needed to rapidly establish itself overseas. Within a 5-year period AT&T had secured 28 international strategic alliances, primarily with European partners. AT&T's strategic alliances with Olivetti and Philips proved especially disappointing for each company. The European MNEs were reluctant to inject capital and research effort into the alliances as rapidly as AT&T expected. At the same time, AT&T was overconfident, taking for granted that its technology would sell its products in Europe.[47] AT&T did not recognize the need to establish a European identity first.

▪ Underfinancing

ISAs have failed due to underfinancing of projects. In some cases, MNEs have been reluctant to supply the necessary capital, as demonstrated by the cases of Philips and Olivetti mentioned above. In other instances, firms may be overextended financially and may also have underestimated the costs entailed in achieving the goals of the alliance. For example, both McDonnell-Douglas' alliances with Europe's Fokker for the manufacture of the MDF 100 and with Aerospatiale/Dassault-Breuget for the Mercure 2000 during the late 1970s and early 1980s were terminated. Neither plane was commercialized, in large part because McDonnell-Douglas was unwilling to commit the necessary funds.[48]

▪ Management Differences

Among the several managerial-related problems that can afflict the formation and longevity of ISAs is the desire by one or both partners to dominate the direction of the alliance as it evolves. While successful ISAs require firms to reach decisions jointly, the tensions inherent in sharing authority can lead to managerial disputes, and eventually to the termination of the alliance. This factor is especially important in cases where there are broad differences in size and corporate culture.

One study of ISAs involving U.S. companies found that "American MNEs believe that power, not parity should govern international collaborative ventures."[49] In contrast, the study found that European and Japanese firms often consider partners as equals and subscribe to management by consensus. One U.S. company involved in highly acclaimed alliances with various Asian partners is Corning. In its partnership with Korea's Samsung, Corning has not insisted on top name billing. As one Corning executive explained, "There's no need for dominance if it's a successful, growing enterprise."[50]

Differences in management cultures, poor interfirm communication and cooperation, unclear or competing lines of authority, and slow decisionmaking can impair ISAs.[51] For example,

---

[47] See Louis Kraar, "Your Rivals Can Be Your Allies," *Fortune*, Mar. 27, 1989, p. 76.

[48] For an excellent overview of ISAs in the aircraft industry, see Keith Hayward, *International Collaboration in Civil Aerospace* (New York, NY: St. Martin's Press, 1986); Mowery (ed.), "Joint Ventures in the U.S. Commercial Aircraft Industry," op. cit., footnote 1.

[49] Howard V. Perlmutter and David A. Heenan, "Cooperate to Compete Globally," *Harvard Business Review*, March-April 1986, p. 146.

[50] Kraar, op. cit., footnote 47, p. 76.

[51] See Harrigan, op. cit., footnote 17.

when Motorola tried to transfer semiconductor technology to Texas from its joint venture plant in Sendai, Japan, the transfer was at best a partial success. According to a Motorola executive, "In Texas, we just could not convince our managers to step aside and let people named Seki or Nishihara run their operations for a year."[52]

Another illustrative example is the failed alliance between TRW and Japan's Fujitsu because of the creation of a "double management system."[53] This system, which required dual managerial approval, so encumbered operational decisionmaking that both companies terminated the alliance in frustration.

Alliance Goals Change

Differing goals between MNEs have caused major conflicts regarding the future direction of an international strategic alliance. Demand changes, competitive pressures, or other factors may necessitate a shift in the alliance's original objectives, which can change the relevance of the alliance to its members. This may create dissatisfaction and conflict among the partners, undermining the viability of the original arrangements. According to one observer:

> As an owner's dependence on its venture's activity rises or declines, the balance of relative bargaining power between partners shifts, especially if resources one partner contributes to the joint venture become more or less valuable than the resources contributed by other partners.[54]

A recent Japanese survey found, for example, that one of the reasons for the slowdown in alliance formation as well as increased rates of termination between Japanese and foreign MNEs was that the foreign partners had gained sufficient knowledge of the Japanese market to go it alone.[55]

Erosion of Competitive Position

Pooling strategic assets is a driving motivation of ISAs. However, such exchanges may have unintended, detrimental consequences on a partner's long-term competitiveness.[56] Cooperation between MNEs involved in pre-competitive R&D alliances tends to be both simpler and more frequent because the gains from eventual sales are distant. However, when collaborative ventures near the marketing stage, "the incentive to cheat on a partner or to benefit at each other's expense may become strong."[57] Lack of trust and fear that the continued participation in an alliance will lead to the erosion of an MNE's global competitive position is a critical reason for the short lifespan of some ISAs.

In some cases, while the partners' overall strategic goals converge, their competitive positions in an industry do not. In its broad strategic alliance with Japan's Mitsubishi Kasei, the U.S.-based Monsanto found that the joint venture company had diversified into a number of product lines that were in direct competition with those of its U.S. parent.[58] Another example where product collisions may produce an untenable balance between cooperation and competition is AT&T's

---

[52] David E. Sanger, "Costs May Be Too High for All-American Chips," *The New York Times*, Jan. 1, 1992, sec. 1, p. 48.

[53] Perlmutter et al., op. cit., footnote 49, p. 150.

[54] Harrigan, op. cit., footnote 17, p. 46.

[55] For example, the German pharmaceutical company, Bayer, recently took over the distribution channels that Takeda Chemical Industries had previously provided. See Gregory H. Feldberg, "Joint Ventures in Japan Suffering Wedding Blues," *The Japan Economic Journal*, Aug. 25, 1990, pp. 1 and 7.

[56] For example, see David Lei and John W. Slocum, Jr., "Global Strategic Alliances: Payoffs and Pitfalls," *Organizational Dynamics*, Winter 1991, pp. 44-62.

[57] Hergert et al., op. cit., footnote 6, p. 106.

[58] Feldberg, op. cit., footnote 55, p. 7.

alliance with Philips to market AT&T's digital telephone switching system in Europe. Philip's commitment to the alliance was clearly strained when AT&T teamed up with Italy's Olivetti, a major Philips competitor in the office machinery sector.

One example of an international strategic alliance that recognized early on the need to develop trust and to limit opportunistic behavior while strengthening the competitive position of both partners is Motorola's partnership with Toshiba. At the center of the alliance is an agreement that calls for Motorola to release its microprocessor technology incrementally as Toshiba increases Motorola's penetration in the Japanese semiconductor market.

Thus far, this chapter has examined the trends in and motivations for the growth in the number and scope of ISAs. It has also delineated how trade, investment, industrial, and regulatory policies of governments shape and condition both the formation and the content of these MNE alliances. Nevertheless, the discussion above highlights the inherent fragility of ISAs due to the various problems associated with underfinancing, managerial failures, and shifting and competing goals, among others. The final section addresses the implications that international strategic alliances may have for U.S.-based MNEs as well as for U.S. Government policy.

■ Implications of ISAs for U.S. Firms and Government Policy

International strategic alliances are a relatively new and multifaceted phenomenon. The rapid expansion of ISAs since the early 1980s, as well as their high failure rate, makes any assessment of their implications for U.S.-based MNEs and policymaking difficult and tentative. To date, studies of ISAs have concentrated on the motivational factors influencing alliance formation.

There are few detailed, comparative industry case studies that focus on the vital question of how ISAs affect the competitiveness of U.S. firms in particular and the economy in general. In the final report of this assessment, OTA will address this question.

The following discussion raises some important issues. While there are no clear answers or prescriptions, ISAs have different and perhaps competing implications for U.S. firms and policymaking. On the one hand, ISAs are part of the transformation to a global economy. For MNEs, international strategic alliances have led to the further integration of the world economy and to the growing interdependence of nations. The consequences, as one MNE manager observed, are that "national borders and corporate nationality are less significant in the increasingly globalized economy."[59]

On the other hand, ISAs raise many tough issues for U.S. policymakers intent on preserving high-wage jobs for Americans and keeping the nation competitive in many high-technology industries. This tension between the interests and needs of MNEs and national governments is inevitable, but ought not to be irreconcilable.

In some cases ISAs enable formerly U.S. domestic companies to become multinational enterprises. Particularly for small U.S. biotechnology and computer start-up companies, alliances with foreign MNEs can provide access to international financing, manufacturing technology, and distribution networks.

International strategic alliances permit MNEs to unbundle their portfolios of various assets and to transfer them to partners. Hence, in deciding what their core competencies are, U.S. MNEs are becoming less vertically integrated. They are allowing portions of their R&D, manufacturing, marketing, and other capabilities to be managed outside the firm through foreign alliances.

---

[59] Toyota White Paper, op. cit., footnote 2, p. 4.

Alliances constitute a new MNE tool for mobilizing in response to high product development costs, reduced time between product generations, and the technological convergence occurring in many industries. As a result, ISAs create shifting, competing coalitions of MNEs, as opposed to competing firms. They allow MNEs to join together in specific products or markets, while retaining autonomy in others. One analyst observes that dominant U.S. MNEs, such as AT&T and IBM, "engage in a network of partnerships, playing a central role that allows them to enter/exit alliances according to their comparative advantages at the moment."[60] Indeed, it is not unusual for MNEs to be partners in one consortia or alliance and competitors in others. IBM and Siemens, for example, have formed their own alliance and cooperate in JESSI in semiconductor development, but compete in mainframe sales. For survival, most MNEs can no longer afford *not* to be involved in international strategic alliances. Thus, ISAs may encourage, in some cases even necessitate, a follow-the-leader strategy.

The complex network of allied firms and competing coalitions of MNEs, engendered by ISAs, is restructuring the world economy. International strategic alliances are leading to further market concentration in high-technology industries, and, in some cases, to mergers and acquisitions, raising the potential of global oligopolistic markets and the creation of international cartels. Referring to the ability of MNEs involved in strategic alliances to set technical standards and thereby reshape existing industries globally, one observer suggests, "In the future, new frontiers

between industries will thus be the result of rules of the game defined within the framework of alliances between dominant firms of technology-based oligopolies."[61]

Finally, there is a concern that ISAs may prove to be a one-way street leading to the transfer of key U.S. technologies to overseas competitors. Some analysts argue that multinational joint ventures are disproportionately transferring technology and other key assets from the United States to Japan.[62] Although there has been little concrete evidence to support or disprove this view, the question nevertheless remains: Can U.S. firms learn to consistently create and manage international alliances in ways that guard against transferring key assets to ambitious partners, while enhancing their competitive advantage?

In reviewing U.S.-Japanese strategic alliances, various studies conclude that Japanese MNEs use strategic alliances more effectively because they make greater efforts to learn from their U.S. partners.[63] In part, this willingness and ability to absorb technology and other resources from alliances may stem from the greater experience Japanese firms have accumulated via their alliances with other companies in their own country. Indeed, some analysts believe that "collaborative research has become the defining feature of Japanese research practice and the *sine qua non* for competitiveness in many technology-intensive sectors.[64]

By contrast, some U.S. firms take a short-term perspective as a way of avoiding investments and regaining competitiveness with minimum effort. One study found that U.S. companies involved in ISAs with Japanese partners were more interested

---

[60] Ciborra, "Alliances as Learning Experiments," op. cit., footnote 5, p. 53.

[61] Charles-Albert Michalet, "Strategic Partnerships and the Changing Internationalization Process," Mytelka (ed.), op. cit., footnote 1, p. 47.

[62] Reich et al. op. cit., footnote 36, p. 79.

[63] Refer to, for example, Levy et al., op. cit., footnote 37; Hamel et al., op. cit., footnote 30, pp. 133-139; Lei and Slocum, op. cit., footnote 46.

[64] Levy et al., op. cit., footnote 37, p. 120.

in reducing the costs and risks of entering new product lines or markets than in acquiring new skills.[65]

While the view that international strategic alliances are weakening U.S. companies and thereby eroding national economic competitiveness has garnered much media attention, the reality may be different. There is evidence to suggest that more U.S. MNEs are effectively mastering ISAs, through the internalization and competitive deployment of assets transferred by foreign companies. An illustrative example of the benefits to be gained from a two-way street approach is the General Motors-Toyota NUMMI automotive alliance in the United States.

This collaborative venture between two leading industry rivals gave General Motors the opportunity to learn first-hand about the Toyota Production System—a key manufacturing technology that is among Toyota's foremost competitive assets. In exchange, Toyota, via NUMMI, had the opportunity to learn whether its manufacturing system, using unionized American workers and U.S. auto parts suppliers, could be transplanted successfully to the United States. This ISA is an undisputed success. The acclaim GM has received with its new Saturn series is a result, in part, of the company's experience with Toyota's labor, supplier, and just-in-time production practices. The confidence Toyota gained through NUMMI was a deciding factor in encouraging greater localization and the establishment of a manufacturing plant in Kentucky.

---

[65] Hamel et al., op. cit., footnote 30, p. 134.

Multinational Enterprises and Global Capital Markets | 6

This chapter highlights important developments in the financial environment of contemporary MNEs. Two interrelated themes run throughout. The first concerns global integration, which is reshaping multinational finance and thereby complicating the task of national economic management. Domestic market openness, the development of offshore money markets, international capital movements associated with large macroeconomic imbalances, exchange rate volatility, technological change, and financial innovation are all working to erode the long-standing structures of national finance. Such policy instruments as capital controls, constraints on the establishment of nationwide banking networks, and limitations on ownership linkages between financial and industrial firms have thus come under enormous pressure.

The activities of MNEs both contribute to this pressure and represent adaptations to the resulting structural changes. Policymakers seeking either to secure the economic benefits associated with MNEs or to address their social and political consequences must therefore take into account the existence of increasingly global capital markets. In such an environment, the effects of various policies directed at the performance of MNEs are now more difficult to anticipate, and the possibility of unintended consequences is greater.

The inherent tension between the multinational logic of firms and the national logic of governments is nothing new. As the second theme of this chapter brings out, however, the tension may not have uniform effects across all industrial nations. The pace and extent of structural change differ at the national level, and enduring asymmetries can skew both business competitiveness and the social impact of global financial integration. National differences in the degree of financial openness and transparency remain. They can stem from subtle regulatory barriers or disparities in tax and accounting systems; they can also reflect the extent to which relatively concentrated national financial networks influence the allocation of capital. Thus, the chapter emphasizes the transitional condition of international capital markets and the need for further comparative research along both national and sectoral lines.

Following a summary of chapter findings, the supporting analysis examines the changing financial structures confronting MNEs. The international rules of the immediate post-war system were clearly aimed at encouraging the free flow of goods and services, and therefore the free flow of short-term trade finance. (Box 6-A provides relevant historical background.) They were not, however, intended to encourage the unrestrained flow of all forms of capital. Countries remained free to control both speculative short-term flows and foreign direct investment (FDI). In order to preserve that right, they explicitly built safeguards into the rules of the Bretton Woods system.

Over time, and especially as a result of U.S. pressure, a movement to promote a new norm of international capital mobility gathered steam. The financial policies of the major industrial countries at the broadest level eventually converged around that norm, a convergence linked throughout the post-war period with the policy underpinnings of expanded direct investment flows and the associated principle of reciprocal national treatment.

It is now evident that, since the end of World War II, a set of explicit and implicit rules impeding the free flow of capital across borders has been replaced by a still-evolving set of rules permitting and even encouraging that flow.

Many reasons for the shift toward increasingly global financial markets have been suggested. The most prominent include:

1. the pressures for regulatory convergence generated by the expanding activities of MNEs themselves and of financial intermediaries (banks, securities companies, insurance companies, etc.);
2. perceived needs to supplement national savings pools with external resources, especially in light of persistent trade and fiscal imbalances;
3. imperatives to accommodate technological change; and
4. shifts in political preferences at the national level.

These changes have opened national financial markets to one another and created a partly overlapping set of international financial markets. Rapidly expanding volumes of capital now flow through those markets, as figure 6-1 indicates.

The nature and extent of these capital flows are altering the framework within which multinationals make their strategic investment decisions. Financing issues must be addressed in a context that presumes exchange rate volatility and international capital mobility. This dynamic financial context adds a further dimension of complexity, as well as new, if risky, opportunities.

Similarly, the tension between the logic of global financial integration and the continued responsibility of national governments for national economic performance is becoming increasingly apparent. The contrasting expectations placed on MNEs exemplify that tension. On the one hand, their performance is increasingly measured relative to other multinationals; they must therefore take full advantage of any new opportunities presented by a changing international environment. On the other hand, governments look to them to provide stable, high value-added jobs, technological innovation, and other benefits. Moreover, nations compete with one another to attract these firms and benefits.

Against the backdrop of burgeoning international capital movements, governments have been trying to coordinate rules in order to harness

Box 6-A—International Capital Mobility in Retrospect

The new regime of international capital mobility represents a distinct change in the normative order developed in the aftermath of World War II.[1] During the discussions leading up to the 1944 Bretton Woods Conference, one of the sticking points between the principal negotiators, the United States and Great Britain, involved the issue of official controls on short-term capital movements in a pegged exchange rate system. Although the chief British spokesman, John Maynard Keynes, had moved away from his own 1933 view that finance was not one of those "things which should by their nature be international," he continued to believe strongly in the right of the individual state to impose capital controls as and when it alone perceived the need to arise.[2] The U.S. position, articulated most forcefully by Harry Dexter White, approached the matter differently. Although willing to concede that "disequilibrating" capital flows were both conceivable and undesirable, White envisaged a monetary order that would actively discourage all types of financial restrictions that "hamper trade and the international flow of productive capital."[3] (The word "productive" here was carefully chosen; it was generally understood to distinguish such flows from "speculative" flows.)

The U.S. position obviously reflected the expectation that, as the major creditor of the post-war order, the United States stood to benefit from as liberal an environment for international investment as it was possible to create. By the same token, however, the Americans were also intent on ensuring that access to the financial resources of the new international monetary institution they wanted to establish would be limited. In the face of undesired capital outflows, the Americans preferred that the country experiencing the problem adjust its exchange rate and/or the domestic policies responsible. They therefore contemplated a central regulatory role for the future International Monetary Fund (IMF).

In 1944, the final Bretton Woods compromise affirmed the priority of adjustment in the event of sustained capital outflows but left the option of controls to the discretion of individual states, provided only that such controls were not intended to restrict trade.[4] In the subsequent experience of the IMF, the difficulty of making clear

---

[1] This box draws on John B. Goodman and Louis W. Pauly, "The New Politics of International Capital Mobility," *International Business and Trade Law Papers*, No. 29, University of Toronto Faculty of Law, 1990; for further background, see Eric Helleiner, *The Emergence of Global Finance: States and the Globalization of Financial Markets* (Ithaca, NY: Cornell University Press, forthcoming).

[2] J.M. Keynes, "National Self-Sufficiency," *Yale Review*, vol. 21, No. 4, 1933, quoted in Charles Kindleberger, *International Capital Movements* (Cambridge, England: Cambridge University Press, 1987), p. 86. For his later view, see the relevant section of his 1942 "Proposals for an International Clearing Union," reproduced in J. Keith Horsefield, ed., *The International Monetary Fund, 1945-1965*, vol. 3 (Washington, DC: International Monetary Fund, 1969), p. 13.

[3] Keynes, ibid., footnote 2, p. 86. The view that all capital controls should be discouraged later became even more prominent in the U.S. position, a development students of the subject have attributed to the resurgent influence of the New York financial community after the war ended. See Marcello de Cecco, "Origins of the Postwar Payments System," *Cambridge Journal of Economics*, vol. 3, 1979, pp. 49-61. As noted below, however, that influence evidently was not strong enough during the 1960s to prevent the U.S. Government from experimenting with capital controls when the need arose.

[4] See Article VI, sections 1 and 3 of the Articles of Agreement of the International Monetary Fund. For his part, Keynes interpreted this compromise as follows: "Not merely as a feature of the transition, but as a permanent arrangement, the plan accords to every member Government the explicit right to control all capital movements. What used to be heresy is now endorsed as orthodox . . . It follows that our right to control the domestic capital market is secured on firmer foundations than ever before, and is formally accepted as a proper part of agreed international arrangements," as quoted in Joseph Gold, *International Capital Movements Under the Law of the International Monetary Fund*, Pamphlet Series, No. 21 (Washington, DC: International Monetary Fund), p. 11.

(continued on next page)

Box 6-A—International Capital Mobility in Retrospect—Continued

distinctions between illegitimate exchange restrictions and legitimate capital controls soon became apparent.[5] Among the leading industrial states, however, tensions related to such difficulties began to ebb after the restoration of currency convertibility in 1958.

The new prominence of the capital mobility objective received explicit expression in 1961 in the founding documents of the industrial countries' Organization for Economic Cooperation and Development (OECD). In particular, on December 12, 1961, the Council of the OECD adopted the Code of Liberalization of Capital Movements, in which the member states agreed to "progressively abolish between one another" restrictions on movements of capital "to the extent necessary for effective economic cooperation."[6] Although the Code represented the most explicit international statement of intent regarding the discouragement of capital controls since Bretton Woods, it left significant room for member states to make exceptions for certain types of capital transfers and to take any actions considered necessary for the "maintenance of public order or . . . the protection of essential security interests."[7] In the event of severe balance of payments problems, the Code permitted a member state to derogate temporarily from its liberalization obligations.[8]

For the signatory states, in short, the OECD Code extended and clarified the fundamental normative consensus of Bretton Woods. But it did not change the essential rules governing international finance. Freer capital movements across borders were to be encouraged in the context of a liberal international economy. But states retained the right to impede that movement whenever conditions warranted. During the decade following the formation of the OECD, the importance states attached to that right would become evident in their actions.

Despite the OECD Code, in the wake of persistent current account imbalances experienced throughout the 1960s and early 1970s, virtually all leading industrial states resorted to various types of controls on short-term capital movements.[9] Even the United States embarked on a series of experiments designed to control disequilibrating outflows and defend the pegged exchange rate system designed at Bretton Woods.[10] Similar

---

[5] To take one example, note that leads and lags in current payments can effectively create "capital flows" that may or may not be equilibrating for a country's overall external balance.

[6] Organization for Economic Cooperation and Development, *Code of Liberalization of Capital Movements*, Paris: OECD, October 1986, Article I. Also see OECD, *Introduction to the OECD Codes of Liberalization* (Paris: OECD, 1987). Furthermore, the signatories agreed to "endeavor to extend the measures of liberalization to all members of the International Monetary Fund."

[7] Organization for Economic Cooperation and Development, *Code of Liberalization of Capital Movements*, ibid., Art. 3.

[8] Ibid., Art. 7.

[9] The current account of a nation's balance of payments records such items as receipts for exports and expenditures on imports. An excess of the former over the latter translates into a current account surplus; an excess of the latter over the former creates a current account deficit. An enduring deficit often implies that the exchange rate is overvalued. If the holders of financial assets expect a devaluation, their attempts to exchange those assets for assets denominated in a currency expected to be revalued upward can compound the pressure on the exchange rate. In certain cases, such capital flows may force unnecessary or excessive exchange rate changes. They may push the rate away from its otherwise "natural" equilibrium. In theory, floating exchange rates might be expected to ameliorate this problem. In practice, unrestricted capital flows, including purely speculative flows, can lead to an exchange rate that continually "overshoots" or "undershoots" the equilibrium level that would bring the current account into balance.

[10] Under the terms of the Bretton Woods Agreement, signatory states agreed to declare a "par value" for their currencies in terms of gold. The U.S. dollar, which turned out to be the key price in the system, was set at 1/35 of an ounce of gold. The par value was to be defended when it came under pressure, but scope was retained for changing it in exceptional circumstances. Exchange rates were therefore neither fixed nor floating, but "pegged." On the U.S. resort to controls, see John Conybeare, *U.S. Foreign Economic Policy and the International Capital Markets: The Case of Capital Export Controls, 1963-74* (New York, NY: Garland, 1988).

controls were put in place by other states in deficit, while various nations in surplus adopted measures to ward off unwelcome inflows. The story of the eventual collapse of the exchange rate system is well-known and not in need of recapitulation here.[11] It is, however, important to note that as the system was collapsing, multilateral discussions on the future regulation of capital movements continued.

In 1972, in an atmosphere of crisis, an intergovernmental forum on international monetary reform was established. Labeled the Committee of Twenty of the IMF Board of Governors, its real work was undertaken by a staff drawn from the finance ministries and central banks of the leading monetary powers. Since capital mobility was a key issue of the day, the staff assigned an analytical project to a group of technical experts, who were essentially asked to examine the problem of speculative capital flows. Despite difficulties encountered in specifying the extent of the problem, their final report conceded that disequilibrating flows could continue to disrupt even a more flexible exchange rate arrangement. It concluded, however, that although capital controls could not be forsworn, they should not become permanent features of a reformed system because of their potential negative impact on trade and investment flows.[12] In this connection, the group also recommended that governments craft a new code of conduct for the use of capital controls and that the code be monitored by an international agency, such as the IMF. In the end, this recommendation was not pursued. For this and other reasons the final report of the Committee of Twenty failed to lay the groundwork for a new "Bretton Woods" agreement.[13]

Since the end of global monetary reform negotiations in the 1970s, myriad strategic and tactical decisions taken by states and businesses created ever deepening channels between the world's financial markets. Those channels, including lightly regulated offshore financial markets known collectively as "Eurocurrency markets," facilitated a burgeoning expansion in the scale of short-term international capital flows. Among the most significant decisions taken to facilitate these flows were those that abolished conventional national controls.

---

[11] See Benjamin J. Cohen, *Organizing the World's Money* (New York, NY: Basic, 1977); Jonathan David Aronson, *Money and Power: Banks and the International Monetary System* (Beverly Hills, CA: Sage Publication, 1977); Fred L. Block, *The Origins of International Economic Disorder* (Berkeley, CA: University of California Press, 1977); and John S. Odell, *U.S. International Monetary Policy* (Princeton, NJ: Princeton University Press, 1982).

[12] Gold, *International Capital Movements*, pp. 37-40. For relevant technical background, see Sir Alec Cairncross, *Control of Long-Term International Capital Movements* (Washington, DC: The Brookings Institution, 1973). (Despite the title, short-term capital movements are also treated.) Also see Alexandre Lamfalussy, "Changing Attitudes Towards Capital Movements," in Frances Cairncross (ed.), *Changing Perceptions of Economic Policy: Essays in Honor of the 70th Birthday of Sir Alec Cairncross*, (New York, NY: Methuen, 1981).

[13] For the Committee's conclusions on the issue of capital controls, which essentially recapitulated the original Bretton Woods principles, see "Final Report and Outline of Reform of the Committee of Twenty" (June 14, 1974), reprinted in Margaret Garritsen de Vries, ed., *The International Monetary Fund, 1972-1978* (Washington, DC: International Monetary Fund, 1985), vol. 3, p. 170, paragraphs 15 and 17. On the ultimate failure of the reform effort, see John Williamson, *The Failure of World Monetary Reform, 1971-1974* (New York, NY: New York University Press, 1977). Note the rehearsal of essentially the same issue in a recent study on international capital movements commissioned by the Ministers and Governors of the Group of Ten in the wake of the September 1992 crisis in the European Monetary System. See *IMF Survey*, May 17, 1993, p. 148.

---

the efficiencies promised by freer flows of capital and to stabilize the markets through which those flows take place. To some extent, this involves trying to come to grips with the broader implications of differences that remain in the underlying structures of major markets.

Recent research suggests that some MNEs, particularly those based in Japan and Germany, may still benefit from regulatory, accounting, and fiscal asymmetries and from privileged relationships with national financial institutions. Although the trend toward globe-spanning markets has been underway for some time, the legacy of traditional financial structures persists to varying degrees. U.S. MNEs, for example, must contend with a system that insists on complete transpar-

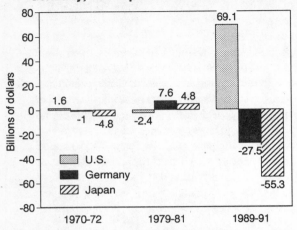

Figure 6-1—Capital Account Balances of the U.S., Germany, and Japan in Selected Periods

NOTES: These aggregate statistics include short as well as long-term capital. A negative sign indicates a capital outflow. Data are in nominal dollars.

SOURCE: International Monetary Fund (IMF), *International Financial Statistics Yearbook, 1992* (Washington, DC: International Monetary Fund, 1992).

ency, consistent earnings, and an arms-length relationship between management and owners—a system conventionally depicted as consumer-oriented. German and Japanese MNEs, conversely, still ought to benefit from less transparent, producer-oriented systems that either provide more stable, longer term, and more patient sources of capital or that endow corporate managers with longer investment planning horizons.

The interplay between forces promoting greater financial openness and residual market asymmetries is reshaping the environment within which multinational managers make their decisions on future investments. In terms of both scale and complexity, financing issues have assumed greater prominence in corporate strategic planning. To the extent that managers are adapting their firms to this new financial environment, their decisions complicate the task of crafting effective new rules to govern the international economy. The evolution of MNE strategies also raises new challenges for governments attempting to preserve traditional social values. Nations thus find themselves in a narrow corner. On the one hand, they seek the

jobs, investment, new technology, and skills that financially adaptable MNEs can provide. On the other hand, they must craft rules that strike a new balance between competitive efficiency, fairness, and enduring social priorities in a political framework still fundamentally centered on the nation.

CHAPTER FINDINGS

1. The major capital markets within which MNEs make their financing decisions developed in different national policy contexts. Financial regulatory and supervisory policies still have the most direct influence on underlying market structures. But a much broader range of policies influence those structures, as well as the amount, cost, and availability of the capital channeled through them. These include monetary and exchange rate policies, overall fiscal policies, corporate tax rules and depreciation schedules, antitrust policies, and accounting standards. Such policies effectively constitute the rules of the financial game within national capital markets.

2. The structure, depth, and operations of national capital markets can provide important advantages to MNEs. In the early post-war period, American capital markets provided U.S. firms with high volumes of relatively low-cost capital. For some companies, this helped fuel expansion overseas and, eventually, development into MNEs. Today, the much different financial market arrangements of other countries may be well-adapted to provide capital advantages to their own firms.

3. From the end of World War II until the 1970s, the structures of national capital markets, and the rules defining them, differed markedly across advanced industrial countries. The U.S. market, for example, was geographically decentralized, distinguished clearly between commercial banks and securities companies, and discouraged banks from owning shares in nonfinancial corporations. The Japanese sys-

tem was more centralized and state-directed, albeit with an American-inspired separation of commercial banks and investment banks. In the German system, principal banks were distinguished by their universal character and their ability to own nonfinancial firms.

4. Certain factors enabled structural differences between the most important national capital markets to be maintained in the early post-war years. Implicit or explicit access rules, for example, limited the participation of foreign banks and securities companies in domestic markets. Capital flows between those markets were, in retrospect, relatively manageable. Indeed, in view of the priority assigned to stable exchange rates, all governments considered control and influence of capital flows not only acceptable but necessary at various times. MNEs could accommodate themselves to different capital control regimes, although with attendendant losses in efficiency.

5. Since the early 1970s, structural differences across national capital markets have eroded, although they have not disappeared. Capital controls are being dismantled across the advanced industrial world and beyond. The forces behind this development include pressures associated with variable exchange rates, changing perceptions of the appropriate balance between risk-taking and market stability, and heightened competition between governments for the jobs, prestige, and other benefits expected to flow from a more developed financial services industry. Thus, the financial planning environment for MNEs has changed.

6. The expanding activities of MNEs themselves significantly compromised the capacity of governments to maintain capital controls. Leads and lags in invoicing and payments, transfer pricing practices, access to funding sources in a range of markets, and the ability to shift some operations to different regulatory jurisdictions—all helped undercut the efficacy of controls.

7. During the 1980s, national markets for long and short-term capital became more deeply integrated as an overlapping set of international markets grew spectacularly. The general deregulatory logic of this movement implied a trend toward convergence in both financial market structures and the capital costs facing MNEs, but the pace and ultimate extent of such convergence remained problematic and contentious.

8. Despite the logic of convergence, differences persist in the structures through which capital is raised and allocated in the major industrial countries. At the very least, the legacy of past differences endures. In the 1990s, individual investors and borrowers still view the U.S. system of capital investment as comparatively decentralized, fluid, short-term-oriented, and efficient. By contrast, Japan and Germany still appear more centralized, oriented toward longer time horizons for investors, characterized by closer links between nonfinancial firms and financial intermediaries, and adapted to provide potentially higher social returns.

9. Global financial trends since the 1970s have had mixed consequences for MNEs. On the one hand, the opening of markets and the development of new techniques has greatly expanded their financing options. On the other hand, financial uncertainties have increased partly because of fluctuating exchange rates and shifting interest rate differentials (figures 6-2, 6-3, and 6-4) and partly because the overall financial environment is more open and complex. In effect, a relatively clear set of nationally based rules of the financial game has not yet been replaced by an equally clear set of new multilateral rules.

10. For an increasing number of firms, multinationalization represents a strategic response to the rapidly changing financial environment. Diversified operations in a number of jurisdictions allow firms to take advantage of remaining regulatory, tax, and other differences and to hedge some of the risks associ-

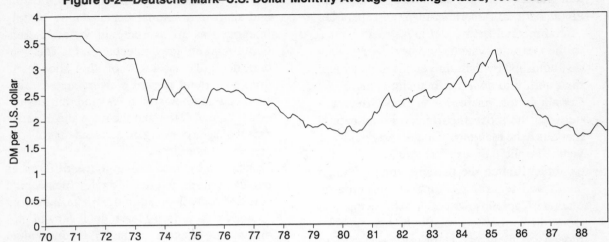

Figure 6-2—Deutsche Mark–U.S. Dollar Monthly Average Exchange Rates, 1970-1988

SOURCE: IMF data as cited in Paul Volcker and Toyoo Gyohten, *Changing Fortunes: The World's Money and the Threat to America's Leadership* (New York, NY: Times Books, 1992), pp. 370-371.

ated with increased financial uncertainty. At least in theory, locating managerial, production, and support facilities in the market of final sales can mitigate the effects of excessive swings in financial variables. Many such facilities represent the diversification of an overall financial portfolio from the point of view of the MNE's home office (see chapter 2).

11. The continuing evolution of global capital markets and the broadening embrace of adaptive strategies by MNEs pose new challenges for national governments. Those challenges arise from the fact that many firms, and citizens generally, hold those governments accountable for ensuring economic growth, shielding particular sectors or particular groups of workers from excessive or unfair competition, and otherwise defending important social values.

GOVERNMENT POLICIES AND FINANCIAL MARKETS

Modern financial markets did not spring up spontaneously. Critical to their existence are public policies that constitute the rules within which they operate. All countries subject these markets to a high degree of specific regulation. Because of their centrality in the overall economy, moreover, they have been heavily influenced by broader official policies and practices. Table 6-1 illustrates some of the most important of these policies.

Governments specify, enforce, and adjudicate the fundamental property rights of market participants. Directly or indirectly, they license intermediaries (banks, brokers, etc.). They may insure savers against loss, or protect investors. Through regulatory, supervisory, tax, and other financially related policies, they establish the rules for savers, investors, and intermediaries. Those rules are influenced by distinctive cultural, legal, and political traditions and have therefore differed from nation to nation. Such differences can create difficulties for MNEs, but they can also provide significant opportunities.

In the decades following World War II, the rules governing national markets for both short-term finance and long-term capital differed markedly across advanced industrial countries. The United States, for example, prohibited commercial banks from underwriting corporate bond or stock issues or owning shares in industrial enter-

Figure 6-3—Japanese Yen–U.S. Dollar Monthly Average Exchange Rates, 1970-1988

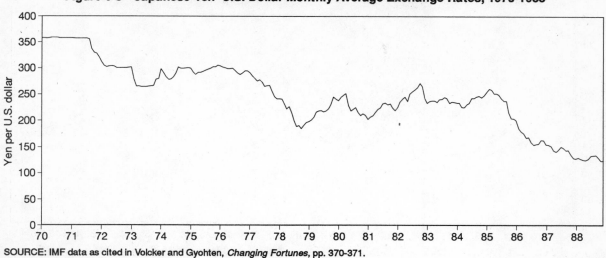

SOURCE: IMF data as cited in Volcker and Gyohten, *Changing Fortunes*, pp. 370-371.

prises; the banking market was also segmented along State lines. Reflecting this geographic and functional segmentation, as well as the size, scope, and mainly domestic orientation of the overall economy, the U.S. stock and bond markets were decentralized but deep. The British capital market shared some of these characteristics, but, the banking system was less segmented and more outward-oriented. The French market was more centralized and state-directed; the role of banks was especially prominent and the government used them to steer industrial development. The Japanese system had marked similarities to the French system, although the links between government and banks were more indirect, with a U.S.-style separation of commercial banks and investment banks in place after the war. The German system was also characterized by relatively underdeveloped stock and bond markets and by a prominent role for banks, but the principal banks were distinguished by their universal character (that is, they were permitted to engage in a wide range of commercial and investment banking activities).

In the period just after World War II, national financial markets were deliberately insulated by the architects of the new international monetary system. Faced with the possibility of extending the principles of global liberalism from the arena of trade to the arena of finance, most countries recoiled. At the Bretton Woods Conference in 1944, the United States, Great Britain, and others finally agreed that countries should be obliged over time only to abolish restrictions on financial flows directly related to trade. They accepted no obligation to open their national financial markets to foreign participation, to liberalize longer term capital inflows or outflows, or to avoid using national financial policies in pursuit of larger political or economic aims.

The reluctance of governments to match trade liberalization with financial liberalization is understandable. Capital is inherently quite mobile, but labor is not. If a national population is subjected to bracing international competition through trade flows, countervailing financial flows might be necessary to cushion the effects, both economic and political. Especially under a system designed to minimize movements in exchange rates, governments needed tools to facilitate necessary adjustments to international payments imbalances. The ability to direct national savings toward national investments ap-

Figure 6-4—Interest Rate Differentials in Japan and Germany vis-à-vis the U.S., Quarterly 1982-1991

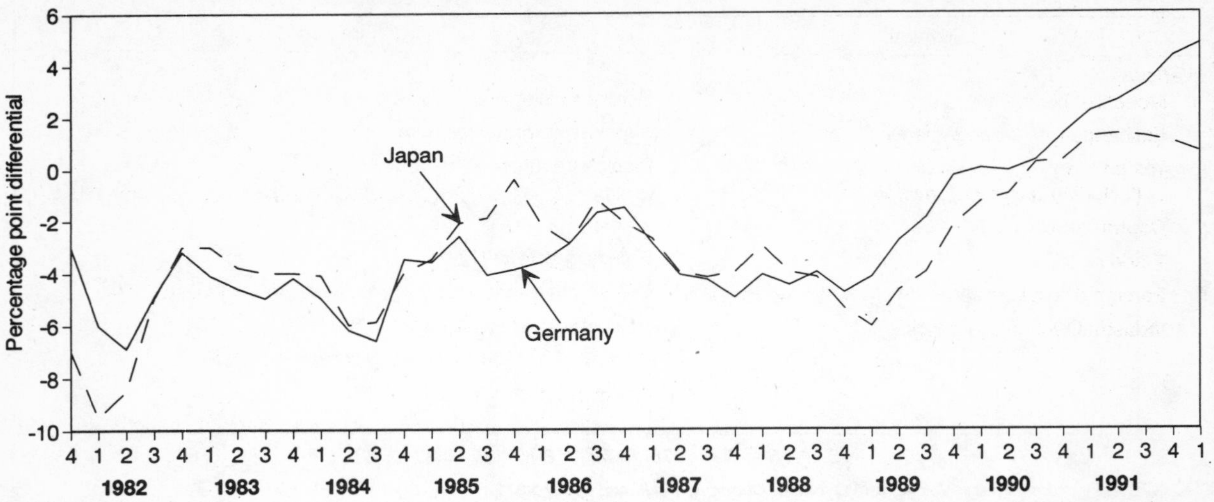

NOTES: Interest rates are calculated on an end-of-quarter basis and are graphed according to how many percentage points they varied from the U.S. interest rate at the time.

SOURCE: Adapted from the Bank for International Settlements, *62nd Annual Report* (Basle, Switzerland: BIS, 1992), p. 144.

peared to be the necessary concomitant to a liberal trading system with fixed exchange rates.

FINANCIAL MARKETS AND MNEs

Firms develop multinational strategies in response to their operating environments; financial markets comprise an important part of that environment.[1] National differences in regulations and tax policies, for example, can translate into differences in the availability and cost of capital across borders. By expanding operations across national borders, a firm can advance its strategic goals. It can often more readily generate capital internally (for example, by broadening the sources of earnings) or externally (through increased access to national or international capital markets). Moreover, if one of a company's inherent advantages is derived from the availability of bountiful amounts of low-cost capital, expanding

into foreign markets where rivals lack such an advantage needs little rationalization.

The fundamental issue related to contemporary developments in financial markets can be captured by the term "financial uncertainty." Conceptually, this is nothing new. Businesses have always had to deal with an unpredictable external environment. But the level of financial uncertainty has been increasing since the 1970s, and has become highly problematic. Extreme interest rate volatility, unstable and highly unpredictable exchange rate movements, and the rapid pace of innovation in financial instruments—these and other developments have made routine planning more difficult and added a new dimension of complexity to long-term investment decisions.

In order to justify a large-scale productive investment, MNEs must minimize financial uncertainty. The development of various risk man-

---

[1] The research assistance of Anthony Perl is gratefully acknowledged. For relevant background, see U.S. Congress, Office of Technology Assessment, *Competing Economies: America, Europe, and the Pacific Rim*, OTA-ITE-498 (Washington, DC: U.S. Government Printing Office, October 1991); "Financing Long-Term Investments," chapter 3 of U.S. Congress, Office of Technology Assessment, *Making Things Better: Competing in Manufacturing*, OTA-ITE-443 (Washington, DC: U.S. Government Printing Office, March 1990); and, *International Competition in Services*, OTA-ITE-328 (Washington, DC: U.S. Government Printing Office, July 1987).

Table 6-1—Selected Policies Influencing Financial Market Structures

General	Specific
National	
Monetary policy	Licensing rules
Exchange rate arrangements	Supervisory practices/rules
Tax policies (including depreciation rules)	Disclosure rules
	Functional restrictions (investment/commercial banking, insurance, etc.)
Capital controls	
Trade policies	Geographic restrictions
Foreign direct investment rules	Ownership restrictions (bank/industry, industry/bank, etc.)
Industrial/technology policies	Payments system practices
	Price controls (interest rate ceilings, etc.)
	Competition policies
	Market access policies (right of establishment, national treatment, reciprocity)
	Accounting standards (often non-governmental)
International	
Exchange rate regime	Central bank agreements on supervisory practices, capital adequacy, etc.
Economic policy coordination efforts (G-7, EC, etc.)	
Tax treaties	Securities/banking markets regulatory coordination (EC single market program, NAFTA services rules, OECD capital and GATT services negotiations, IOSCO work programs)
OECD capital and investment instruments	

SOURCE: Office of Technology Assessment, 1993.

agement techniques and tools has become a growth field both for MNE managers and financial intermediaries. But hedging techniques are costly and fail to eliminate all financial uncertainties. Indeed, they may create new ones.

No one fully understands the risks inherent in contemporary global financial markets. Paul Volcker, former chairman of the Federal Reserve Board and no radical critic, saw fit to conclude a recent book with the following observation:

> The economic case for an open economic order rests, after all, largely on the idea that the world will be better off if international trade and investment follow patterns of comparative advantage . . . . But it is hard to see how business can effectively calculate where lasting comparative advantage lies when relative costs and prices among countries are subject to exchange rate swings of 25 to 50 percent or more. There is no sure or costless way of hedging against all uncertainties; the only sure beneficiaries are those manning the trading desks and inventing the myriad of new devices to reduce the risks—or to facilitate speculation . . . . But these risks and costs seem to be driving more of the industrial investment of operating businesses in developed countries toward producing for local or regional markets. In other words, the decisions in the real world are often defensive and are designed to escape exchange rate uncertainties and protectionist pressures rather than to maximize efficiency. That inevitably leads to diluting some of the important benefits of open markets, which is maintaining tough competition among the world's dominant producers.[2]

Although MNE managers may hope for the day when excessive exchange rate and other financial

---

[2] Paul Volcker and Toyoo Gyohten, *Changing Fortunes: The World's Money and the Threat to American Leadership* (New York, NY: Times Books, 1992), p. 293. Also see C. Randall Henning, *International Monetary Policymaking in the United States, Germany, and Japan* (Washington, DC: Institute for International Economics, forthcoming).

pressures subside, few expect it soon. U.S. firms with significant revenues generated overseas, for example, must be concerned about potential losses caused by an unanticipated fall in the value of the dollar. If they have significant physical or financial assets overseas, they are also concerned about valuation changes that can translate into net losses on consolidated balance sheets. In addition, they must take into account the possibility that they or their foreign rivals may gain an edge through the relative depreciation of national currencies.[3]

Intermediaries have responded with a dizzying array of new products. Most involve some variation on the future sale or purchase of financial assets or liabilities, options to engage in such transactions, or the swapping of future cash flows with another party.[4] All such techniques, of course, carry a cost that must be borne by the firm or its customers, and few allow firms to cover longer term uncertainties at an acceptable cost. Excessive caution with respect to longer term investment can still be the consequence. Moreover, the financial volatility associated with those uncertainties can encourage firms to initiate risky financial transactions extraneous to their core business in pursuit of speculative gains. But it is the prospect of longer term losses that can incline firms toward excessive caution in their long-term investment planning. While firms have been learning to deal with the more immediate consequences of financial volatility, there remains the possibility that such volatility can exert a deleterious influence on the long-term investments that create the jobs, incomes, and substantive innovations of the future.

Beyond financial engineering, MNEs can consider a range of strategic options for dealing with excessive financial uncertainties. They can try,

for example, to limit their financial exposure through deliberate strategies of global diversification. By spreading plant, equipment, supply networks, and costly personnel to their final markets, MNEs can attempt to hedge their cash flows and their balance sheets. Longer term productive investments may still be discouraged by the expectation of future monetary and financial turbulence, but the prospect of competitive losses associated with such turbulence can be reduced by embedding such natural hedges into the firm's structure. The actual impact of financial volatility may therefore vary by industrial sector.

Governments accountable for developments within national economies and national capital markets, of course, might view the consequences of financially driven strategic decisions by MNEs differently. The kinds of market imperfections that contribute to exchange rate volatility and financial uncertainty might be the result of deliberate policies; the cross-border arbitrage activities of MNEs might appear as unwelcome threats to the integrity of those policies.[5] Conversely, if a government presides over broad and deep national capital markets and sees it as important to maximize the resulting benefits for its own citizens, the multinationalization of firms obviously threatens to transfer at least some of those benefits abroad.

Critics of MNEs have long held that this transfer of national capital advantages is exactly what U.S. firms accomplished in the decades that followed World War II. In effect, they contend that those companies combined relatively cheap U.S. capital and technology with cheap labor in production facilities abroad. It arguably followed, from such a view, that such activities eroded both the relative capital advantage of the United States and the relative international competitiveness of

---

[3] See Judy Lewent and A. John Kearney, "Identifying and Hedging Currency Risk at Merck," *Journal of Applied Corporate Finance*, vol. 2, No. 4, winter 1990, p. 20.

[4] For a recent analysis, see Group of Thirty, *Derivatives: Practices and Principles* (Washington, DC: 1993)

[5] Arbitrage involves undertaking simultaneous and opposite transactions in separate markets in the hope that profits will result from temporary price differentials.

firms that stayed home. Implicit in such a view, however, is the assumption that the returns to the nation from the activities of MNEs—for example, through dividend flows—did not adequately compensate for this erosion.

Whether the ultimate returns on multinational activity are in fact adequate from a national point of view is a matter of perception and political judgment. The advocates of multinational enterprises have typically argued that the transfer of U.S. capital advantages abroad promised to redound to the benefit of the United States. At the possible cost of shifting some jobs abroad, it promoted the development of a more open world economy, increased options for American consumers and investors, and ultimately addressed traditional U.S. security concerns. However, questions have arisen concerning the extent to which such benefits are contingent on the assumptions that the policies of leading countries are all converging toward liberal norms and that firms competing in global markets are not playing by different rules.

Such differences in rules can arise from structural distinctions in the markets through which domestic and multinational firms raise their capital. For most of the twentieth century, those markets have been recognizably national in their fundamental structures. Although such distinctions are eroding, partly through the normal operations of MNEs, they have not yet disappeared.

FINANCIAL MARKET STRUCTURES: A PRIMER

With words like "flow," "liquidity," "deepening," and "spillover" rampant in the vocabulary of bankers and economists, it is no coincidence that hydraulic analogies frequently enter discussions of international finance. National financial markets have often been depicted as reservoirs for national savings and investment; international markets and cross-border sales and purchases of financial assets and liabilities (financial intermediation) as canals linking those reservoirs; national financial controls as dams designed to stop flows into those canals; and broader national policies as locks constructed to regulate flows both within national reservoirs and into cross-national canals.[6] The contents of national reservoirs may be described as more or less fluid; the faster changes in one part of the reservoir cause accommodating changes elsewhere in the same reservoir, the more fluid are those contents and the more unified is that reservoir. The more fluid are the contents of neighboring reservoirs, and the more open the canals between them, the faster will changes in the level of one reservoir move to another. Similarly, as long as closure is the rule, turbulence in one reservoir matters little to those depending on other reservoirs. But when the reservoirs are open, turbulence can spread quickly.

In the early years of the post-World War II era, only one national reservoir was reasonably full, that of the United States. Moreover, both in the United States and elsewhere, the contents of national reservoirs were quite viscous. Interest rate controls, geographic restrictions on the operations of intermediaries, and functional barriers— for example, between the operations of commercial and investment banks—all increased viscosity. In addition, by deliberate policy design, the dams between national reservoirs were formidable; they could be replaced by canals only slowly, and the locks in those canals were carefully regulated.

Figure 6-5 gives a rough idea of the resulting structural differences in the most important national banking markets during much of the post-World War II period. The key differences highlighted are the degree to which a relatively few banks (as opposed to securities companies and other types of intermediaries) were allowed to

---

[6] Here and elsewhere, the chapter was inspired by Ralph Bryant's *International Financial Intermediation* (Washington, DC: Brookings Institution, 1987).

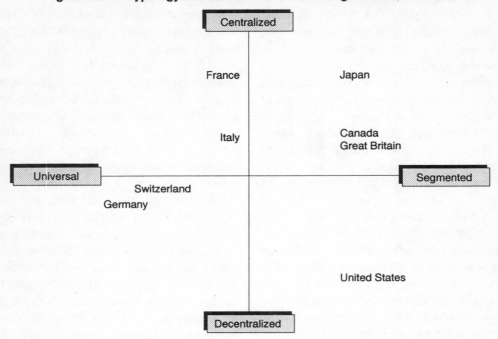

Figure 6-5—A Typology of Post-World War II Banking Market Structures

SOURCE: Office of Technology Assessment, 1993.

dominate the national financial system, and the degree to which direct linkages were permitted between commercial banking (essentially, taking deposits and making loans) and investment banking (among other things, underwriting the issuance of stocks and bonds).[7]

Today, the picture is much different. Inside the national reservoirs of advanced industrial countries, fluidity has been greatly increased by the deregulation of interest rates and the breakdown of barriers between financial intermediaries. Especially since the late 1970s, dams have been dismantled at a rapid pace, canals have been widened considerably, and locks have progressively been left open. Highly regulated banks have been losing customers, especially MNEs, to stock, bond, and commercial paper markets. In some cases, nonfinancial MNEs have even become their competitors. In response, banks have sought riskier customers in their domestic markets and pushed aggressively for a loosening of traditional regulatory constraints. As geographic and functional limits have eroded, there has been a gradual movement across most banking markets toward more universal-type banking structures. Most dramatically, banks have also expanded their involvement in international markets (see figures 6-6 and 6-7).

Although it would be stretching the facts to depict the dismantling of dams and the opening of canals as having created a truly global reservoir, a disturbance in one reservoir can generate crashing waves in another.[8] In fact, since the 1970s the turbulence associated with persistent

[7] Universal banks are able to engage in both sorts of activities; in addition, they may be able to buy and hold for their own accounts the securities issued by industrial firms.

[8] For an accessible survey of developments and a summary treatment of relevant economic literature on the subject, see ''Survey of the World Economy,'' *The Economist*, Sept. 19, 1992, pp. 5-48.

Figure 6-6—Deposit Banks' Foreign Assets by Residence of Bank, 1977-1991

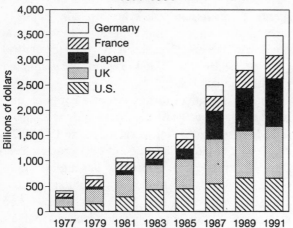

SOURCE: IMF, *International Financial Statistics Yearbook, 1992*, p. 61.

Figure 6-7—Cross-Border Bank Credit to Non-Banks by Residence of Lending Bank, 1977-1991

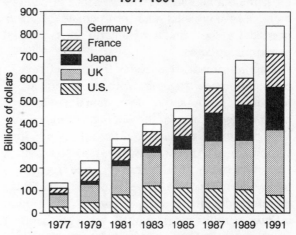

SOURCE: IMF, *International Financial Statistics Yearbook, 1992*, p. 67.

macroeconomic imbalances and various specific events (the failure of the Herstatt Bank in Germany, the collapse of Continental Illinois Bank, the October 1987 Wall Street panic, and the BCCI case) has often combined with this new openness to engender financial crises that demand coordinated international responses.

This is precisely what some policymakers feared after World War II, leading them to construct a post-war monetary system that left countries free to retain and strengthen the dams and locks of the war years. But perceptions soon changed and governments effectively began encouraging the vast expansion of international capital movements through their fiscal, monetary, trade, and financial regulatory policies. They were also pulled along, either by the actions of other governments[9] or by the activities of MNEs and financial intermediaries. The outcome has been the adoption of policies aimed at capital decontrol and the integration of financial markets.

CAPITAL DECONTROL AND FINANCIAL INTEGRATION

Capital controls were a response to the political sensitivities associated with international capital movements (see box 6-A). During the early decades of the Bretton Woods system, all advanced industrial states resorted to them at one time or another and all approached their eventual liberalization cautiously.[10] They included a broad range of explicit restrictions, special taxes, or tacit arrangements designed to discourage certain kinds

---

[9] For instance, in the 1980s the United States targeted Japanese financial liberalization as a key to resolving trade disputes.

[10] Much debate surrounds the reasons for this caution and the potential consequences of its apparent abandonment. Harkening back, explicitly or implicitly, to such seminal books as Karl Polanyi's *The Great Transformation* (Boston, MA: Beacon Press, 1957), much of that debate concerns the resurgent chimera of the "self-regulating market" and, ultimately, the changing dimensions, effects, and implications of interdependence in the financial sector. Relevant works include: Susan Strange, *Casino Capitalism* (Oxford: Basil Blackwell, 1986); Robert Cox, *Power, Production, and World Order* (New York, NY: Columbia University Press, 1987); Robert Gilpin, *The Political Economy of International Relations* (Princeton, NJ: Princeton University Press, 1987); James Hawley, *Dollars and Borders* (Armonk, NY: M.E. Sharpe, 1987); Charles Kindleberger, *International Capital Movements* (Cambridge, England: Cambridge University Press, 1987); Jeffry Frieden, "Invested Interests: The Politics of National Economic Policies in a World of Global Finance," *International Organization* vol. 45, No. 4, autumn 1991, pp. 425-51; and Michael C. Webb, "International Economic Structures, Government Interests, and International Coordination of Macroeconomic Adjustment Policies," *International Organization* vol. 45, No. 3, summer 1991, pp. 309-342.

of financial transfers between residents and non-residents.[11] In an era of pegged exchange rates, most maintained such controls either to achieve balance-of-payments goals or to create the space needed for the pursuit of autonomous national economic policies.

Capital flows are critical to the balance of payments since, together with developments in the current account, they determine the volume of reserves available for defending a pegged exchange rate or influencing a flexible rate.[12] Free capital flows can also frustrate monetary policy. A government conducting a more restrictive policy compared to the rest of the world may therefore decide to impose controls on capital inflows or to lift them on outflows; a government conducting a relatively expansionary policy may decide to impose controls on outflows or to lift them on inflows. All of the measures adopted in such a context directly affected MNEs and financial intermediaries. They also encouraged those firms to pursue evasive strategies in response.

Since the late 1970s, governments in the advanced industrial world have moved decisively to facilitate international capital mobility. More countries moved to abolish capital controls and dismantle associated bureaucratic machinery. To be sure, capital flows continue to encounter frictions at national borders.[13] Still, it is clear that state policies that formerly accommodated the possibility of controls on short-term capital movements have lately converged in the opposite direction. Such policies suggest a fundamental break with the practices through which the central rules of the Bretton Woods system were adapted and implemented.

Capital decontrol forms part of a complex and interacting set of public policies adopted across the advanced industrial world since the 1970s, the end-result of which has been to encourage a freer flow of capital across borders. Through transfer pricing practices, leads and lags in managing their accounts receivable and accounts payable, and participation in offshore currency markets, MNEs played an important role in that dismantling process. In addition, the domestic financial deregulation that swept throughout the world during the 1980s reduced the viscosity of financial flows.

Britain initiated this trend in the late 1970s. Adoption of a variety of liberalization measures followed in subsequent years in the United States, France, Germany, Japan, and other industrial countries.[14] Governments thus sought to address some of the more acute difficulties that had come to be associated with controls.[15]

Domestic deregulation complemented, and was partly driven by, the deepening that occurred in

---

[11] See Organization for Economic Cooperation and Development, *Controls on International Capital Movements* (Paris: OECD, 1982).

[12] This discussion draws on John B. Goodman and Louis W. Pauly, ''The Obsolescence of Capital Controls? Economic Management in an Age of Global Markets,'' *World Politics*, vol. 46, No. 1, October 1993.

[13] See Ralph Bryant, *Money and Monetary Policy in Interdependent Nations* (Washington, DC: Brookings Institution, 1980). Also directly relevant are Martin Feldstein and Charles Horioka, ''Domestic Savings and International Capital Flows,'' *Economic Journal* vol. 90, June 1980, pp. 314-329; Martin Feldstein, ''Domestic Savings and International Capital Movements in the Long Run and the Short Run,'' *European Economic Review* vol. 21, 1983, pp. 129-153; Tamim Bayoumi, ''Savings-Investment Correlations: Immobile Capital, Government Policy, or Endogenous Behavior,'' *IMF Working Papers*, WP/89/66, Aug. 22, 1989; International Monetary Fund Staff, ''Determinants and Systemic Consequences of International Capital Flows,'' *IMF Occasional Paper Series*, vol. 77, March 1991; Martin Feldstein and Philippe Bacchetta, ''National Saving and International Investment,'' in B. Douglas Bernheim and John B. Shoven (eds.), *National Saving and Economic Performance* (Chicago, IL: University of Chicago Press, 1991), pp. 201-220; and Jeffrey Frankel, ''International Capital Mobility: A Review,'' *Papers and Proceedings of the Annual Meeting of the American Economic Association*, 1991.

[14] Such measures included the abolition of controls on interest rates, the relaxation of exchange controls, permission for intermediaries to introduce new instruments (e.g., bank certificates of deposit, money market funds), the relaxation of barriers to the participation of foreign institutions in national banking and securities markets, and the dismantling of cartels that traditionally managed local stock and bond markets.

[15] Examples include the movement of funds (and the best corporate customers) out of banks and into less-regulated securities markets, the crowding out of private investment by rising governmental financing needs, the inefficient allocation of available financing, and the need to compete with other countries for the jobs and investment promised by a burgeoning financial services industry.

Table 6-2—International Financial Transactions, 1978-1990 (in billions of dollars)

	1978	1980	1982	1984	1986	1988	1989	1990	1991
International bank lending (net stocks)	530	810	1,020	1,285	1,790	2,380	2,640	3,350	3,610
International bond financing (net stocks)	NA	NA	NA	390	700	1,085	1,252	1,473	1,651
New international bond issues (net flows)	29	28	58	90	163	144	166	122	163
Euro-commercial paper outstanding	NA	NA	NA	14	53	59	70	80	

NOTE: NA indicates that data was not available.

SOURCE: Bank for International Settlements, *Annual Reports,* various issues; International Monetary Fund, *International Capital Markets: Developments, Prospects, and Policy Issues* (Washington, DC: International Monetary Fund, 1992).

the cross-national Euro-currency markets. Capital decontrol, financial deregulation, and the expansion of international financial markets worked together to widen and deepen the canals that link national financial reservoirs. More concretely, this translated into a remarkable expansion of cross-border bank lending, a growing movement of corporate bond issuers into new offshore markets, and the development of new commercial paper markets wherein MNEs, in particular, could raise funds from investors without going through banking intermediaries. Table 6-2 charts these trends in international financial transactions.

Although such data obscure the fact that the capital flowing through these markets is far from uniform—for example, obligations denominated in U.S. dollars have historically dominated most market segments—the overall picture is of a startling rise in the volume of cross-border financial transactions. A recent survey by *The Economist* puts the numbers into perspective.[16] In the early 1980s, the ratio between the cross-border lending of banks and the aggregate gross domestic product (GDP) of Organization for Economic Cooperation and Development (OECD) countries was 4 percent; 10 years later it stood at 44 percent. Partly reflecting a rising fiscal deficit and a search for new financing sources, the proportion of U.S. Government bonds held by

foreigners rose from 7 percent in 1970 to 17 percent in 1988. (For Germany, comparable figures were 5 percent in 1970 and 34 percent in 1988.) Between 1980 and 1990, the annual volume of cross-border transactions in stocks ballooned from $120 billion to $1.4 trillion, a compound growth rate of 28 percent a year. Table 6-3 provides an indication of the expanding foreign participation in national stock and bond markets.

The rate of expansion in other financial markets has also been dramatic. Daily turnover on foreign exchange markets in the mid-1980s was estimated at just over $300 billion; in the early 1990s it is estimated at over $900 billion. As table 6-4 shows, during the same period cross-border markets for various types of financial derivatives mushroomed in both absolute and relative terms as MNEs, other investors, and financial intermediaries sought ways to hedge their financial risks or to profit from financial volatility.

This growth in international financial transactions has occurred while governments have been seeking a new balance in their financial policies. While aiming to maximize the efficiency gains promised by open, competitive markets, they must also attempt to minimize the potential costs associated with increased market instability. In contemporary financial markets, the interests,

---

16 "Survey of the World Economy," op. cit., footnote 8, p. 9.

Table 6-3—Cross-Border Transactions in the Stock and Bond Markets of Selected Countries, 1970-1990
(as a percentage of GDP)

	1970	1975	1980	1985	1990
United States	3	4	9	36	93
Japan	NA	2	7	61	119
(West) Germany	3	5	8	34	58
France	NA	NA	8	21	53
Italy	NA	1	1	4	27
United Kingdom	NA	NA	NA	368	690
Canada	6	3	10	27	64

NOTE: NA indicates that data was not available.
SOURCE: Bank for International Settlements, *62nd Annual Report* (Basle, Switzerland: BIS, 1992), p. 193.

operations, and inherent structures of MNEs are at the center of this balancing effort. By linking national markets, they effectively embody the conditions of financial interdependence currently confronting all governments. In such a context, governments face incentives both to cooperate and to compete with other governments in structuring and overseeing the markets within which MNEs operate.

In principle, mechanisms for advancing their competitive impulses are relatively straightforward; governments can regulate or deregulate, tax or subsidize, open or close the markets they oversee. As those markets become more deeply integrated, however, mechanisms for cooperation, unavoidably intergovernmental in character, become more difficult to create, just as the risks they must address become more complex. As financial markets expanded during the 1970s and 1980s and greater numbers of corporations and financial intermediaries embarked on multinational strategies, a disjunction became increasingly evident between the global logic of financial integration and the continuing reality of decentralized political authority over financial markets. In 1974, for example, the failure of Herstatt Bank in Germany and the Franklin National Bank in the United States sent regulators around the world scrambling for ways to insulate

their national markets from the potential fallout in the worst case or to stabilize their interdependent markets in the best case. The dilemma became even more acute with the onset of the developing country debt crisis that followed Mexico's near default in August 1982.

In the absence of clear international governing arrangements, regulators have been concerned about the widening of potentially dangerous regulatory gaps that can distort competitive conditions to the detriment of national or global welfare. Internationally linked financial markets and the continued responsibility of national political authorities for both market stability and macroeconomic management have highlighted a need for more coordinated prudential oversight in the financial sector.[17]

The results of intergovernmental efforts in the financial regulatory arena have thus far been uneven. Some successes have been achieved in promoting the norm of capital mobility, encouraging higher and more common capital requirements for international banks, and enhancing the safety of cross-border payments-clearing systems. More difficult have been efforts to coordinate the treatment of other kinds of banking risks, regulations governing securities firms and markets, tax policies influencing financial flows, and approaches to managing the systemic risks poten-

---

[17] See Franklin R. Edwards and Hugh T. Patrick (eds.), *Regulating International Financial Markets: Issues and Policies* (Dordrecht: Kluwer Academic Publishers, 1992); Joan Spero, "Guiding Global Finance," *Foreign Policy*, No. 73, winter 1988/89, pp. 114-34; and Ethan Kapstein, *Governing the Global Economy: International Finance and the State* (Cambridge, MA: Harvard University Press, forthcoming).

Table 6-4—Selected Financial Derivative Markets, 1986-1991 (in billions of dollars)

Instruments	1986	1987	1988	1989	1990	1991
Interest rate options	516	609	1,174	1,588	2,054	3,231
Currency options and futures	49	74	60	66	72	77
Stock index options and futures	18	41	66	108	158	210
Interest rate swaps	400	683	1,010	1,503	2,312	2,750
Currency and interest/currency swaps	100	184	320	449	578	700
Other	NA	NA	NA	450	561	630
Total	1,083	1,591	2,630	4,164	5,735	6,900
Ratio of total to OECD GDP	0.10	0.13	0.19	0.29	0.35	0.40

NOTE: NA indicates a non-applicable category during these years.

SOURCE: Bank for International Settlements, *62nd Annual Report*, p. 192.

tially created by new financial products.[18] Complicating such coordination efforts is the possibility that MNEs and intermediaries will seek to avoid the higher costs that can be entailed. If all leading states are not included in the coordination process, business activity might drift to those not included. Similarly, if less tightly regulated or less heavily taxed markets exist within smaller jurisdictions (e.g., Luxembourg, Cayman Islands, Netherlands Antilles, Channel Islands), opportunities for circumvention can remain.

Global financial markets are thus evolving in a context defined, on the one hand, by increased openness and innovation and, on the other hand, by the efforts of governments and central banks to find new ways to ensure overall market stability and safety. Together with the effects of fluctuating exchange rates, this context confronts MNEs with both incentives and opportunities to engage in hedging strategies.

The MNE structure itself provides the surest and most enduring mechanism both for coping with financial uncertainties and for taking advantage of new financial opportunities. Having operations in an expanding number of jurisdictions can offset various financial risks. Firms may also establish multicurrency credit lines, issue bonds and equity shares in offshore markets, decentralize the funding operations of foreign

subsidiaries, and bypass traditional financial intermediaries. Firms can accomplish this by issuing their own securities in a broadening range of foreign markets. As figure 6-8 suggests, this has reduced the direct financing role of banks across the industrial world, although there remain striking differences among particular national cases, a matter examined below. In very practical terms, the pursuit of such activities furthers the process of global financial integration.

FINANCIAL INTEGRATION AND NATIONAL STRUCTURES

While various indicators and the experience of MNE managers attest to the broadening trend toward financial market integration, significant room for debate remains on the question of how far that trend has actually progressed across specific markets and sectors. Economists typically measure integration in terms of the convergence of prices. France and Germany, they would argue, may be said to have an integrated capital market when the effective cost of capital for investments of equivalent risk is the same in Brest as in Stuttgart.

In fact, intense theoretical and empirical debate surrounds the issue of how far financial integra-

---

[18] See International Monetary Fund, *International Capital Markets: Developments, Prospects, and Policy Issues* (Washington, DC: IMF, September 1992), pp. 10-24.

Figure 6-8—Indicators of the Relative Importance of Banks in the Financing of Corporations in the U.S., Germany, and Japan

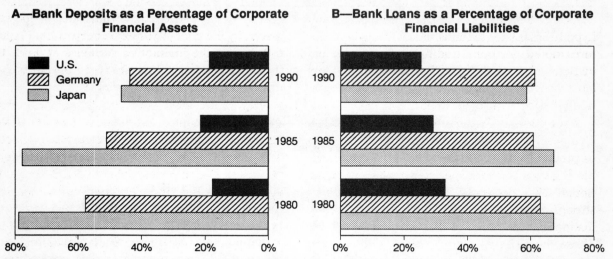

A—Bank Deposits as a Percentage of Corporate Financial Assets

B—Bank Loans as a Percentage of Corporate Financial Liabilities

SOURCE: IMF, *International Capital Markets: Developments, Prospects, and Policy Issues* (Washington, DC: International Monetary Fund, 1992), p. 3.

tion measured in such terms has progressed.[19] On one side of the debate are those who argue that differences in national capital costs are more apparent than real. Measurement problems account for much of any obvious difference, they contend, and the erosion of national barriers to capital mobility should eventually close any residual gaps. On the other side are those who argue that systematic differences remain in the effective capital costs facing, for example, similarly situated U.S., Japanese, and German corporations. Despite difficult definitional standards, proponents of this position often conclude that at the heart of the matter are enduring differences in the time-horizons of the ultimate providers of capital to such corporations.

Beyond the theoretical debates of economists, analysts have tried to gather data on the percep-

tions of corporate executives concerning comparative capital costs and investment time horizons. One recent study surveyed senior officials in 15 capital-intensive U.S. firms under significant competitive pressure from Japanese rivals. Views about the availability or importance of low-cost capital to the Japanese were deeply divided. Executives perceiving themselves to be slightly ahead of their rivals minimized the importance of capital cost differences, while those behind emphasized the issue. Across the board, however, came the view that their Japanese competitors behaved "as if" they had lower capital costs. The authors of the study concluded: "Once leadership is lost in a particular market, the firm that is able to behave as if it has a lower cost of capital—whether or not it actually does—has an obvious advantage. It will be willing to invest at a more

---

[19] See U.S. Congress, Office of Technology Assessment, *Making Things Better: Competing in Manufacturing*, op. cit., footnote 1, chapter 3. For a comprehensive and timely review of the analytical literature on the issue, see W. Carl Kester and Timothy A. Luehrman, "Cross-Country Differences in the Cost of Capital: A Survey and Evaluation of Recent Empirical Studies," Michael Porter et al., *Capital Choices* (Boston, MA: Harvard Business School Press, forthcoming).

rapid clip than its competitors."[20] But what factors can contribute to the perception of firms that they can behave as if they had lower capital costs than their rivals? One of the most prominent hypotheses relates to fundamental financial structures rooted in national traditions of corporate and market governance.[21] At that level, the widely hailed phenomenon of financial market integration takes on a different look.

A recent study for the private-sector Council on Competitiveness points out that the wellsprings of productive investment are complex and variable.[22] Beyond project-specific circumstances, national macroeconomic factors clearly exert a strong influence. Also influential are nationally distinctive mechanisms for allocating capital. These mechanisms may be seen as having two interactive dimensions, one external to the business and one internal. The external dimension refers to the structure of the major capital market within which the enterprise operates, usually its "home" market. The internal dimension refers to the ownership structures, management practices, and behavioral norms embedded in the firm itself. Capital for specific projects is effectively raised from either or both sources. In an aggregate sense, such systematic differences exist in the capital allocation mechanisms available to U.S., Japanese, and German firms that two distinct types may be drawn. The study characterizes the U.S. mechanism as a "fluid capital" system centered around transient owners and the need for corporate managers to maximize narrowly defined investment returns (e.g., stock prices). Conversely, the Japanese and German systems are labeled "dedicated capital," with their centers of gravity being permanent owners and managers driven by the goal of corporate perpetuity. Figure 6-9 depicts the interactive variables at work in these two systems, while table 6-5 sketches broad distinctions in ownership patterns.

Viewed as ideal types, each of these two systems of capital allocation has its own strengths. In theory, the U.S. system more quickly allocates resources and captures emerging opportunities. It also provides higher returns to individual investors and produces fairer, more transparent financial markets. The German and Japanese systems, conversely, tend to boost productivity in existing businesses, promote internal diversification into closely related fields, and promise what one analyst terms "higher social returns."[23] Arguments concerning the negative consequences of both systems abound, but the most common accusation is that the U.S. system can encourage firms to underinvest in their core businesses and leave shareholders with few instruments for disciplining corporate managers, while the German and Japanese systems can tend toward overinvestment and inefficiencies that make it difficult to redeploy resources into emerging sectors.[24]

Both systems are under some pressure from the trend toward more open and interpenetrated national markets. For this reason, many economists expect the value of the respective benefits

---

[20] Joseph Morone and Albert Paulson, "Cost of Capital: The Managerial Perspective," *California Management Review*, vol. 33, No. 4, summer 1991, pp. 9-32. Also see James Poterba and Lawrence H. Summers, "Time Horizons of American Firms: New Evidence from a Survey of CEOs," Porter et al., Ibid.

[21] See, for example, John Zysman, *Governments, Markets and Growth: Financial Systems and the Politics of Industrial Change* (Ithaca, NY: Cornell University Press, 1983); Michael Borrus et al., *The Highest Stakes: The Economic Foundations of the New Security System* (New York, NY: Oxford University Press, 1992); and Allen B. Frankel and John D. Montgomery, "Financial Structure: An International Perspective," *Brookings Papers on Economic Activity*, vol. 1, 1991, pp. 257-310.

[22] Michael Porter et al., *Capital Choices, Changing the Way America Invests in Industry*, a report presented to the Council on Competitiveness and co-sponsored by the Harvard Business School, June 1992.

[23] Ibid.

[24] Ibid., p. 13. Also see Alfred Chandler, "Competitive Performance of U.S. Industrial Enterprises: A Historical Perspective," Porter et al., op. cit., footnote 19.

Figure 6-9—External and Internal Capital Allocation Mechanisms

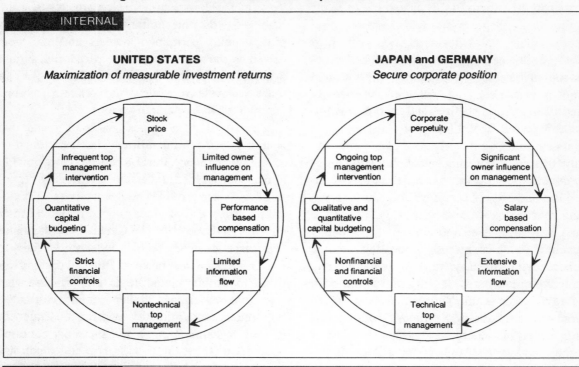

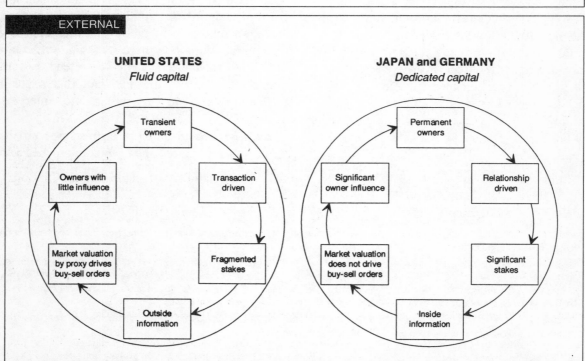

SOURCE: Adapted from Michael Porter et al., *Capital Choices*, A Report to the Council on Competitiveness and co-sponsored by the Harvard Business School, June 1992, pp. 9-10.

they provide to firms to be equilibrated eventually. For MNE managers, however, "eventually" can seem a long time. Even though figure 6-8 indicates a broad shift away from banks in the field of corporate finance, it is noteworthy how bank-centered the Japanese and German systems remain.[25] It also bears underlining that the extent of actual regulatory change varies across countries, a variance that can have protectionist effects.[26]

During periods of heightened financial uncertainty, as well as when facing very long-term and large-scale investment decisions, an MNE belonging to a relatively less open, bank-centered network may have a distinct and lasting advantage over MNEs more dependent on decentralized and open capital markets. To the extent that the bank at the center of such a network becomes fully engaged in dynamic international financial markets, the associated MNE may have the best of both worlds: access to leading-edge financial innovation and information as well as credible assurance of fall-back capital resources for both emergencies and new opportunities.[27]

MNEs AND MULTILATERAL COOPERATION

Multinational enterprises are inherently adaptable. As long as they can establish themselves in different national jurisdictions, they are capable of adapting to any feasible international capital regime. When capital controls and rigid regulatory structures were in place, they had little difficulty funding their operations in separated national markets or in incipient offshore markets.

Table 6-5—Estimated Comparative Pattern of Ownership and Agency Relationships in U.S., Japanese, and German Industry
(In percent)

	U.S.	Japan	Germany
Individuals	30-35	20	4
Institutional owners	2	40	27
Institutional agents	55-60	6	3
Corporations	2-7	30	41
Government	Negligible	Negligible	6
Foreign investors	6	4	19

SOURCE: Michael Porter et al., *Capital Choices*, A Report to the Council on Competitiveness and co-sponsored by the Harvard Business School, June 1992, p. 42.

But when capital decontrol became the norm, their financial options expanded and their dependence on banks generally declined, albeit to different degrees. Because of this enhanced flexibility, and despite the increased risks involved, MNEs appear to prefer an open international financial system.

Nevertheless, MNEs cannot themselves ensure the stability of open financial markets. For this, they must rely on governments and central banks. Beyond financial oversight functions, they also seek more specific governmental assurances (e.g., in support of large-scale investment in leading-edge high technologies) and, often, indirect assistance in underwriting health care, pension, and other costs.

The costs of such governmental services must be borne by someone. Fully open capital markets and the availability of multinational options potentially work to ensure that the most mobile, creditworthy, and externally oriented firms, sec-

[25] Michael L. Gerlach has recently presented extensive evidence on this score for the Japanese case. See his *Alliance Capitalism: The Social Organization of Japanese Business* (Berkeley, CA: University of California Press, 1992); and "Twilight of the Keiretsu? A Critical Assessment," *Journal of Japanese Studies*, vol. 18, No. 1, winter 1992, pp. 79-118. Also see Louis Pauly, *Regulatory Politics In Japan: The Case of Foreign Banking* (Ithaca, NY: Cornell East Asian Series, No. 45, 1987).

[26] The U.S. Trade Representative's Office recently challenged Japan on just such grounds. See Office of the United States Trade Representative, *1993 Trade Estimate Report on Foreign Trade Barriers* (Washington, DC: U.S. Government Printing Office, 1993), pp. 158-160.

[27] See Alfred Steinherr and Christian Huveneers, "On the Performance of Differently Regulated Financial Institutions: Some Empirical Evidence," *CEPS (Centre for European Policy Studies) Research Report*, No. 12, December 1992. Universal banking structures, the authors conclude, may provide better support for the long-term investment strategies of the nonfinancial sector than the segmented structures characteristic of the United States and the United Kingdom.

tors, and factors of production avoid their full impact. In other words, taxes imposed directly or indirectly on national firms to help pay for new social programs now have more direct effects on the international competitiveness of those firms; they can also more readily prompt them to pursue multinational strategies. In the absence of countervailing action, this suggests that the least mobile firms, sectors, and factors will bear most of the burdens created when governments respond to pressures for expanded business and social guarantees.

If consequent political tensions provided an impetus to efforts aimed at reversing the trend toward capital decontrol, unilateralism would hold little promise of success. The erosion of national political influence implied by the greater openness of contemporary financial markets and by the jurisdiction-spanning activities of MNEs and financial intermediaries now makes it necessary to address such tensions above the national level. This is the logic that has driven policy planning within the European Community and that has lately pushed central bankers to collaborate more intensively in other settings.

To the extent that global financial developments have distinctive and asymmetrical conse-quences for individual nations, the implications go beyond issues of financial regulation and firm competitiveness. If modern democracy may still be said to rest on a social contract between government and the governed, the twin and related forces of global financial integration and multinational corporate expansion undermine many of the traditional ways in which that contract has been satisfied. They make much more problematic, for example, the effective targeting of subsidies, and they diminish the capacity of governments to control the pace and direction of adjustment to economic change. In short, while they can both open new avenues for enhancing economic growth and innovation, they make it difficult to direct financial resources drawn from a national base toward the solution of national problems. Given the costs and uncertain benefits of attempting to reverse the trend toward global financial integration, and mindful of the enhanced ability of firms to circumvent such an effort, the political dilemmas that result from its potentially uneven impact imply the need to craft new bargains at the multilateral level.

Index

Academic research. *See* University research

ACCJ. *See* American Chamber of Commerce in Japan, Trade Expansion Committee

Acquisitions and mergers, Japanese attitude toward, 73-75

Administrative guidance by Japanese government, 16, 83, 84-86

Advanced Micro Devices, Fujitsu alliance, 100, 124

Aerospace industry
government support of, 31
ISAs and, 121, 123

Aerospatiale/Dassault-Breuget, McDonnell-Douglas alliance, 130

AIDS drug research, 124

Airbus, 123, 126

AMD. *See* Advanced Micro Devices

American Chamber of Commerce in Japan, 72, 75, 76

Antitrust laws, 127-128

Apple
Sharp alliance, 124
Toshiba alliance, 124

Asia. *See also specific countries*
industrialization strategies, 33-34

Asset pooling, 124

Asymmetries in government policies, ownership, and control
influence on new competitors, 33-36
ISAs and, 126-129
trade friction and, 38-41
U.S.-based MNEs and, 33, 36-38

Asymmetries in national policy regimes
competitiveness and, 7
description, 4, 15-16, 68-71
Japan example, 71-79

AT&T
divestiture, 128
international competition and, 13
Olivetti alliance, 125, 128, 130, 132

Philips alliance, 124, 128, 130, 132

Automotive industry. *See also specific companies*
automakers with plants in the United States, 63-64
domestic content issue, 84, 94-99
EC-Japan agreement on Japanese auto imports, 69
FDIUS and, 51-52
ISAs and, 121
Japanese Government encouragement of investment in the United States, 84
keiretsu and, 75-76, 86-87, 91-93
labor costs, 25
protectionist policies and, 30
Section 301 filing, 85
voluntary restrictions on Japanese automobile imports, 33

Bayh-Dole Act, 107, 109-110

Biotechnology industry
ISAs and, 118, 119, 121, 123, 124
Japanese investment in, 99, 104-106

Bluegrass Automotive Manufacturers Association, 93

BMW, 63

Boeing, 13, 126

Bretton Woods Conference, 8, 137-139, 143, 149

Britain. *See* United Kingdom

Bull, 32, 128

Bush administration
FDIUS policies, 62
national treatment policy, 48

Business Global Partnership Initiative, 84

CAFE. *See* Corporate average fuel economy

Canadian Free Trade Agreement, 94, 98

Canon, 103

Capital decontrol, 149-153

Capital flows, 136, 150

Capital mobility, 137-139

☆ U.S. GOVERNMENT PRINTING OFFICE:1993-343-283/96951

ISBN 0-16-041943-3

9 780160 419430

90000

Superintendent of Documents **Publications** Order Form

Order Processing Code:

*7162

P3
Telephone orders (202) 783-3238
To fax your orders (202) 512-2250
Charge your order.
It's Easy!

☐ **YES**, please send me the following:

_____ copies of *Multinationals and the National Interest: Playing by Different Rules (176 pages)*, S/N 052-003-01338-0 at $10.00 each.

The total cost of my order is $_____ . International customers please add 25%. Prices include regular domestic postage and handling and are subject to change.

_____
(Company or Personal Name)   (Please type or print)

_____
(Additional address/attention line)

_____
(Street address)

_____
(City, State, ZIP Code)

_____
(Daytime phone including area code)

_____
(Purchase Order No.)

Please Choose Method of Payment:

☐ Check Payable to the Superintendent of Documents

☐ GPO Deposit Account ☐☐☐☐☐☐☐ — ☐

☐ VISA or MasterCard Account

☐☐☐☐☐☐☐☐☐☐☐☐☐☐☐☐☐☐☐☐

☐☐☐☐ (Credit card expiration date)

Thank you for
your order!

_____
(Authorizing Signature)   (9/93)

                YES NO
May we make your name/address available to other mailers? ☐ ☐

Mail To: New Orders, Superintendent of Documents, P.O. Box 371954, Pittsburgh, PA 15250-7954

THIS FORM MAY BE PHOTOCOPIED

Superintendent of Documents **Publications** Order Form

Order Processing Code:

*7162

P3
Telephone orders (202) 783-3238
To fax your orders (202) 512-2250
Charge your order.
It's Easy!

☐ **YES**, please send me the following:

_____ copies of *Multinationals and the National Interest: Playing by Different Rules (176 pages)*, S/N 052-003-01338-0 at $10.00 each.

The total cost of my order is $_____ . International customers please add 25%. Prices include regular domestic postage and handling and are subject to change.

_____
(Company or Personal Name)   (Please type or print)

_____
(Additional address/attention line)

_____
(Street address)

_____
(City, State, ZIP Code)

_____
(Daytime phone including area code)

_____
(Purchase Order No.)

Please Choose Method of Payment:

☐ Check Payable to the Superintendent of Documents

☐ GPO Deposit Account ☐☐☐☐☐☐☐ — ☐

☐ VISA or MasterCard Account

☐☐☐☐☐☐☐☐☐☐☐☐☐☐☐☐☐☐☐☐

☐☐☐☐ (Credit card expiration date)

Thank you for
your order!

_____
(Authorizing Signature)   (9/93)

                YES NO
May we make your name/address available to other mailers? ☐ ☐

Mail To: New Orders, Superintendent of Documents, P.O. Box 371954, Pittsburgh, PA 15250-7954

THIS FORM MAY BE PHOTOCOPIED